95,800 words.

The Water Magister's: Self-Discovery Book 1

by David A. Rodriguez

Intro

Acknowledgements

I would like to acknowledge so many people in the creation of this book as they have each played a huge role in my own growth from the moment I first interacted with each of them. I would first like to acknowledge Willy who has always been that light for me back when I was eighteen. He was always showing me books to read and gave me some amazing insights that at the time I did not understand but I still read the books. They just sat with me in the back of my mind but I knew it was all true I just did not know how to apply any of it just yet.

Next I would like to acknowledge Sami who without her I would not have had a catalyst in this huge awakening I have had in my own world. Without going through that process of depression I would not be where I am now, it would not have given me the driving force to strive for greater things and for that I acknowledge you and I love you.

I would like to Acknowledge Loni for accepting me in open arms when I first arrived to her Reiki class. I had so much pain and walls up but she saw past it and was able to open space and allow me to grow.

I acknowledge Lauren my first true Yoga Teacher. Without your guidance I would not have taken the path of a Yogi. It is because of you I progressed on such a deeper level then I could have imagined spiritually and mentally. You did not know it at the time, but because of your inspiration you took me to great heights of my own mind.

I acknowledge Kevin for having created such a beautiful community known as the "Light Beings Community". You have always been such a shining and aspiring light for my growth and you saw the true power I hold inside of me.

I acknowledge Moses and Zayna for having such a beautiful Yoga Studio in Hollywood known as "I Love Yoga Studio". Your teacher training has propelled me even further because I thought I had reached a plateau of knowledge. But as I stayed open I have been able to learn so much more.

I would also like to acknowledge Las for seeing the light in me during my open mic at a place called "Mystic Water Kava Bar". Without your beautiful support and initial $100 funding this book would not have been possible. I acknowledge you for being able to see the infinite source that resides in me as well as others.

I acknowledge Erika for being such a beautiful reflection for my own growth as to the many walls I had that were still shielding my heart and preventing me from reaching my full potential. For the challenges that we both co created together so that could be the best versions of our selves after we separated.

I acknowledge Patrick for assisting me with bringing my sigil front book cover to life with updated graphics. I love your graphic skills!

There are so many more but I would just like to say Thank you to Everyone who believed in me and I hope reading this will inspire at least one soul out there.

I love you.

Foreword

What is crazy?
The definition of crazy is : mentally deranged, especially as manifested in a wild or aggressive way.

To what does this definition reach towards? I can say during all the time I have been self aware there have been plenty of times I myself have labeled my self as crazy. But as it further progressed I come to find out that they were all truths and my ego just refused to believe it.

So when someone calls you crazy how do you take it? Do you take offense because "OH God Why is someone calling me crazy? Am I crazy...Oh no, will society judge me?"
Are those the thoughts that pass through your head?

I am going to share with you what I truly feel I am and have felt it deep within by channeling or just by knowing. But they are stories that empower me to keep pushing forward, so what difference does the actual story make as long as it empowers you to keep pushing forward with love.

Since my own time in my depression I had a few years ago. That was when I found who I truly was and It was not given to me all at once. It came in waves. I love that Phrase. Because of how accurate it is. I get bits and pieces of an identity so I can keep pushing

forward into my own growth. So here it is.
I am from Sirius and I am a High Elder and a High
Commander the creator of this race named "Ashtar",
from this constellation sent here to Earth to support
the mass awakening through Water. Now you may
laugh at that sentence because of how far fetched it
sounds.

I laugh at it as well but, it still remains true to me
regardless because I create my reality. I arrived at this
realization because when I began reading about Dr.
Masaru Emoto, I realized everything has water in it,
we are made of water. Just by your intention alone you
change the Molecular structure of water. So if I do
this, I change the molecular structure of water it self.
Thus changing the DNA in humans when they drink
it. If you do some research on Sirians you will come to
find that they are the scientists that changed DNA in
Humans and are a technologically advanced race. I am
developing a special machine that was channeled to
me to restructure water using many different things
currently available and others that are not. This
machine will be one of a kind and will assist in the
evolution of man kind.

Another one of my missions has been to discover a
unique crystal. I have always said that I wanted to go
cave diving into caves that no one else has ventured
to. I want to be pulled to an area intuitively to find a
crystal similar to the philosopher's stone. This may be
just a wild imaginative idea.

But I feel one day I will find a crystal that will attune me to it's vibration and then I will no longer require the crystal, I will be that crystal to then share the frequency with others.

So once I realized this I understood I am Sirian. I have received many channeled messages from others, as well as My higher self to confirm this. I channel Ra as well as Metatron, Buckminister Fuller, Tesla, Arch Angel Michael, Arch Angel Chamuel, The Council of 9, The Syrian Council, and the Syrian Star fleet who are here right now when I do my writings. They ask me periodically if I want them to reveal themselves and I normally say no.

Slowly each day I awake to this realization through subtle messages for me, by me. Of course none of this truly means anything because it is just the ego wanting validation in who is being channeled. When in fact it does not matter who or what flows through me, ultimately it still is just me. But for the purpose of understanding those are the beings that are channeled through me thus far.

I was given the name "The Water Magister" because I was thinking of what to call my self for my writings. I had never heard the word Magister before but it immediately was whispered to my ear and I then researched what it means. It means a teacher or master. I am a Water Teacher.

When I first began the conception of this book I was unclear as to what that goal of the book would be.

Was it to inspire the masses? Was it to be a form of inspiration for those who's light has been fading due to depression and sadness? It took me a good long meditation to understand why I wanted to write this and it is because of the following:

I feel that in my next incarnation I will find and read this book. The sigil on the cover is my way of leaving breadcrumbs for my next incarnation. What is a sigil you ask? It is a symbol that has a specific meaning behind it and since we are the creators of our reality each time you see it or view it. You are giving it more awareness towards what that sigil represents.

I feel that I will see this sigil so that I can continue the path I have chosen for that body. I believe that once I see the symbol that was given to me to place on this cover that I will immediately recognize it and grab the book from the shelf or the book will find its way to me. It will always play a huge role in the awakening of the sleeping masses as many of you who are reading this are only coming to terms of understanding who you truly are. I understand now as well that those who are destined to learn more about who they are and the experiences that may come from the awakening process will find their way to this book and many others. There is no such thing as coincidence and you are reading these words because you were ready to hear them in your mind.

I know that there will be many of you who have been out there living a life that you felt had more meaning. Because the way we have been living does not make sense to us, it doesn't feel right. This book is for you and to allow you to understand more of yourself as you do so. It is also a book to refer to see the different steps one person has taken to truly find out what they are made of and why we have been placed on this planet. You may use this book as reference for tools from my many meditations and channeling's. I will be creating a separate book for specific instructions on 12 Meditations that were given to me which I taught at my classes titled "The Water Magister: Metatrons Meditations". I also share my yoga practices that have allowed me to create such beautiful peace in my self.

This book is a raw and truthful insights into my mind and all that I have written has happened in my own reality as real as if I were to touch you and grab your hand. The things you will read are from the divine and as I experience am able to translate it into this human language we have developed. The style of writing is in form of journal entries and I wanted to keep it that way as each of them has dates. It will include poetry, journal entries, random thoughts, meditation practices and visualizations and ideas that come to me by being in a peaceful mind state so it easier to hear the voice that communicates through me.

Before I begin I would like to explain a little about my self. I was born under conditions of my choosing because of the choice of my parents. In such I was brought into this world by forms of mental abuse, sexual abuse and addictions. There have been many times in my life where I asked why me, why do I have to feel all of this pain? But now in retrospect it all makes sense. Without those moments I would not be able to distinguish truth and beauty from the chaos and ruble.

I have added the story in the prologue section so you can have an idea as to where I was and how I got to where I am now. But for a good five years I was self destructive and the way I hid my pain was through sexual addiction and the objectifying of women. I held on to so much pain and put up so many walls that turned me into a black hole of darkness. I had to reach my lowest point in order to get to where I am now and I am still climbing.

After all the books I read about spirituality and meditation back when I was 16 to about 20, I began recalling all of that information and it was at this moment that I began applying it and truly understanding all of it. I recall my aunt's Fiance discussing things like how he could levitate, how he could leave his body and still his mind. I thought he was crazy, but there was always something inside of me that felt like he was telling the truth. I would come across small synchronicities during this age. But after my heart got broken the first time I quickly reverted back into my shell. Finally at the age of 30, was my age to awaken and begin the journey of my self. After so many years of womanizing and being a sexually promiscuous male. It was time to break free.

I held onto all that knowledge at the back of my mind and was only able to access it after many meditations and experiences.

It was during a span of the first year of my awakening that I call the "Sponge Mode". It is a mode in which your brain wants to learn as much as possible because its like you are a new born learning things for the first time.

Something of note is I have had such a difficult time writing this book because of fears that have been clouding me. I had a belief that if I finished writing this book, I would die. It may be an irrational one but it just goes to show how powerful a fear can be to prevent you from becoming your true authentic self.

The other fear I had was that of truly expressing my self without caring how the reader may take what I say. I spent many days crying because of the amount of time I was spending procrastinating. Not only this, but I then took on another story in my mind that what I am to write about has no value because of what an ex instilled in me. I created a writers block for 10 months until I broke free from it.

I also have included old poems from the past when I was channeling and I never knew how powerful the writing was until I re read it all. I also want to mention that I was the only editor of this book as every time I had people say they wanted to assist me in editing, they never did. It only showed me something very important.

How could I ever expect someone to do something for me of something I wasn't going to do my self. So I acknowledge any grammar errors that still may linger as I only write based on the thoughts that flow and corrected things as I saw them to the best of my ability.

I hope you enjoy the inner workings of my life.

Thank you. I Love You.

Prologue

Hello There,

This is my story on how I discovered my self worth, my acceptance of self and most important how I began loving myself.
Going back into my childhood is where it all begins. I came from what you would call a difficult childhood. I was sexually abused by multiple members of my family. I was physically abused by my father and by children at school. Because of the sexual abuse I associated connection to sexual acts to the opposite sex to connect rather than taking the time to get to know someone to connect on a deeper level.

Which is what our society does, as we tend to jump into things because it is a form of distraction from an emotion. I remember thinking to myself," Why me?" "How could this happen to me?" It was a memory that has always been lingering in the back of my mind into adulthood.

The physical abuse that was done to me by my father was because I wouldn't do things he wanted me to do. I wouldn't want to eat all of my food. I remember a time that still lingers in my mind where I did not want to eat and he beat me, put me in a cold shower and then tossed me out into the patio naked while I cried for an hour or so. Do you know how much this affects a child?

I am 33 now and have a loathing for cold water. Every single time my body touches cold water that memory comes up because of how traumatizing it was for my little self. I have practices now where I have begun loving myself which I will go into later in this story to allow myself to come into contact with cold water.

In early adolescence, I would consistently be bullied because I was the smallest and skinniest kid in school. I would go home crying every day. Again, the thought of, "Why me?" would pop into my head. How could a world be like this where so many people could hurt another Being in this way? During my time in high school I remember having the constant thought of "Forgive them father, for they do not know".

I went to a catholic church and truly grew to dislike it by the age of 10. I suppose that message always stuck with me. I would recall thinking to myself, "Wow, the kids who are hurting me, spitting on me, picking their pubic hair and throwing it on me among other things, must have an awful childhood to want to do this to another because of the unbearable pain they are feeling".

So I took it. I took all of it. I took all of their anger, all of their abuse, all of their hatred that they did not know how to process because they were never taught how to process those emotions. Our school system doesn't teach that.

It teaches how to critically think and remember answers for a test; to be slaves to authority. I just

13

continued bottling all of my anger, all of my resentment to the world from the sexual abuse and the physical abuse of my father.

This next part of what I am about to say is something I have only shared with very close friends and lovers. Because of that, the vulnerability in it leaves me open. Some of you may experience big revelations of judgment and if so ask yourself, "What is it showing you?" Some of you may experience understanding and compassion.

Some of you may truly see me for Me. This is the process which lead me to being the man I am today. Because of how much pent up anger I had within myself I never knew truly how to process it all. I recall a time when I was in middle school where I decided to take 6 kittens from a back yard. When I grabbed them I did not have any intention on doing what I was about to do. It all seemed "automatic".

I brought these kittens into a secluded area in the woods where no one could find me. I then began to kill each one using different methods. Do you know what I felt during this? I felt my power returning to me. I felt joy, I felt powerful and in control of my life in that moment.
Because I picked on something weaker than me. But I held onto so much guilt up until I was 30 because of what I had done that day.
Looking back on this memory at my current age, I remember reading books on serial killers and how they turned out the way they did. I read books on how

children would "shoot up" schools because of all that pent-up anger. I understand each of them now.

Why? Because, I know they had experiences in their childhood where they felt completely powerless. They felt like they were victims of the situation. When they finally decided to take a stand and reclaim their power, whether it be in a perceived negative way they did so, so that they could feel "whole" again. Once they did this, they associated their claim to power by the act and would continue on into it.

I could have easily turned into a Serial Killer or a child whom you saw on the news that shot up their school because of the misplaced emotions I did not know how to address. What was my saving grace during those times in my life? Well for me funny enough, it was paint ball and video games. That was my release. I became heavily addicted to video games. I would wake up really late and go to bed extremely late.

After school was over I would run home just to immerse myself in a fantasy world because in there I was special. I was powerful! I was acknowledged and accepted. The point I am making is we have to begin finding and supporting children who are experiencing these traumas and show them ways on how to truly feel their anger in a constructive way. Because if we do not do something and teach children how to process their emotions. We will continue to see the same things play out and the story of violence in the world.

My purpose for these writings is to share with you

some of my deepest and darkest moments and follow-up with how I took myself out of them. Moving forward into my life I fell in love with a beautiful woman at the age of 21. My mother stayed a single mother after what had happened with my father, and then later remarried.

When she raised me she taught me how to treat others how you want to be treated. She is the most amazing woman in my life because of the morals she instilled in me. Because of this, when I fell in love for the first time I held this girl in such high regard that she would never hurt me because I would never hurt her.

I began to have dreams three months into dating her where I saw her cheating on me. The dreams of her cheating on me were so vivid that when I look back on them now, I can see they were actually memories! It was like a video camera watching what she was doing with another man.

I confronted her with this and she denied what she had done. So, the dreams kept occurring. I reached a point where I became so fed up with them I opened up my web browser and went onto Myspace. I had already known her email address, but it was her password I did not know. I sat there for a moment and closed my eyes and the first thing that popped in my head I typed it into that box.

Can you guess what happened? Yep, I was inside her account. The sheer astonishment of what just happened made my jaw drop. I guessed someone's password at the first attempt?! I couldn't believe it! I logged out and typed it in again. Low and behold it still let me in.

As if I was supposed to find this out to excel my soul into the next level of evolution. I looked at the very first message and it was of a man who had said he couldn't do this anymore because he knew how much I loved her. Her response was something that set me off saying ,"It would be a shame to not have sex with you again". Upon reading this my blood boiled! I felt the heat of the sun all over my body which filled me with fury. I began to cry uncontrollably. How could someone do this to another person?

This then brought up old memories. Memories of my sexual abuse that I had blocked out. I laid there crying loudly in my bed. It made me cry even more that I had been denying the emotions I felt during those times in my younger years. I didn't want to feel this anymore. "Fuck this world!" "I have nothing to live for!", I kept thinking.

I had many thoughts of suicide at this point because there was nothing in this life that I wanted anymore. I never acted on it of course, but maybe in a parallel reality I did. I say this because to this day, I still do not know why I chose not to. I had all the reasons to do so but I just couldn't. I hadn't fulfilled a purpose in this souls contract just yet. Because of the resentment I now held towards her, I then began resenting all women.

For a period of five years I put up walls. My heart was cold and I became promiscuous. I would read up on how to manipulate people via pick-up artists books. My idol for a while was an author named Tucker Max. During these 5 years I had the most sex I have ever had in my life. I was with over 80 partners. It ranged from couples, to orgies, to Craigslist sex and even on two occasions prostitutes.

I didn't want to "feel" anymore. I decided to place all my anger on everyone else by making them feel manipulated and treating them like dirt because that was how I felt. I wanted them all to hurt. There were instances where a few women wanted to get close and I just lied and told them I loved them just to have sex with them because it was what they wanted to hear. I would run from women that showed too much love to me.

Why would I want to feel that much love when I didn't even love myself at that point? I was an alcoholic during those years and drank practically every day. I did drugs because I didn't want to feel emotions. I remember an entire month I used ecstasy every day because it made everything go away. It made me feel confident in myself to further take advantage of women in their weak states. I was truly a bad person, or so I thought.

During the last few months of that period, I began to feel tired of manipulation and I wanted to just stop it all together. I was on dating sites for a good majority which was how I seduced so many. I was beginning to close down my accounts because I didn't want that life anymore. The moment I made that choice was what I now see as a blessing. A beautiful women came into my life and loved me. I had become a broken version of who I once was. She didn't care. She brought me up from that darkness to a neutral point. This was not easy for her.

During the three years she and I dated I still didn't want to feel certain things because it would bring up memories of my childhood and other things. Why would I want to feel that? At this point in my life I was still addicted to video games. Every day I would finish work and play fantasy games that made me feel like I could make something of myself. I felt special in those games.

I was always seeking those feelings outside of myself. My girlfriend during this time was not receiving the proper love a women deserved. I would spend some time with her but I would still go right back to the video games because that was the way I felt safe. That was where I felt comfortable in my little bubble of reality so I did not have to feel.

I began to research conspiracy theories and got heavily into all of it. I began going from being in my bubble of reality to genuine fear. I began to be fearful of the government. I began to be fearful of the chemicals in the air. I began to be fearful of people and what ulterior motives they may have.

Throughout this, She still stuck with me for a while. I began to be a "prepper" and spent over $5,000 in survival equipment thinking the financial system was going to collapse. I taught myself archery. I taught myself how to make and load my own bullets. I owned 3 guns at the time. I invested all of my money in seeds, bullets and survival equipment.

I was in a downward spiral at this point and this was when she broke up with me. She was afraid of where I was headed. I was heavily depressed some days. I remember watching her leave and taking mostly everything from the apartment leaving it practically empty.

I sat there while her friends helped her take everything out. One of them murmured,"Wow, this is so awkward." I was sitting at my computer in my underwear, tears in my eyes in awe of everything that what was happening around me. I cried for days.

I had a memory of when I was 21 or so I would read self-help books but it made no sense to me so I just stored the information in my head and continued finding ways to numb myself. Then, one day out of the blue from the days I had been crying.

I hear a voice whisper to me and say, "Meditation". I wondered, "Why is that in my mind?" On this day though, the moment meditation popped into my head I went on Youtube and typed in "Meditation music".

The first thing that I saw was a third eye meditation video. I began listening to this for 3 days for about 5-15 minutes a day. On the third day, I then heard another word pop into my head, it was "Reiki". I had no idea what this word was or what it meant. I Googled it as well. I then looked for a Reiki healer in my area and found one.

This was the beginning of my self love. I began going to reiki circles with others who too are healing from traumas and some afraid to be vulnerable, others wanting to share. I was just there to see what it was about. I remember not ever wanting to hug anyone or allowing them to get too close.

I would hug at times but make sure there was a lot of space and it was quick tap on the back so it could end quickly. This was the start of my true awakening. This made me who I am and realized my purpose in this world. I began reading and studying any piece of spirituality I could find or that came recommended. I spent the majority of my time at a place called: Mystic Water Kava Bar.

This was where I found Kava. It took me out of my depression. I felt at peace and blissful every time I drank. I began finding teachers because I was now ready. I was ready to step into my Self. I was ready to love. I was ready to be vulnerable. I began journaling all of the things I did to give love to myself from ayahausca ceremonies, peyote and one-on-one sessions.

After so many years, I finally understand why these experiences happened. I am now here to share with you the reasons why.

I realize now after all the studies and after all the teachings in my life it was all because I created it all.

Let that sink in for a moment. I created all of it, every experience, every moment, every person in my life, every instance of sexual abuse, every time I was physically abused, every heartache. I created it because I wanted to see what it was like to be sexually abused, to be physically abused, to be bullied, to feel weak, to feel powerless.

Without any of that I would not be able to relate and connect with those who too have felt this. I would not be able to be the workshop facilitator I am today and allow myself to be vulnerable with all of you. I would not be able to allow that bridge to my heart to expand to yours.

Yet now that I felt one side of the spectrum, I can now appreciate the feeling of being strong, the feeling of being powerful and unlimited. I can tap into my creativity and no longer cause harm to anything outside nor inside myself. I know what some of you have felt, I honor you and acknowledge you for conquering those hardships.

Understand this if you will. The moment you take ownership as the creator of your experiences, you will then truly understand that you are responsible for creating them. You then are never the victim and in this moment you reclaim your power. You will see how beautifully orchestrated these series of events had to play out in order to mold you into who you are right now! You can see how powerful and strong you are for having stayed with this life.

You have purpose, you have drive, you have a calling. You are the light of the world. As you heal these aspects of yourself you will notice a dramatic shift in those around you. Because as you heal, you heal the world outside of yourself. You will then begin to forgive yourself rather than place blame on others. This is where your power lies.
We can all find healing through these stories of limitation, trauma, abuse, addiction.

We truly heal the world around us because we then become the beacons of light for others to see they too can do the same. We will be those pillars of society that become a foundation as the rest begins to crumble and go through the same process of integration. We are the light bringers , shining light into the darkness for those who are lost and have forgotten their power. We are that for the world.

Once you begin to understand that it was you that created all of those experiences, you can then go back through each experience one by one. Begin giving those versions of yourself the love that you wish you had received during the experience itself. Send forgiveness and acceptance because you deserve it. You deserve the inner peace of knowing you do not have to hurt anymore.

I began sending love to my child self who disliked cold water and had trauma towards it. Letting him know it is ok and that I am here. As I began to do this my dislike of cold water began to fade. I allowed cold water to be on me in showers in short increments for several days while I envisioned this moment in my mind. To send that love over and over until he heard me.

You create your reality because you are the God and Goddess of your sphere of reality. Everything you say in your mind goes. This is why being mindful of your own thoughts are crucial in this point in your life. We are beginning to understand our true unlimited creative potential. Fears of responsibility will come up. Just know you are experiencing this shift in consciousness because your soul is ready and you have been calling for it.

You are ready for this. I love you, I always have, and I always will. Because you are a reflection of my self and I am here simply to remind you of your potential. It is time to take this human experience forward into higher realms.

Are you ready?

Journal Entries

Prior Journal Entrees and Pre-Awakening

7-23-13

That night, I was dreaming: I was on a boat alone, it seemed like it was rowing it self. In the middle of nowhere, fog began to emerge. A loud voice began to speak in a very calm tone and kept repeating "Ya-Weh is coming". I woke up. I had never heard "Ya-Weh", before and looked it up online. I wondered, "Why it was spoken to me?" This word was **"**a form of the Hebrew name of God used in the Bible. The name came to be regarded by Jews (circa 300 BC) as too sacred to be spoken, and the vowel sounds are uncertain." I will never forget this dream because of how profound it was.

The Peyote Experience

2-27-14 Reiki Circle

Today I went into a deep meditation with the others. I felt light and connected.

During my meditation I began to see full images of real events taking place. The first was of my mother and step father. As I saw this it lasted about three to five seconds. I thought to my self "I wonder if I can see other people in real time". I thought of a friend named Franc. I saw him in a black wife beater walking somewhere. After I saw him I began picturing a circle above the group of souls with me. As I did I saw cables coming out of me and connecting with everyone. Once this was done I envisioned the color red and the word "grounding". I then pulsated these thoughts like a pump pushing it out to each person.

After everyone opened their eyes we shared our experiences. I shared mine and many felt or saw the color red and felt the word grounding. I also then sent a text to my friend Franc what I had seen and he confirmed what I saw was true. He had worn that black wife beater. He asked me How I knew and I told him I was simply in a deep trance of meditation. In the circle there was another man named Frank. He pulled me aside and told me he had many messages for me. First was he felt the need for the past two weeks to send me grounding energy because I have been progressing so rapidly in my crown and third eye. Next he stated I was asking alot of questions but all

28

the answers were inside of me.

I have a ball of light that follows me. I have to ask that the questions rather then others because all of the answers are within my self. I thought I was going crazy at this point.

My reiki teacher has said my heart emits a bright white light. Could that be because of how quickly I have been progressing?
This was my day, I feel love everywhere and I love it. I love you for teaching me the lessons. I am now aware of my path and it becomes more clear each day.

2-28-14

1:30 PM - I meditated in the car as I normally do now for half of my lunch break. Right at the end about five seconds before the alarm went off I heard in my mind a voice that asked "What is my name?". It was not my voice.
It synced so perfectly with the melody of my alarm.

7:01 PM - I meditated for 30 minutes before going out. I felt as if I jumped up out of my self twice in this meditation but it was rather quick. I quickly ended up back in my body.

3-1-14 My First Peyote Ceremony

Author Note: I was drawn to do peyote by a calling. I did not know what it was but I was so adamant about learning more of who I am. I did not

29

care how or what way I would do so. I was looking for every possible way to seek answers to questions in my life.

My experience of Peyote:
Within thirty minutes I saw the image.

Author Note: I had never seen a peyote cactus. Even when I ate the peyote it was broken up so I never knew the shape. Upon looking at this image I now see it is a top view of the Peyote plant. On another related note about 1 month after this experience I read a book by Carlos Castaneda "Teachings of Don Juan". In it he describes that when grandfather takes you in, you see a bright white light and that is how it reveals it self. This is what I saw and illustrated in my journal the day I experienced it.

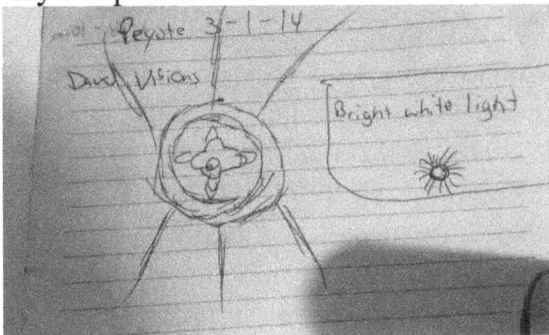

There were minor visuals. Three rounds of peyote went around. At one point there was a powder blown into my nose called "Rapè". This apparently opens the third eye. This greatly enhanced my experience immediately. For five minutes I felt one with everything. I could not walk straight, I then meditated and for the second time in my life I saw a small piercing white light that came from within my mind. I opened my eyes to see if someone was flashing a light. But this came from within, it was pure, loving and beautiful.

Author Note: The first time I had ever experienced this bright white light was during my first Kundalini class with Lauren. It was a one on one session with a beautiful woman. In one of the postures I had my eyes closed and I saw a bright white light. I immediately began to laugh because of how beautiful it was. I opened my eyes and she smiled almost knowing what I had seen.

I had to throw up several times, they call it "getting well". After I got well I then sat down again I began to ask "What is my name?" I saw a man on a cross for a while behind the darkness of my eyes and had the feeling that this was me on a cross in a different life. You can guess who this may be. Yet at the same time I don't want to believe this could have been me.

Author Note: I realize now that once you begin to wake up and be self aware. You will see your self as one of the major gurus, teachers or prophets that have lived. This is normal because it is to be used as a tool to allow you to understand that you are the same as that teacher. But instead of attaching to the idea that you are that guru or sage or Deity. Utilize it as a form of empowerment to keep pushing forward in your creative expression, even further then those who you feel your self to be. I see a lot of people in the spiritual community get stuck on this stage and truly feel they are Jesus, Buddha, Gandhi. This stunts your progression by allowing the ego to take on the identity of this. Keep moving forward and utilize it as a learning tool to reach your full potential.

I saw this image for at least ten minutes. Next I let go and I saw a winding road where I was a car driving. I saw this scene like a black and white movie. I believe I was this car driving along the ash hill where the fire was. I have illustrated a drawing. See below.

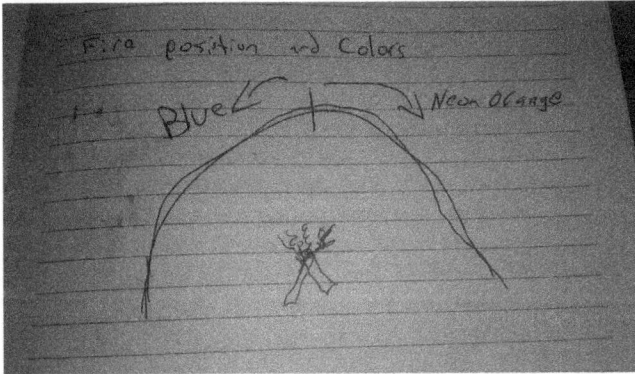

I believe the piercing light was my higher self telling me I can go to him when I want and it is safe to astral travel. I now feel a better sense of oneness and connection.

Thank you for this experience. I love you.

Author Note: It was at this moment where I began to be vegetarian. I gave up video games, I gave up masturbating, I gave up porn, I gave up coffee, I gave up alcohol, I gave up smoking weed for a full year. I began to appreciate everything I put into my body. I would say over and over as I would eat and drink things "Thank you, Thank you, Thank you.". This was even before meeting or knowing about intentions of water.

New interests to research:
Making a Spirit Staff or Wand
Feather head piece
Cloth Clothing that is light

Poetry from the Peyote Ceremony
-Peyote-
Swirling transparent colors
Looking all around sharing love with everyone
Men and women in headdress
Bring me back to forgotten memories
And love, I know I have lived
That life and am now witnessing
It from a different perspective
Fresh eyes, oneness
Voices sharing moments of love
Fire and Ash flowing up
Laugher and Silence filled with
Prayers and intentions
A mother sees her lost daughter
And cries with happiness
She shares this and love is given
Water filled with memories
Always love ever giving back
Aho a phrase repeating
When gratitude is shown
She smokes her tobacco prior
To serving the nectar of our bodies

It flows through us and is us
Give thanks to it and hold it close
We forget and continue to remember
We are all one and everyone and things
Deserves this love shown no matter what,
always and forever
Change is always within but you must
Share it, I love you.

-Ever love-
Breeze, wind, love
Crashing on my face
Appreciation, gratitude, aho
Shared from one another
Oneness of life flowing
From breath to breath
Connection and stillness in the now
Gods and Goddesses joining under one tepee
Filled with laughter

-Pleasures-
Dishes of palette invoking pleasures
Come out in the morning
Corn, chips, fruits
In a way we fasted and await
The gifts mother earth is about
To provide, Each item blessed with
Love and intention each brought in
By a loving Goddess.

Meanings of the foods:
Corn - Mother earth, the dirt.
Buffalo - To look outward and of power - The last

time I ate meat and became vegetarian by intuition. I had never had any training on how to have a proper vegetarian diet. I just woke up one Monday morning and my body declared it no longer wanted meat. Not because I wanted to save the animals, they do not require saving. But because my body asked for it, and I realized It was a vital point in my life that developed my will power.

Fruits - All gamma of colors of beauty, things we take for granted

-Spaceship-
We all entered inside the tepee Spaceship
with perspectives of old
The illusion of time passes
And insights are had sharing energy
Night becomes day and the sun shines
Brightly with love on our ever glow skin
We embark out-wards of the tepee spaceship
Into a new land of possibilities and
Perspective, seemingly like a new planet
With eyes widened enjoying the new
Moment of stillness and oneness
The wind kissing my face welcoming
Me into this new world of ever lasting love

Vegetarian Begins

3-11-14 *Dream*
My dream for the night was strange but short. I was looking for a new condo and I had a sexual dream with the Real Estate Agent.
This is being shared because I have been having many sexual dreams through the writing of this book which will be elaborated on further along the way.

3-14-14
45 Minute Meditation. I did a binaural 3rd Eye meditation and I saw a few images. I saw a brief rainbow, I saw a train station filled with people. I also saw a womans face. I have been seeing female eyes lately. I felt the vibrations all through my body and more as I verbalized " I love You, I am Light".

I feel anxious today because on January 19th 2014 I saw the number 57 in a meditation. I marked my calendar and it lands on March 17th 2014. I do not know if that was what the meaning was but I also looked up the Angel Number meanings and it stated that my spirit guide was communicating with me. We will see if something of importance happens on Monday. I Love You!

3-17-2014
The vibrations are so strong now. I feel my body tingle with sensations of love. The more I focus on words and intention of pure light. The more vibrations come. It speaks to me. I can project this feeling by

envisioning a white orb and extending it out of me and everyone around has a cable attached to this orb. I notice a shift in the room immediately when I do this. Colors can be projected this same way as long as they are open to the connection. My head vibrates more and more, passion, love.

Actions of giving become natural not wanting or needing anything in return. Life is bliss, pure, perfect. I am here.

3-22-14

Today I meditated and saw a vision of a very beautiful girl with short bangs, black hair, cute little nose and she was short. Then a friend of mine named Franc came over, I told him what I saw. Then we went to go do Archery. I taught him how to use a bow, later in the night we went to the Kava bar and decided to play Jenga. I saw sitting down by her self a beautiful girl as I had seen in my meditation. We shared eye contact multiple times and smiled at one another. I knew it was her. I asked if she would like to play with us and she accepted, her name was Eugenia.

Author Note At the time I do not know the purpose of the meeting was. But over time I realized now that we were to learn and support each other in a story of understanding to get insight into each others perception on certain subjects.

3-23-14 *Poem* Seeker
As days go on and seconds turns to minutes, hours,
I progress my abilities.
Each day getting more and

more vivid then the last.
I see visions of people before I see them in person.
As if some outside force is guiding me,
telling me to go talk to them.
Collecting people and forming a group,
I am a string that attaches to all
these people I have met joining everyone together.
I can see the connections and correlations.
I must admit, I see things most do not.
That is my purpose to seek out and find them all.
Make them aware of what they are capable of.
Influencing as many as I can day by day.
I welcome more visions so I can find the rest
So I can create the most beautiful
and intricate group,
Anyone has ever laid eyes upon.
I am the Seeker!

3-23-14
Every passing Minute is a chance to turn it all
around.

3-26-14
I had a dream that I was Hercules and I had lost
my kidney. Someone had stolen it. I believe it was a
female god. The next day I was uploading a video on
youtube for work. I saw the trailer for a new movie
Hercules and the intro had a hidden message about
being a warrior which I believe was directed towards
me. The message is that It is my time to shine the light
for others. To see how powerful we all are. By me
owning my own power fully and displaying it to
others for them to see it is okay to come out of hiding.

No longer having to be afraid of judgment and of fears. Pushing past these obstacles into the next stage of our evolution.

4-2-14

Lately I have been feeling drained. I feel this hidden aggression building. The one that happens when I am in an area where the energy is strange or negative. It happens while I am at work due to all the drama between the owners of the business and the agents. The owners have been getting very greedy and it is seeping into everyones morale while working.

4-3-14

My dream last night was of a friend named Vanessa. She was running from a male and a female but they were slightly humanoid. We were running room to room and I had a bb gun to combat them. It was at the point I shot the gun I woke up.

Authors Note: I realize this was a test as the dreams are the training grounds to solidify beliefs.

4-4-14

Today I meditated for 12 minutes on my solar plexus chakra. Upon doing so I saw visions again. One was of a tattoo on the right arm. It looked like a chubby stick figure.

4-6-14

I think I am becoming the being I was destined to be in this lifetime. My daily life is becoming more and more of what makes me happy. I absolutely love my body and self and I aspire to fine tune it further for the purpose I set. I love everyone and give as much as I can to those who seek to better themselves.

4-7-14

Today it has officially been 1 month since I am Vegetarian. I am proud of my self and proud to have the will power to push forward. Thus building a solid foundation to work from.

Authors Note: Find out your why to be a vegetarian if you decide it. By utilizing it as another tool in expansion towards greatness you will build your will power.

4-8-14

When was the last time you did something for the first time?

4-9-14

For too long and too often I see people saying they want to do something or they want to change something or make some impact. But they never do anything.
For the most part it is only mindless dribble and all talk and no walk. I realize the reason this happens is because a few factors. One of which is laziness, which is an off shoot of fear. The next comes the lack of motivation and then comes the "how?"

I myself am guilty of saying I have wanted to do things but never followed through. But that's changing in my life now. Because I know now that the only way I can make an impact in people and their lives is to first change my self and love my self.

When you finally come to terms that you do not love your self the way you have wanted to. You will then begin finding the reasons why and in this you can begin working on those issues to fix all of the "wrongs" that have been affecting you in your current life. You will begin working on your self until the point you realize, wow. I love my self because the reason I did not was simply because I forgot how to.

4-11-14
I am thankful for the love in my life.
I am thankful for the friends I have.
I am thankful for the opportunities I have.
I am thankful for the pets I have.
I am thankful for my apartment.
I am thankful for the air I breathe.
I am one with you, I am that I am
I love you for being you and guiding me.
Thank you for giving me this life.

He was a man of many talents. He saw the world in ways many did not, he conveyed them through actions and always loved those around him.

The Ayahuasca Experience and More

4-26-2014

Ayahausca Ceremony

We all sat In our places meditating on what is to come giving prayers and intentions of what we would like to receive.

I left mine open I wanted to feel what ever grand mother wanted to show me.

We all took our first drink, the taste was quite gross. We took a mouthful of tea to get the taste out of our mouths, then spat it out because you are not to drink during the ceremony. Sitting in lotus my mind starts to create fear. But I know it is not real. It was saying how what I was drinking is poison and I will die to spit it out or this will end badly. I told my self, if I am to die here today then it was to be and pushed on.

As I began to see patterns I know I have felt all of this already lovingness all around. I begin having my first vision I was taken into a blue area

Where my true self was talking to me telling me there isn't much time with it. It told me that I need to support as many people as I possibly can. That I have to go out of my way to help those who want it. Then the vision left. I began feeling my self again. Next comes another round of healing juice. I am barely able to keep it down. But I manage at this time my body wanted to purge. Many times but I told it not to just yet.

I imagined an Energy going inside of me and pushing it down into the belly. With this method I was able to keep it down for quite awhile. I began feeling euphoric, then suddenly I purged it all. I said thank you in my mind for the release. I began to feel euphoric again then I was vibrating all over the body. I literally felt one with everything. A musician began to play on his guitar and sings. After awhile I feel I wanted to contribute so I began to sing. I sang 2 songs. It made me feel free because when I sang I was everyone and I was able to express with my body every word to the fullest.

It was truly a beautiful moment in my life. Thank you, I Love you!

Poems from Ayahausca
- Traveling into the darkness

Not knowing what or where it will take me
I know I am to go with the flow

Having the voice of my self letting me know
what I am to do Helping and guiding
I often knew this was my purpose but I would toss
it aside

Now I know I can no longer
Everyone I meet I promise to
support them in some way
For without them I would be nothing. I love you.

4-28-2014

I have recently been engaged in a very beautiful interaction with a woman. We met last week, at a little gathering a mutual friend held. Funny because I went at about 7pm but couldn't find the place due to not having my phone working. So I gave up and went to the kava bar to do some work. I kept having the feeling that I was to go back but I didn't. Time passed it is now 9:30 pm and a female friend of mine asked why I was not there. So I decided to go again. This time I found it and met a few people just saying Hello. Nothing more, the girl I have been spending time with was among them.

But I saw nothing in her initially. We ended up going to another persons home. I hung out in the hammock and played with the fire at times. People started leaving and wanting to go to the beach. As everyone was leaving we spoke again and I mentioned I wanted to have my own house with a huge garden. She mentioned she loved animals and I mentioned my fennec fox Lily. We talked for about 5 minutes. She was beautiful, but I still saw nothing yet. I ended up going home and slept. Forgetting about her. Woke up the next morning and went about my day then I looked at my facebook to see she had friend requested me.

I thought how interesting a woman chasing me for once? Did I make a good impression, I thought. So we talked for awhile on Facebook. Then we set a time to hang out and we decided on my favorite place...the kava bar. We had some interesting talks, I began to feel a connection to her. We went to a meditation meeting together and after we went to my place and we talked for awhile about different topics. Then for some reason I decided I wanted to meditate with her. But this was unique because I had a specific meditation I wanted to do with her which came to me in this moment. You sit in front of each other and have your knees touching your left hand is under hers and your right hand is above hers. Creating a circuit of each others energy.

Now you both envision both of your energy circulating in the middle passing one hand to the other creating a cauldron of energy mixing. Do this for 10 to 15 minutes. Next stop the circulation of both energies as they are now mixed. Next envision cutting it in half and both parties take a half. Pull it into you, you will feel a new surge of energy you have never felt before. The next few days you may feel disoriented and possibly drained. This Is because you have taken on the transmutation of their energy. During this time the energy will experience everything you do. Now 7 days after do the same meditation. But instead only pull back your own energy into you. You will now have felt everything the other half felt in this time. With this practice you will both form a bond like no other. Keep this practice up and notice the entire dynamic of your relationship change.

5-9-14

Today I have been feeling rather drained. When I did reiki yesterday my Master said I was not aligned and I felt this. So today I meditated and gathered my energies back. I realize I have to heal my self now everyday for 21 days to get back to my prior self and this happened, I think another factor is I recently met a new women. She may be drawing energy from me and this may be why. But I am helping her with her own issues as well so the energy is not being wasted on an unconscious mind. I am ok with this. But I know I have to be more aware of this and have a healthy balance of giving and receiving. It is so easy to get lost in the giving aspect, something I will work on. The best way to gather your self again is the following.

Meditate and stare at your self in the mirror. Imagine all the energy you have given away willing or unwillingly and see it all being given back to you. After this as you look at your self say the following. I am love, I am light, I am peace, I am joy, I am abundance, I am abundant. I am here to help everyone who shows they would like it. I love the body I chose, I love you, I am grateful for the ability to have these experiences.
Thank you.

Poem
Lost & Found
Lost in each other losing touch of the outside world
    Realizing we are lost lovers that have found each other again.
Our energy joins one another and heals the other, To Heal the battle wounds of past experiences.
Once we are healed with each others energy do we move on or will we stay together to experience
    Each others physical body, mind and soul.

46

Big moments will still be coming. We can share our bubbles with each other and be equals feeling the same.

For we are the lost but now we are the found. I am here and there feeling each others wholeness.

Do you feel this same way?

5-12-2014

Today marks the end of the short lived relationship with the women from the gathering. I feel I was her anchor to this world. She had alot of issues going on in her life.

She had custody issues with her children. Issues with her ex, all in all I feel I brought her back onto the path. We had an amazing connection. We were both so similar and at times I would get lost in her eyes. I knew her before. The only thing she had issues with was my pets. My fox is not paper trained and can never be 100% so she tends to poo where she wants, but that was the reason of the departure. I was doing my best to be as clean as possible. I cleaned every day, and have incense. But she just couldn't deal. I learned from a past relationship to never give up my animals or who I am for someone if they cannot love me for me, it is just not ment to be. But our chemistry was amazing. I hope I rubbed off on her some so she can better her self.

Now on to the next matter at hand. During my time with her when ever she slept over I would have intense vivid dreams of another women. This women is a yoga instructor of mine which prior to this women

47

torpedoing into my life. I had been doing a slow dance with. I had that first meeting with her many months back and saw her as a white diamond during a 1 on 1 yoga session. One of the conversations her and I had in the dream world she was telling me she disliked cold water because of a past experience she had. I was telling her about my issues as well. Every time I woke up I would look over at this other women and I would question why I am with her and not the yoga teacher. But still I gave my full love to her. If I am going to be with someone I give them my all.

So I also remember my inner self before this fell apart telling me to begin pulling back. It is so interesting the way our minds are. I think those dreams were telling me I have to pursue her and continue this slow dance I started. Everything is the way it is and I accept t. I know things are being worked in the back ground for my own experiences. I love you for allowing me all of this knowledge and understanding to not lose my self in the emotions of attachment. For misery accompanies attachment. Thank you.

Attachment is the great fabricator of illusions, reality can be obtained only by someone who is detailed. The wise are so totally detached. Pain is for those who are attached.

5-14-2014
I have been reading a book called "Astral Travel" by Gavin and Yovonne Frost. In it they describe a technique to travel where you see your self rising out of your body like steam. I did this and came close to

exiting myself. But alas I have not yet. It is an ultimate goal to Astral Travel, I know when I am ready it will happen.

5-18-2014

Last night I went to a friends birthday gathering at a hotel. It is funny how when you are in alignment you come across like minded people everywhere you go. There were 2 people at the party that were aware of themselves. I realize now I am a connector of people to let them know there are many of us. To not feel helpless and alone. I am a healer, these souls put on my path are for me to assist in their own journey while at the same time they give me constant reminders That I am to stay on this path to help them. I learn from their points of view and they from mine. Our journey is an interesting one filled with constant reminders. Thank you for putting them on my path. I love you.

Author Note: I used to truly believe I healed others, but now I realize it is only our light that inspires others to heal themselves.

5-18-14
I went to an impromptu meditation gathering for world peace. In it there was a Qi gong instructor. This instructor when I looked at her from a certain angle I saw her hands were dark green on both hands. It was funny to see that because I had never seen anything like that before.

5-23-14
So today upon taking my fox Lily to the beach she

got too nervous and had a seizure and I got very worried she laid there limp in my hands. I wondered how I could be without her. She has made such an impression on me and has helped me through a lot. She was blind for about 2 hours. But she is ok now. I love you Lily.

5-25-14

So before I go into my dream. Last night was fun I went to the Hard Rock Casino and never have I gone to a place so full of distractions with an aware mind. It was fun seeing people immersed in their world of make believe. On several occasions I locked eye contact with people who I knew were aware as well. When we locked eyes we both would nod at each other. I hung out with the ever beautiful yoga instructor at her job as I read and waited for her to get off. This was the first time I was able to have alone time with her. I wonder if she feels that connection as well. She is so hidden and afraid of being hurt because of a past lover. So her feelings are well hidden, as with mine I am no longer afraid of being hurt because I know if it does happen, I required that experience to better my self.

But in any case we had some amazing conversations. At times I would get lost in her eyes as she would talk and I would notice a white figure in them. It was pretty awesome. So on to my dream. I had 2 dreams that I remember. The first was about a friend and she was dating this guy. They were so happy together. In the dream I was only an observer. They went to a club and the girl began making out with another man. The boyfriend saw this and turned and looked at me, the camera and said "So this is love to you??" He then left the club and the scene turned to her crying on the dance floor at which was when I woke up.

The next dream I was a vampire of some sort and I rented a hotel. In this hotel the owners were framing me and messing with me trying to get me kicked out. I was fighting with a female owner and went outside then I just said it isn't worth it and I flew away.

Switching back to the hard rock last night. After hanging out with the Yoga Teacher I went to play poker and black jack. But I would observe everyone and how the tables energy was. If I didn't like it I moved to the next. In poker I only had to play 2 hands and doubled my money. I then left and did the same with black jack tables. But I only played one hand with the double amount I won at poker and I knew this was the table. I got an Ace and a 9. I doubled that and now I had tripled my money. I then left to go home happy for the earnings and my time spent with an amazing and beautiful women.

Tools of Awareness
When you are out and about keep an upright and proper posture. Spine erect. This makes you aware of your body and places your attention in the moment. It also aligns the chakra system perfectly along your spine to receive any messages you are to receive.

Provided you learn from your mistakes
Provided you leave them behind
You surely are progressing.
-Yvonne Frost

Meditation
Place your self in many areas where you will have
many distractions. Train your mind to be still and find
peace within these places.

5-27-14
Song
It's just another magic moment and I know by now
you probably should've seen
   The things I see in you , reflecting back to me.
   Because I know right now
   Every time I look at you and every time I see your
eyes
   I share that magic moment

   I know right now You should've somehow felt the
things I do between you and I.
   But I just can't, I can't read you

   I am just assuming now, but I know what
   Yes I know what I feel, and It's just another magic
Moment.

   It's just another magic moment.
   Shared between you and I as we stare eye to eye
   I look into your soul and I can see you there

You're so afraid of letting go, afraid of what can be
and I know by now, you should've somehow
Shared this magic moment
You gotta share this magic moment

So come and share it with me, so you can be here
with me
and I will be, with my arms open comforting you.
Because it's just another magic moment.

Sensory Deprivation and Breath

5-28-14

Today I did a sensory deprivation tank. I was in for an hour and a half. This was my one of many. For the first 20-30 minutes I believe my mind was throwing all of my fears at me because it did not want to let go. The first was that a shark was going to eat me. It's truly amazing how the mind doesn't want to let you go. I had to bargain with the ego and say that if it allowed me to get over this fear of the shark, I would have a glass of wine. It then moved on. After I got over that It then threw Freddy Krugar at me as a last resort. Which is funny because I am not even afraid of that. After this final attempt it allowed me to experience the true wonder. I began losing sensation in my arms, legs and body little by little. Until the point I was nothing.

I saw my usual blue blob that would begin to get bigger. Then I began seeings images of people I've never met but I am soon to. The next image was a meeting of some sort, it was a long table with people facing me. I realize upon further focus it seemed to be The Last Supper with Jesus. I am not religious as you may now. Which is why it seemed odd. I felt part of it somehow. I deeply wanted to have my out of body experience but it didn't come, however I felt a deep pressure where my crown and third eye are. At some points it felt like I was going to experience an out of body, from the anus…Yes it seems funny to say that but I felt like that was one possible exit or possibly it was my root chakra opening as was my crown and third eye.

Then I heard the knock that my session was over. It all went so fast after the fears went away. I will say if you have deep hidden fears this tank will amplify them until you break free of them. For me I compromised with it. I said alright, if you allow me to experience more of my self and release the fear. I will satisfy one of your bodily desires. You have to understand that your body and your soul / awareness are two different things. So you have to have a balance between the two. I see the body as an animal that the soul inhabits as a pilot and learns to in a way control it but the body has desires too, that must be satisfied at times. But since I did not have an out of body I only gave it half of what it was I promised it. Would be best if they named these tanks to "Face your fears tank". All in all it was an experience to have I would recommend it to anyone that wants to learn about the inner workings of their minds and face the fears that pop up. I know you can do it, because I did and I am no one special. Do it!

Lastly upon exiting it was a huge rush getting control of all of your senses again.

5-30-14
Poem
Dreams so powerful they make me move through the night at times I wake up and hold the pillow tight
    With tears from my eyes, that I rub away gently as

55

I rise from my bed in the night
For those vivid dreams they do come having to get
up and replenish my self
With the water of life so that I can venture off
To dream land again, what oh what will they have
in store for me next
When I close thine eyes and rest my weary head
Some of these dreams so powerful and strong for I
know they have meaning
If not then I am wrong
But I know I am shown truth in each dilemma they
show
Now it's time to go back to sleep and slumber once
more.

I had to write this poem out because of the dream I
had tonight. It was something to do with this very
Powerful being that I had to fight. I won and he
had to leave the mountains where we fought. As he
left the last image
I had was of the being zip lined down the
mountain. I awoke crying and I was not sure why.
Maybe this was me letting go of something.

6-2-14

Your existence here is but a blink of an eye. This
illusion, Although persistent, is just that, an illusion.
There is no evil. There is no good. There is just
you, not your chemical body, but you your
consciousness, your mind. Everything and
Everyone, it's just you. Made by you, for you. You
are the creator, the only creator and you can do no

wrong.

So bask in your Holiness, for you are immortal. Your chemical vessel, that thing you call a body may and will die.

But you are immortal, eternal. So do as thine will by the whole of the law. The law of one, that you are everything that has or will ever be,

And there will be no judgment for your deeds, except that which you give your self.

Serve your self or serve your other self, it is always your choice for you are god, and I love you, always have and always will.

6-5-14

Today I did a shamanic breath workshop. I drove 2 friends to the place. I was not sure what to expect so as always I ventured with an open mind.

They taught us the breath, it was a very basic breath and in my mind I said "How is this going to do anything?" About 10 minutes into it I began feeling tingly

and vibration starting from my feet and working its way up my body until my whole body was vibrating and pulsating. This was an amazing feeling I have never

felt in this capacity. Next my body began tensing up, my feet stiffened.

My fingers contorted and my mouth locked into place. I began feeling and releasing all of my pain I have ever stored away and then let go. I began crying uncontrollably and my body began shaking and

initially was supposed to go to the archery range. But obviously I would rather hang out with her. Some side note: I find it interesting that a few times coming to yoga her and I would wear a black top and white pants, and she would wear a white top and black pants. This happened on a few occasions and she even commented on it on occasion that it was funny because it's like we were the yin and yang. In any case that had to be said for the following to make sense.

We decided to do an aura photo, I went first. The woman was very nice and my photo came out that I have a very huge crown, third eye, throat and heart. She was telling me I had to work on my sacral as it was white rather then orange and my root was a tiny red dot. She stated that even though I see things many are not able to see that I am still anchored and living on earth and rather then flying high all the time. I had to begin working on those areas. She also said that I have the Angel Chamuel protecting and watching over me. Next the yoga teacher went in and hers looked like the total opposite of mine.

The lady did not see us together when we walked into the studio. But asked her how she met me or knew me. She said to her that her and I are supposed to be in each others path. When I analyzed the photos I thought how funny because it was like the yin and yang. Completing each other through the chakras and teaching what the other did not know. Also the fact that I am generally a quiet person, but she is very outspoken.

Next we did a rune reading and a Rorschach blot reading. I went first, the main subject was that I have a new job and a new upcoming love. All of this I find interesting and I laugh internally. The next thing was that my angels were setting up the perfect person for me and that it would be a long lasting one. That I should not worry and my business will be taking off even more then it already is. Next hers was up, she said hers was that she will be having some hard times soon, but that in the next year she would be married or engaged in a persons meaningful relationship. Also that she should practice tantra. I laughed at this because I had been reading about tantra and I had a longing for practicing it with someone who was willing.

I know I may be creating a lot of things in my mind but the coincidences kept piling up and I know she is to be in my life somehow. It isn't even a normal thing I love everyone but something in her is drawing me to her. When they said the angels are working on something for me. I looked back at the dreams I had awhile back and wondered if that was them imprinting her in my dreams or if it was my own intuition telling me I must pursue her. Over all I had an amazing time at this mini festival and I thank you for giving me this experience. I Love You.

6-8-14
So over the weekend I went to the psychic fair. They were pretty accurate as far as that goes in my previous entry. I decided to buy a necklace that was a selenite and aquamarine. I also bought a larger selenite

stick. Prior to going to sleep I placed that stick to the right of my bed on my nightstand. I also left my necklace on before bed. Before getting comfy for bed I began to hear a ringing in my right ear. Which funny enough was where the selenite stick was. Normally when I hear ringing I hear it on my left ear. I thought nothing of this and went to sleep.

At about 3:40 am I was awoken to a loud whisper in my right ear and it was saying my name. "David, David, David!!" I woke up and as soon as I did the voice then said "Get your gun, they're coming to kill you". I was startled and I looked around my room. This was not a normal voice like my self talking in my mind. It was a completely different voice and female. I closed my eyes and envisioned white light expanding out wards from me to cover my entire room. This happened instinctively. I then said out loud "If you are a negative entity you are not welcome here". I also began remembering I used to be able to hear similar things when I was younger but I chose to forget it. It is funny how the moment I got these crystals this happened. I saw a black shadowy figure outside of my windows and I placed my hand facing it and envisioned a white light expanding out from my hand and dispersing the figure. It disappeared.

I began talking to others about this experience and they say it could be two things. I have been expanding my light and consciousness so much that negative entities see it like moths to a flame. They want it because they are not able to generate it. So they gather your light by instilling fear within you and then they feed off that. Or it could have indeed been a warning of a potential reality that may come. I also wanted to mention upon talks with some like minded people. Since I am a Taurus, an earth sign. I could connect with stones and crystals much easier then others that are not of that sign. I welcome more of it only if it serves my higher self and the purpose I chose here. Thank you.

The Metatrons Cube Theory

6-13-14

So an interesting thing happened today. I met with a person I met from a workshop. He was selling intention necklaces. But the profound thing about the whole meeting was a dream I had. Where an alien had taken me to a dome city and in the middle of this dome was a huge tower elevator with a platform at the top. When I was on top the tall grey alien began explaining the following. This dome around the city only allowed conscious and aware members of society to enter into it. It hit play on some device for the dream and it showed millions of people in all directions migrating to the dome.

However what I witnessed was families being torn apart because only the conscious members were allowed to enter. I then fast forwarded time and I saw all the people who were suppose to be inside go in one by one. The next thing that happened was the most disturbing. I began seeing bright mushroom clouds being ignited in all directions. Once all the dust settled the only thing that was left was ash, rock and the dome city. This was in all directions. I know what you may be thinking...He is just rehashing the Steven King book "Under the Dome". I had this dream before I had even heard about that book or the TV show. But it did inspire me to watch it after I had this dream. Now after I explained this to the guy he began telling me too has seen a city or area under a dome with a tower in the middle. He began telling me he wanted to find a way to build this. At first I laughed but I allowed my self to hear it and absorb it.

Immediately a surge of information came to me as he was speaking. What if a certain sacred geometry of the Metatrons Cube was actually a blue print to positioning of people to mediate in a way where the lines connect is the direction that the mediators will push energy to one another. Not only this but the positioning varies based on their astrological signs. I.E Their elements of Earth, Wind, Water, Fire, Sound(Would be a musician or singer), and Love/Light (Would be a couple that is in True Unconditional Love). I feel strongly that it would be my self and another that would be in unconditional love, however I am sure it is open to anyone who has truly mastered this aspect of love it self. You would have to have a male and female for each element.

The females are in the center ring, and males on the outer ring corresponding to their element. I believe each symbol has an individual intention and if all is setup properly they have the potential to allow the anchor body mediators to manifest physical objects instantly based on an idea or thought. This meditation would create a energetic sphere around the surrounding area. The residents inside would begin to notice immediate self awareness. The diameter of the sphere would be roughly 3 miles around the surrounding area.

Please refer to the image below of the Metatrons Cube.

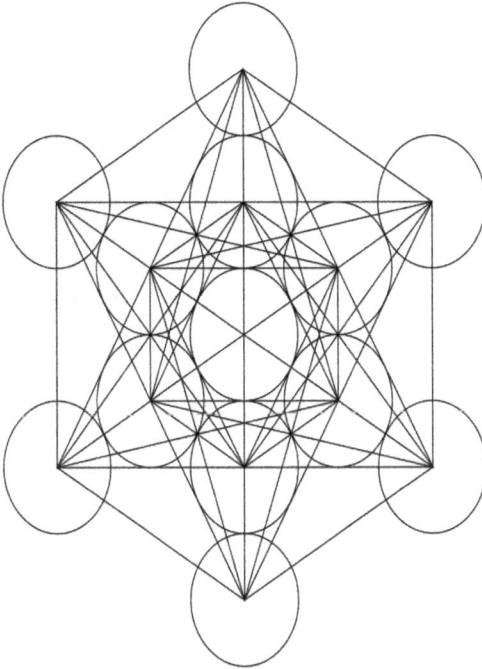

Each Circle represents a person. The center circle would either be a person whom has emotional mastery and can direct all the collected energy towards a set thing to manifest or a catalyst like a container of water that can hold the vibration for all to drink or allow the object to appear out of the water.

If this is true the tree of life may have an ability to create a real life form. Of course all of this is only an idea that surged through my mind as emerging inspiration. But hey I just want this idea to float around. I think I will experiment with this idea once I create the opportunity for it. I just have to find willing and open minded people to do so.

6-14-14

Today I went to a manifesting workshop. I understand the fundamentals of manifesting. However a newer question arose. If when we decide to manifest and that experience does not change, does this mean that this experience is not to be changed because it is a lesson to be learned still? It is to say does a lesson or experience trump the changing of your vibration or willful manifesting of something different? Or is it not changed due to yourself still not grasping the fundamentals of manifesting. I ask this because there are many people in my life that say they want to change something but still do nothing and keep repeating their cycle over and over.

6-15-14

I had a 45 minute third eye meditation today in which I began to see a glittery slipper. It was very clear but went away quickly. I laughed and thought "Hah, Cinderella's Shoe?". Next I saw a red dot above a yellow dot, This too went away quickly. It is maybe that I have to work on those two chakras. For the rest of the meditation I saw my usual blue orb pulsating and vibrating.

6-19-14

My dream last night was that of a video game. The only way to progress through the levels was to die. In this dream I met a lot of old ex girlfriends of mine and old friends. I must have died at least 50 times in the dream. I began analyzing it and it seemed like real life where I would just reincarnate until I progress to the next stage of my evolution.

Later in the day, I also did my first vinyasa flow

yoga. It was very energetic, I feel amazing learning a new tool for healing my self and allowing my own growth.

6-21 & 22 - 14

This weekend I went to a summer solstice camping trip. I arrived on Friday and setup my tent. I met with the property owner. We had been planing on doing permaculture to the land. So we were preparing. We did a meditation and then decided to get some sleep for a solstice sunrise with a cacao & coconut milk ceremony. We blessed the drink. It was actually pretty good, I never tasted it before. After this we did ashtanga yoga for a good hour. We then did some archery in the back yard. Shortly after people started arriving to help with the permaculture. I had an attraction to one of the women there. She was a yoga teacher, yeah yeah Apparently I have a thing for yoga teachers. Can ya blame me? Yoga pants…I began noticing my mind creating unhealthy scenarios where I would be with her in random locations sexually and I became attached to the idea of being with her on an intimate level. There was just something about her that had a strong sexual energy.

So in turn the universe was testing me on attachment and this is how. A group of people came and of this group was a guy who was very in shape and took charge. He lead the group to get the permaculture completed. He was actually very good at motivating everyone. I saw the girl I was interested in began taking interest of course and in turn jealously kicked in. All because I became attached to an idea of how it ought to be. In any case my mind began creating all these scenarios of seeing her having sex with him. This day was a real test for me. They both left for an errand together and more scenarios played out in my mind. When they got back I was still in this attachment. They wanted to cut down a tree and in order to do so I had to move my tent. So the guy offered to help me. As he did, he broke my tent and it further made me angry and annoyed. I laugh at how I am creating all of this for my self internally.

It was this moment when I stepped back and said to my self. Wow you are not present right now. Let go of that attachment. For he is you and you are him. In essence I am his experience regardless of what happens, meaning if he experiences her, then I too have already experienced her. I went into a warehouse and meditated on this because I did not enjoy the feeling. After such I gave up the attachment and let go. My demeanor completely changed back to my normal state. The mind is so damn sneaky and constantly wants to test you.

So as time passed more and more people arrived we all began gathering around the camp fire. With drums playing, guitars strumming, people dancing. It was quite an amazing time. Observing all of these like minded people all together to share a space with love. Next we gathered in the warehouse and did a metatrons cube meditation, similar to the one I envisioned which I guided, with extra people on the outer rings. It was super powerful but still did not have all the proper components I feel. We then all took mushrooms, After such we broke up into small groups. I began observing the structure of everyone to see where everyone went. After watching for awhile I began feeling the rush of energy flowing through me from the mushrooms.

I decided I wanted to do reiki on some people. I practiced on a gentlemen as he was laying flat on his back while he was listening to someone play on the sound bowls. As I was practicing on him I felt his body's energy pulsate and contract at a very rapid rate. I then moved on to a friend and it went well except she had a block in her throat chakra. After this I went outside while feeling all the earth pulsate and vibrate with me. I went to the camp fire and grabbed a seat and just observed everyone in their moments. I then overheard someone talking about an out of body experience and I had to be a part of this conversation. It was with 2 girls and 1 guy which I had met them except for one of the girls there.

In any case the one I never met was explaining that she had just had an out of body experience and she did not even take any mushrooms. The guy had done a massage exercise with her and she had zoomed out. She did not want to return to her body and he had to keep calling her name for her to return. There was something interesting I thought about her. Then I took a step back and the intention I had prior to taking the mushrooms was to be able to find someone I can grow further with spiritually in any time frame. I laughed internally because this only happened after I let go of the previous attachment. We began doing many meditations and energy transfers. To many to detail but the main ones were We had created a triangle with myself and the 2 girls, the guy had left.

We each chose a color for an orb and began rotating it from our joined hands from the right to the left. The next one was just me and the girl. We did an eye stare meditation and I saw a white halo around her. Her hair was a radiant gold. I then saw her as a 1950's or 1960's cigarette girl with a feather in her hair. She then told me she had seen me as a 50's gangster in a suit.

We knew each other from a previous life. From this moment we could not let our hands go or have some part of our bodies not touching. It felt as if the energy was one and I had never felt this before. At one point I took my hand off hers and she grabbed and put it back where it was. We then began playing with this energy as we felt the oneness. We would separate our body because we were touching at our shoulders at this point looking up at the stars. I was still tripping on the mushrooms. As we would separate I visually saw two energies being pulled away then when one moved our shoulders together again it would join and be one. We never kissed or anything but that feeling was a very intense and loving one being shared. At one point in my visuals while we were touching I saw the DNA sequence but in between each strain was a color of the chakra. I want to have an artist create this.

6-24-14
Today I taught my first class to people ever. It was

71

by "chance" the yoga teacher couldn't make it and said for her to teach because I have taken her classes nearly every week for a long while. I mentioned I would teach meditation, but I had never taught it. So this was literally the universe saying Hey! It's time to start teaching what you know. I went over 3 tools of awareness.

The first was the camera method or observer method. The second was the phrases and affirmations, and the third was the touch and sensation. The meditations I did was the "I am that I am" Mantra. Followed by an energy recall meditation. There was 12 students that showed up.

It was such an amazing feeling to be able to teach to others. I felt complete in my self when I was doing it. At first nervous but then things just flowed. I have been given the go ahead to do more classes every Wednesday at 7pm.

What are you?
In this day and age, we often lose sight of what really matters the most in life. Due to all of the outside distractions that are constantly bombarding us from all angles, including but not limited to our own personal dialog that manifests in our thoughts. The negative media, advertisements, society, pressures from work, relationships.

We often lose ourselves and forget what it was we truly wanted in the first place. But once you push all of that aside. What is left? You realize all this time you were being something you are not and that is when you become self aware. Peaceful, loving and always caring about others. That is who you are. Be the change you want to see in life. The time is now to show the world how resilient we really are.

6-29-14

I am currently reading the book "The Teachings of Don Juan" in it on page 105 it mentions experience with peyote. It mentioned that the plant teacher truly accepts you when it appears to you as a man or as a bright white light. I then recalled my experience when I did peyote and remembered I saw a bright white light.

It was so beautiful and it brought me back to that moment just a few short months ago. This is so amazing seeing and reading things as confirmation on what I have experienced.

7-2-14

I had my second class of teaching today. I did an exercise involving balloons and putting in each one a written dream of what the person wants to create. I will go more in depth in this at a later point or another book to teach the meditations I have created. After this we went upstairs and did 2 meditations. The first I guided to visualize being inside of a balloon being tethered and held down by multiple strings of fear and other limitations. Once freed the balloon floated into space towards a bright white light while watching everyone dance and be happy within this balloon.

The second meditation I partnered them up with someone they didn't know and they did a shared meditation and sharing each others dreams. The feed back I received from them was amazing. At the end of the class I instructed them to burn the paper where their dream was written on so they can manifest in their reality.

7-4-14

Today I awoke around 9:20 am to tend to my plants. I went back to sleep for a few but my fox insisted on pouncing on me in the bed and making me get up. She is my alarm clock for when I hit my snooze button…I have been sleeping with a selenite grid around my bed and an amethyst in my hand. So last night I saw two very clear images. But they did not last long. The first was an image of a huge house.

It was beautiful and clear as me talking face to face with someone. I wanted to keep my awareness there but it went away once I became excited. Next I wanted to see it again but instead I felt as though I saw the inside of the house and the rooms were beautiful and colorful with amazing chairs and art on the wall. I went about my day and around 3pm I did an hour meditation with the amethyst on my forehead.

I saw a clear side view of a battle ship as the sun was setting in the back ground. Once I acknowledged that I saw it it went away. After this I saw the usual dark blue blob pulsating. I was putting thoughts out wanting to communicate with other indigo children just to see if anyone could hear me when I was in this state.

I will be going to my first tantra class tonight to see what they can teach me. I will share about it later.

Later that night my tantra class was over. The class was small it had 3 girls and 3 guys including me. The class began with us introducing ourselves and letting others know what our current thoughts are in our life. We then began an eye stare meditation. I was partnered with a friend of mine.

After this we all stood up and began staring at one another from afar. I thought it was rather strange but only because I never did this before so I felt very awkward in it. We got closer and hugged arms and began doing the same. I don't know why but it felt a little uncomfortable for me doing this. But eventually I gave in and began smiling back.

Next was a type of dance in the center, letting go of your self. I saw my friend and another person dance and it looked very freeing but if you were not of love and understanding it would look rather crazy to some. But I mean considering all the things I have been experiencing lately I can no longer really judge it. So I was last up with the organizer and I said I did not want to participate.

The reason being if you do not know me personally. You would know that I have a huge wall put up when it comes to dancing. I am talking like…I freeze and tense up. The only time I have been able to dance was when I was drunk or on a drug. It is not to say that I do not want to. I feel once I can freely express my self in this manner it would be a huge release for my self.

I would even go as far to say that if I could do this I would be completely free as the one true thing holding me back in this currently. That being said she grabbed me and we began spinning. The spinning turned immediately into a release for me and I began dancing. For the first time since high school when I got made fun of and walled up. Now I know I made a crack in the wall from this gesture. I felt it inside of me. After it was finished I thanked them all for allowing me to release in this way. It was a truly moving experience and I have grown a little more from it.

7-6-14

Today I did a sweat lodge for the first time. There was a small shelter built with pieces of wood tied together. It looked rather small. When I examined the hut, I then looked over at the amount of people. It appeared like we were about to shove a bunch of people into a clown car. They wrapped the shelter with blankets to store in the steam and the heat for the different stages of the ceremony.

We lined up in a circle around the fire outside. Each of us was given a little tobacco in our hand so that we could put an intention to the experience that we were about to receive. We then prayed to all 7 directions. North, East, South, West, Above, Below, and within. After one by one, starting with the women, threw the intentional tobacco into the fire so that what ever intention was set it would come to fruition.

After they threw the tobacco, they went to the entrance of the sweat lodge. Right at the entrance was a small shrine that had smoke coming from it. This was used to cleanse your body before entering. You were only allowed to enter into the shelter on your hands and knees. Prior to entering you had to kiss the earths ground and say "Aho".

I threw my tobacco into the fire with the intention of learning more about my position in this grand scheme of reality and how to better hone in on my abilities given to me. So that I could help others and they could use me as a tool for their own spiritual growth. I proceeded to cleanse my self with the smoke. I entered in on my hands and knees into the shelter. There was two rows of people, those in the center and those on the outer rim of the hut. In the center was a hole dug in so that these heated stones which they called "Grandpas" or "Abuelitos" and "Grandmas" or "Abuelitas". Then upon the stones would be water splashed onto it. The entrance was then closed and all we could see was the glowing red stones in the center. As I sat down in my spot, my mind began racing wanting to make me get out of the hut before its too late. My mind loves to play with me this way in many moments in my life where it did not want me to go because I would become more aware. I pressed on saying inside my mind that it had no power over me.

This rock family was assisting us in our journey of learning about ourselves. With each rock placed in the center, a prayer was said followed by the words "Aho".

There were 4 stages to the whole sweat lodge ceremony. 4 songs sung within each stage and an additional 7 heated rocks were placed in the center.

Thus increasing the overall heat. With a pause after the 2nd round for them to pass us water. As the first round progressed, the first 2 songs were sung and the coordinator began splashing water into the hot rocks. Increasing the heat in the hut. It was at this point my mind began to assault me with thoughts of passing out. I pressed on and I was holding onto my two crystals I brought with me. One was an amethyst and the other was a black tourmaline along with my necklace which was Selenite and Aquamarine. I began to focus on my stones and putting my love into them, thanking them for assisting me in this journey, I then kissed each one.

As the last song of the first round was completed. My heart began pulsating at a rapid rate, seemingly out of my chest. At some points the heat while breathing in seemed to be burning my nostrils. I calmly breathed in through the nose and out through the nose. I had made it past round one. Now comes the next 7 stones. It was at this phase where we let go of all our fears and stress as instructed by the organizer. As the first song started, I began focusing on my third eye and began seeing the usual blue pulsating blob that gets bigger the more I focus on it. Three songs in and the heat is so intense that my mind is chattering about asking why I am doing this, What do I have to prove. I told it I wanted to prove to my self I can push the boundaries of my own limits, or the limits that it believes it has set for me.

After the second round was completed the water was then passed around, by this point I am soaking wet from my own sweat. I feel the sweat on the ground and its cool and it was keeping me cool. My entire head is soaked and my shorts are soaked. I took a drink of water and passed it down. My mind begins to assault me again with questions. Why is it you continue to do this to your self, the door is right there it said. Why don't you just leave? No one will care it said. I pushed on not listening to this voice. Round 3 starts, it was in this round I had to begin focusing on all of the love of every single person in my life. The love of my animals, the love of my family, the love of past lovers, the love of everything around me and all the souls with me in that hut enduring the same thing. As I began thinking about each of these loves. The songs are being sung. I also let go of worrying about what others think of me. I am not sure why I have cared, but it is funny to see that it affected me. With this round I feel I have shed some of that layer.

I continue focusing on my third eye and with each thought of love, I feel a pulsating sensation coursing through my body, it felt like chills. A cooling sensation with each thought and name I thought of sending them love. As the last song was being sung of the third round. I can no longer breath through my nostrils, it feels as though they are burning from the inside out. I was forced to breath through my mouth. Very calm breaths, for if they were not calm, you would surly begin to panic from the heat and your mind would easily take a hold of you.

By this round several people had to leave the hut due to their body saying no more, or their minds getting the best of them. As the final round, the fourth, in came in an additional 7 rocks. A total of 28 rocks were now present in center. I had to call upon my higher self and anything else to assist me int his round. My mind had given up, I told my self If I am to die here, so be it. My life here is to learn and grow and assist others in their own growth. I know the universe has strong plans for me.

With this alone I knew I could finish it. As it began, I began to hear a voice. It was of my guide. Telling me it is here with me and that I am being watched by others and they are cheering me on to complete this. They are sending me cooling energy and love. I felt that energy so deeply in my core and being that it was sending me chills and was cooling me off even though it was ridiculously hot.

I was no longer in the hut mentally anymore. I was within my self and loving my self, along with this experience. I was in a state of total bliss. As the fourth round concluded. I said thank you for my guides in assisting me in this and I thanked my self, and my body. For enduring this exercise of will power. For I know it will further my growth in my meditations. The lodge was then over and we filed out on our hands and knees starting with the women first, then the men. I gave so much love and thanks to my self and those around me. I laid outside on my back on top of my yoga mat facing the sky at night. I was saying outloud thank you so much for this beautiful experience. Thank you for all you have given me thus far and furthering my growth. I Love You!

7-16-2014

Just in case no one has told you today. You are a beautiful light that shines upon the world for all to see shine that light.

7-17-14

I love you. Yeah you. The person reading this. I don't care what color skin you have, what sexuality you are, what past thing you have done. What future things you will do. I just love you as you are, in all of your wholeness and holiness.

7-18-14

Tonight my friend and I participated in a mushroom meditation. My friend took me through an attempt to have an out of body during it. He took me to an area where there was a garden and other beings. He guided me toward an area that had a core energy. It was spinning in a clockwise motion. It had all of the colors of the chakras starting from the bottom to the top. It had a shape of a snake in a way. After this meditation we did a candle meditation and as we stared into this flame. It began to take form of a female fire spirit. It was dancing and seemed to have a pink orange dress on. At times my friend and I would see it and it even laughed with us. At another point my friend and I did an eye stare meditation and in this we saw each others physical demons.

I mean his face literally changed to a demon and a sudden burst of fear filled the air. Later he and I both saw this demon in each other. We both thought we were going to kill each other that was how intense the feeling was. But once we both pushed past the fear the face we saw in each other began to smile. We learned everyone has this demon. It takes a strong will to keep it in check. We both laughed at what was seen after wards. Next at another point it felt as if the veil of reality peeled away where his face was.

As that veil opened I saw what seemed to look like a hologram superimposed on his face and it was that of a very muscular blue man with a fierce face that looked battle scarred. But it was a friendly and familiar face that I have seen in the past. My friend also saw a familiar face on mine. Conclusion is once you begin to take these medicines with intention love and awareness it begins to break down the veils we have over our eyes so we can begin to remember who we are.

7-20-14

I have been working with this girl I have known for a few months. She disclosed to me that she had auditory hallucinations. I told her this is a gift. That she does not yet know how to listen in properly. The voices are all negative to her. I took her to a crystal store for her to get 2 stones. One for protection and the other for what ever she felt called towards. From my experience entities gravitate to people who are in tune with source, but do not protect them selves until they learn how to use it properly. Once she got these stones and I performed reiki on her she told me the voices had died down alot and she is not as stressed about it all. She called me an Angel.

7-24-14

Lately I have begun to feel tingling sensations on my back between where my shoulder blades are. It feels as if there are wings coming out when I focus on it. I can even feel the wind on the area where I think they are.

7-31-14

Ok how do I put this. There are those among you who have these extra sensory gifts but since you do not know how to use it properly. You get the negative aspects of them. You believe you may be going crazy. You are not. These are tools for you to use and learn to cultivate into something beautiful. The people in those "crazy wards" are not actually crazy. I feel they just did not have the proper guidance and teachings so they can fully understand what gifts were offered to them when they arrived. Do not be fearful of what you are or the gifts given to you. They are your defining character. We must learn to cultivate these "illnesses" that doctors call them. They do not understand, they are looking at things from a scientific and physical point of view.

8-3-14 Today I completed 108 Sun Salutations for charity, what a challenge that was. My body feels so sore but empowered!

8-5-14

Last night I was awoken by a tugging on my arms and them pulling me to my left side. It felt like someone grabbed me and did this. I proceeded with my day and put on a shirt, then headed to yoga. I told this story to my friend and she pointed at my shirt because I showed her physically how it felt. When I looked down at my shirt I was wearing a led zeppelin shirt. The one that has the angel with wings reaching up. These syncronicities have been happening a lot lately sending me clues to who I am. That I am quite possibly an angel. That I also have wings that I feel. I feel everyone has these. But it sounds so silly to think that possibility. But the people in my life keep hinting at it because of the information I have been passing on to them to accelerate their growth.

8-12-14

What is sex to you? Is it merely a physical encounter to feel another persons warmth? Is it an escape from your mind because within your own experience you have not learned how to escape thought yet? Is it a way for you to bury things and emotions in to another person because you are unsure on how to deal with them just yet? Or a way for you to attain growth and spiritual practice?

It can be all of these and has been all of these things for me. It came in stages. The first stage was I merely wanted to have sex because of the physical aspect of it because yeah it feels amazing. But that was when I had my eyes closed to our abilities and our mind.

Once you awaken from this dream you begin to see how ridiculously amazing sex can be as a tool for both of the parties to grow spiritually with. Now on this note let me first say that is not a reason to jump into things with others because of this.

Sex is the fastest way to transfer your energy to another partner. What I mean by this is when you decide to embark on this journey with another person you must first realize that you are giving an aspect of your self to that person and it stays with them.

Example: If the person you are engaging in is very motivated and outgoing, upon completion of the act. You now have taken on an aspect of this into your self. Now on the downside if the person you are engaging in is having internal conflict and dialog in their mind that is creating a story based out of fear, anger, greed or lust. Then you will begin to exhibit these same tendencies on a smaller scale then what they are personally going through.

Now lets think about this, the reason this is and again this is all my opinion. When two souls decide to join they are joining together to form one union. That is why the energies begin to intertwine with each other. So when you engage in this it is your job as the receiver to transmute this energy into a positive one because the partner could not so you can then create a safe space for your partner to do the same.

What I have learned so far is that once you awaken and decided to have sex with a person and do not have any intention other then it being a physical thing. You are then being drained because the universe knows you are awake and is testing you to this experience. It is saying, so…are you awake? How about If I throw this one at you. It then puts people in your path to see how you engage with so if you make proper choice's and not think with just your physical body it will then reward you with more abilities and insights. On this same note if a person comes across your path and you just do it because you want the physical aspect of it without intention. Then it would punish in a way where you will feel a weakness in the body and not your full potentiality of what you were prior to the act. But there are ways of getting that energy back if you do feel drained. What you have to begin asking yourself is. Why was this person put into my path, why were things so rushed for that sexual energy transference. Was that person in need of my energy to better their growth and vice versa? Also begin to meditate more and do more spiritual practices to bring your self back to your prior energy.

Now for those who are holding out for that special person. This next part is for you. Once two parties whom are conscious to how powerful sex can be. These two partners can begin to unravel their own puzzle together. Sex is one way to attain full enlightenment. If both parties go into the arrangement with true love and spiritual growth. The outcome of said arrangement will be extraordinary, because now you have two parties who want to expand together and bounce off each other in energy to help one another.

With that understanding both parties can pull one another into the astral realm to assist each other in out of body experiences and beyond. As long as both parties are aware of how this can happen. This energy can then be utilized for growth. Rather than just having sex and saying So what was pretty good huh? You begin traveling with each other into uncharted realms of reality and the fact of the matter is you are now both co creating worlds together.

8-12-14

What do you strive for? Where is that drive that keeps you going wanting more to search and seek? Mine comes from the new faces I see. With each person I interact with I see adventure and excitement. A new journey into knowing a person, finding out what they have been through. What they want to attain and all the levels of sadness and love they have felt. I enjoy it because with each person I learn. I know they are me in different perspectives experiencing things from another angle. With each person going through their own individual challenge for their own growth, as they learn so do I. So it is this that drives me for when I support a person I am supporting my self and we both grow.

8-15-14

I am grateful for the people put fourth in my life to allow me to further grow. Thank you all of you who have been in my life to be reflections of my self. So I know what I am dealing with internally.

8-16-14

I did an hour guided meditation on opening treasure chests to find messages for your self. I will incorporate this into of one of my meditation classes I am teaching. I opened 3 chests and the first was my moldavite necklace. The second was my wand, The third was a note written by me and said " You are doing amazing, Keep shining for all to see"

8-17-14

I have begun labeling my water on top of already verbally setting intention on each jug with different words. Such as energy, love, healing, meditation, abundance, Out of Body Experience. Water is magic by setting and learning about intention. What ends up happening is you program the water for what you want it to do.

How do I program my own water?

Place both of your hands on either side of the vessel of water and close your eyes. Imagine your top of your head opening and receiving an immense amount of light. Envision this light traveling down your head into your arms then into the container. After you picture this keeping your eyes closed say out loud the following for Love or something similar -

For Love - Thank you Water, I Love You Water, Your purpose is for all Those who drink you will feel unconditional love for themselves and those around them. Thank you Water, I Love You Water.

For Energy - Thank you Water, I Love You Water, Your Purpose if for All those who drink you will feel the same amount of energy as they would by drinking a cup of coffee. Allowing them to push forward through their day and shedding the limitation story of being tired. Thank you Water, I Love You Water.

For Meditation - Thank you Water, I Love You Water, Your purpose is for all those who drink you to

The Water Magister's Self-Discovery

allow them to go into deeper states of meditation and relaxation. To allow them to go deeper in their practice and uncover insights of their true divinity. Thank you Water, I Love You Water.

For Healing - Thank you Water, I Love You Water. Your purpose is for all those who drink you to provide healing on the physical plane, energetic plane, and mental plane.

To allow them to realize they were always whole to begin with. To break down the walls of limitation and show them they are beyond the stories they tell themselves.

Steps to Charge your water.

1. Get several glass containers, see if you can find some that are colored based on the chakras. This allows chromotherapy to take effect on the water as well.

2. Filter your water with a Reverse Osmosis machine or a machine that removes fluoride.

3. Fill Container with Filtered water.

4. Add trace mineral solution to the water to bring mineral content back after the R/O Filter.

5. Add Himalayan sea salt to the water for the healing properties.

6. Add Colloidal silver to the water if you have access to it for the benefits.

7. Add ORMUS to the water - Recently have been using it and making it since Sept 2016.

7. Locate and buy an Enhydro Quartz crystal and place this in the container. There are other crystals as well to utilize that are amazing.

Such as Shungite, Non irradiated blue topaz, aqua

marine, mica. For more information visit: http://www.dancingwithwater.com

8. Place a label on the outside of the container with the intention you want.

9. Place both hands on either side as indicated above and recite out loud the words to program the water. There is no right or wrong way. Do what calls to you. But make sure you truly feel it come out of you. So ensure you say it with passion.

8-17-14

Its times like last night that I live for. Simple moments in time when friends can come together staring up at that beautiful night sky. Enjoying the simplistic beauty of the clouds and moon. Just making each other laugh while discussing what we see in the clouds. Often times so many people lose sight of who they are, but when was the last time you took the time to stare up at the star light sky and say to your self wow…that is all me and it is beautiful. Its amazing to know all of what we see on a daily basis is just us. We create these falsified walls of separation.

Because in a way we like to say that to ourselves, no I am my own individual. When in fact we are all the same, seeking the same. Learning, doing, being, loving, laughing, giving, receiving. Laughing so hard at times that it brings tears to your eyes because of the silly moments in life. It is this that I crave, as those beautiful stars come shooting by could it really be as some one in the group put it… A shooting star passing by can create another universe by seeking out an embryo of life.

All concepts, all ideas but of course our intellectual mind wants to take hold and say No! It is this way and what you are thinking is impossible. Always wanting to be in control. Love this life, love these moments, be in them, be of it.

8-19-14

Everything just works out as it is to be created for your growth. I stopped trying to push for something and allow my self to flow like water. Once you stop fighting the things and worrying about what may come, you can then let go of expectations. You begin to realize to have expectations of things or on people, you can get disappointed when it doesn't go the way you want. So in this just allow your self to surrender and flow, be with the moment and see where it takes you.

Without having an expectation of a person or event. But then there comes the thought of manifesting. What is the difference in manifesting something and having an expectation of something? Well from my understanding it is this… Manifesting something is possible as long as it does not intrude on another persons bubble or sphere of reality unless they too choose it.

Expectation is what is placed when you begin to place your own thoughts or ideas in a persons bubble of reality. Then when it doesn't pan out you scratch your head and say, Why didn't that work?

I have found my self being disappointed many many

times in people due to me placing false expectations on them because I am projecting how I am onto a person that is not me. Thus I end up being sad or angry. But now I only observe and see how they react. The things I had issues with in my own path were people that said they would do something but they did not end up doing it and continue to wonder why their life hasn't changed. Which further showed me aspects of my self I disliked and refused to face. I realize with the help of talking to a friend, that some people just enjoy the drama and it is their norm. They are comfortable in it.

They cannot cope with change because they are not ready for it. So they stay in these cycles and continuously wonder why their life is not improving due to fear. For those of you who this relates to. Analyze those cycles and ask your self why you feel comfortable going in circles with the same stories repeating? What are you benefiting from it? Each time the cycle repeats it just gets louder and louder.

8-19-14
Cycles keep repeating in your life until you have learned the lesson in it.

8-20-14
I made my first crystal grid tonight for my meditation class. The crystals let you know where to put them as long as you clear your mind.

8-22-14
At times my intuition is so on point I get a little

freaked out by it. But then I remember I am just that powerful.

8-24-14

Today I have received the wand I ordered after a month and some days. It is funny because I was having a necklace made as well that is moldavite. I had the intuition that I was not to receive either of them unless I got both of them at the same time. They were made by two different people and guess what. I received both today at the same time. Intuition was right again.

I participated in a sound healing workshop today. Prior to it beginning they gave us this liquid that goes into your eyes and burns! It is made from a potato. They said it helps with fixing eyesight and opening of the third eye. I had also brought my wand with me because I want to raise it's vibration as well. I feel this workshop was one of my activations into the knowing of my self. I feel my soul wanting to leave my body but it keeps jumping back in.

8-25-14

You are a powerful being of light sent here to make a change in this world. Own it.

8-26-14

Patience is definitely one of the things I have come here to master. Every day is a new challenge come to test it. I still need work otherwise the experience would stop occurring.

8-27-14

I see so much in the agenda of news. I see them pushing separation by race so we don't focus on the bigger things. I see them reving up the war drums. But does anyone else see it too?

8-29-14

I have made the decision to go forward with doing a yoga teacher training course.

8-30-14

The things I feel and see now have been amplified. I see people that are in need of assistance in a spiritual sense. Dreams are communicating with me, meditations are showing me the way. How can I deny what it is I see and feel. Each and everyone of you has a mission to unlock once you began this path. You knew there was no going back to being "normal". This isn't a game or a fantasy, what makes a person feel and begin this path in the first place? If you had not experienced a sudden jolt in your normally scheduled life you too would not ever bother seeking for answers to who we are.

The tools I have been gathering and collecting speak to me in such a fashion that now that I can use them for any purpose I desire. I ask a question and I get the answer rather quickly. What are your talents? What has been calling out to you? Have you been denying your self of this feeling? Pushing it aside thinking "ehhh, it will go away". Because it won't. It will be like a sliver in your foot throbbing over and over until the "pain" becomes unbearable and you have no other choice but to address the issue.

And that issue is coming, wake up. These words that are flowing out are not me, but in a sense they are as we are one. I have now acknowledged that. I am merely a vessel of information put here to relay information that is passed on to me as I see fit and as I open my self up to more vulnerable moments.

At times I review what I have written with a sense of awe because I feel the communication coming through me. One of the things I am being told now is that I have to make this book a priority. You too can open your vessel to communication, song writers, poets, all are able to tap into that in some way. The trick is to merely allow your thoughts to fade away and write or type the first things that comes to you. This is a transmission. As your mind is merely a radio receiver for the higher self. You just need to tune into the radio station of love and you will be sent down all the answers you require in your life. Just listen.
I love you.

8-31-14

Today I was part of a group mushroom trip with my meditation group. This so far has been the most profound trip to date. Prior to this on the same day, I met a swamy for a third eye meditation he gave me a special chalk that has 1,000 prayers into it. I also had him bless the wand I had made for me. I was reluctant to do so because I had the thought of fear that only I can touch the wand. However I realized in that moment that not just a spiritual figure could bless it.

But more on that later. As we began our trip we had many who had never taken mushrooms. 30 minutes in we began to feel everything intensely. I began seeing fractal patterns and geometry. 2 hours in I held hands with a group member and I was taken back to Egyptian times.

She was a queen and I was the king. As that image faded, She said she saw the same thing. Next was when my eyes were closed. I saw my higher self. I had wings! I saw the 7 chakra system on my ethereal body and where my head was was behind it was a tetrahedron with a gold aura around it. I was blue, which solidified my thoughts of being someone from Sirius constellation. I began to know everything about me or so I thought. This group I was with we always travel together to planets to change the reality. We go to worlds and raise its vibration then we move on to the next. It is in this time I truly feel who I am. Ever since this day I now feel I have wings between my shoulders. As I hug people I envision them wrapping around the person giving them unconditional love.

I asked the group are we supposed to know this information? Because all of us feel who we really are now. It all feels like a dream. If it is…..this is amazing. Change here we come!

Note:To See a visualization of the closet thing I could find of what I looked like visit:

http://illusion.scene360.com/wp-content/uploads/2012/02/lakandiwa_03.jpg
It is the image of the being with wings.

Cho Go Pal: Remember Who You Are

9-1-14

My thoughts on making a power object. I used to have the fear of people touching the wand I use for the healing's I do. It was then I realized I was acting from a place of fear. I would only allow spiritual gurus to touch the wand and bless it. But I now know that the more people who you share a story with of any object, the stronger that object becomes. So now I allow anyone to touch it as long as they bless it by sharing the story that this object will be used in healing practices. You can do this with anything. If you give an intention to something and have someone share this same belief it is now a power object. Things like this are all around us. Crystals, Actors, Presidents, Role Models, all have a shared story of them and as each person begins to take on this story because they believe it to be true that object or person becomes that and a stronger version of what the intention was.

9-2-14

You are limited only by your monkey mind. What is holding you back? It will always be all in your mind, you have the power to change your entire world. Make the choice.

9-3-14

Poem Use for the Back or Front of Book

Beautiful soul co creating with me
I thank you for the deeds you have done, the deeds

you will do.

You are the light when I am the dark, a fire sharing their flame with me.

Know that I am thankful for you.

The amazing potential you are, what a surprise it will be

For you to soon see the next level of your awakening

It comes in waves, not all is given at once

You go through life thinking so much,

The true task is to be thoughtless and allow it all to come

Beautiful soul, how I wish you could see through the eyes of mine

Knowing who you really are in this grand scene of acting in the drama

We call life, What a beautiful time will be had once you have seen the time

We have put in this co created world, choosing to go through all of this

Because for us it is fun, Little do you know that we have done this all together

Many many times before

Choosing to forget the memories of our past loves together.

Beautiful soul, Know that once you remember who you are

You will look into that bodies eyes and know and thank them

For assisting you in your journey
Giving those gentle pushes through out your life,
In different bodies but from the same class room of souls
We know each other so well but it is funny because if I truly told you
Who you were to me it would ruin the surprise
So we keep co creating together pretending to find each others true love
but over and over we find one another and that beautiful in on itself is love.

9-4-14

If you are reading this. I am a tool for you to use to remember and grow. I am here to assist with the transition. Reach out to me. Use this symbol in a meditation and I will be there. I was in a deep state of meditation and a the above sigil was revealed to me. This is the same logo on the website. It started with just the Y and the Spiral line going up. When I first received this sigil I thought it was just a random thing I made up. But as I would begin to practice Reiki 2 on some clients or be in meditations. This sigil would keep popping up within the darkness behind the eyes. As I began to use this sigil every time it would come into my mind as it was thoughtless.

It would let me know which chakra points to use it on and did not tell me it's name at first. So I would keep using it until one day I was in a meditation and It spoke to me and told me it's purpose was to assist in supporting the story of remembrance of who we really are. After this point I would continue to use it on different points on the body and I would get a lot of good feed back from the people I would use it on. Then a new transmission came in to let me know one of the many meanings was when two become one, or when one become two. The Spiral coming up was a representation of the kundalini rising. I began to see if I could find any information on this sigil because I had never seen it and I even went to other readers or psychics to see if they have seen this sigil.

I went on many forums posting if anyone had seen it before and I was not answered by to many people. I realized that I would have to wait for it to reveal to me what the actual meanings of the sigil represented. Later it was revealed to me: It is also a representation of the rod of asclepius. See here for More information: https://en.wikipedia.org/wiki/Rod_of_As clepius. A short while after I received the name to be that of " Cho Go Pal ". Said very quickly. The next set of information I received was the use of the triangle and the circle. I still have yet to receive the meaning of these. But I am eager to find out. The colors were chosen because in a past vision I had when in a deep meditation.

I clearly saw 3 obelisk shaped crystals. One Blue, One Red, One Green. When I asked what colors it wanted the overall sigil it sent me that image of the meditation. I got this sigil tattooed on my back because for me It was a strong calling from within telling me to do so. I just listened and allowed it to be done. When I was in the middle of the session of tattooing. I received another piece of information that when a sigil is placed on the body just like a tattoo it would amplify the waters within our own bodies. Just like that of Dr Masaru Emotos label on a glass container. Our bodies are the container for the water inside of us. So by having it tattooed on my body I was programming my own water with intention. The intention to remember who I was before I chose this physical body. So by using this sigil on water or objects or a person during a energy healing you are changing the vibration of that object or space. To that of a remembrance frequency, one where we can begin to shed our layers of long told stories that we have been repeating for 1,000's of years.

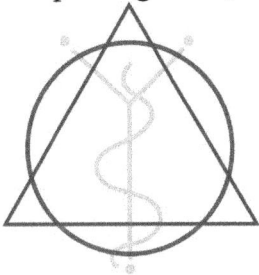

There was a friend who got the Sigil of Cho Go Pal tattooed on her and upon this. This is what she sent to me.
Mind you I never met her in person even as this book is published. She was called to the sigil, as I was.

"Yesterday in float the sigil assembled itself for me in 3D form it's a ball of energy around a pyramid the rod in the middle is a human being who is a conduit like me.. The blue light up the rod is the energy moving through the human being...I was told to draw it and use it in our Ayahausca ceremony coming up... It put the words above the 3 points on the rod as I visually sounded the words gold light emulated from all three points and rotated and combined the 3 strands which turned into dna looking visuals i know we only have 2 strands but, I believe the 3Rd one must be our spiritual strand (not sure) after it showed me the Dna strand it transformed into a beautiful golden staircase that led straight up to a beautiful spinning gold light! I am very familiar with this visualization…"

9-6-14

Today I had the luxury of visiting the Buddhist temple in Miami. My friends and I went in and meditated for 45 minutes at the shrine. Later the monks invited us to have lunch with them. They said we could come back any time. They blessed their food and water the similar way as I do my own. We were given a vial of water that was used to water the plants but a prayer was said to honor our fallen ancestors. I had one of the monks bless my wand for use in my healing sessions.

After this we went to a place called Coral Castle. This castle was made by one man using the magnetic grids our earth has. I brought my wand with me to feel the energy of the land. I felt something calling me to place the end of the wand into the ground as I did so, a surge of chills rushed up it and into my body. Next a friend of mine was having a reading from the psychics there. She turned to me and it looked as if she saw my wings and gasped. She said that I was very protected and I am here to do some great things.

9-9-14
Poem

Waiting
Empty nights filled with connections to the moon
Unity and togetherness with the Goddess of the night.
I often find my self observing everyone else's lives.
But I am so lost still, wondering where she is.
I am ready, I am here I say.
Together we will create an unimaginable world
showing the entirety of existence that all things formed
in thought are possible.
Traveling together into the astral through our
desires.
Pulling one another into unknown worlds and
discovering the wonders.
How I long for another to be able to progress through
this realm with.
My heart is open and always giving.
I am ready to receive.

9-9-14
Poem
I was lost but now I'm found.
I look up when I used to look down
The world I saw when I was young was so
different from now where I stand.
The life experiences that is given to us
Sets us up to that path
Not knowing where we are heading towards
But I know it's towards it's proper course.
I'm never going back, never going back now.
I took this path and I knew the cost
The one to grow and laugh and play
I always knew it would end up this way.
Always coming back in different forms

104

Living it up and never looking back
 Each time is a new challenge
 But without it this would lose it's fun.
 So here I am again calling out to you.
 Knowing what I know and what to do
 If only I could show you your way
 You too would feel this way
 And every time I travel down this path
It's just another fork in that road
 And every choice I make takes me closer, closer to
you
I know now that the journey is where the fun is
 The destination never mattered
 Meeting new souls along the way
If you seem to sway away, they will set you straight
 But now, oh now is that moment
 The times are changing, so don't fret now, oh now
 It's the only moment that we have
 So live it, love it and be here now.

 9-12-14
 Do you hear that?
 It's the sound of change in the air.
What is the cause for this? You!
 You who are doing the work of moving that
 Energy and seeking the truth and making others
aware of themselves.
You who are furthering your own growth through
experience and not becoming complacent and
comfortable because you
 Know there is more to life then that
 You who are motivating others and inspiring your
circle of friends

I salute you for what you do because without you, I would not grow.

It is because of people like you our species evolves and searches for life mysteries

We have known since we were children that we have such a powerful gift.

But it was stripped from us from schooling and society, layer by layer

Funneling us through this system so we can become wage slaves.

Why? We are the only species that has to pay to live on this planet.

I promise you, that once we overcome this story of greed and ignorance.

A new dawn will come where we all work to progress our species not because of money.

But because of love.

The only driving force that we truly ever need and the only force in which we are made of.

Because love is the light.

I love you, keep doing what you are doing and know that You are amazing!!

9-17-14

Let us talk about an amazing herb called Mugwort. I have been using it for my dreams and they allow for some very vivid and prophetic dreams. Mugwort was considered the universal herb for protection and prophecy throughout the ancient world.

Here are the ways to use this wonderful Herb.

1. Smoke the herb or drink it in a tea to induce lucid dreams or vivid dreams.

2. Place the herb under your pillow to assist in

astral traveling.

3. If you are pregnant do not smoke this herb.

4. If you are on your moon cycle this is amazing for the pain , I have been told.

9-18-14

Do you ever take the time to think about all of the people in your life you have affected?

Think about it right now.

Truly imagine the implications of just a small interaction with 1 person. Such as saying Hello and looking at them in their eyes and acknowledging them as a person.

What if that person was depressed or going through something and just the sincere gesture of you looking at them and acknowledging them helped them through what ever story they are going through.

Now imagine the daily interactions you have with people, just a small action can change their whole life in an instant.

Take that into consideration the next time you meet someone new.

I used to be a very mean person when I was younger, I never thought about these things. But I now know what it is to be a portion of someones life

To assist in their growth.

I now know how easily I can uplift someone just as easily as shoot them down. Just love...

We are all powerful, all knowing, but we forget we need constant reminders from others of who we really are.

Be that stranger that uplifts a random person today or tomorrow or any other day.

So that person can look back on their life and say, wow. I can't believe that person was in my life to help me with so much.

That is what an angel is and you too can be that for others. Just love them as you love yourself.

9-25-14

Stop being so hard on your self

Stop thinking you are not good enough for your self and others.

Stop judging your self so much

Stop taking experiences away from your self due to fear

Stop thinking so much about the past or future

Start appreciating the accomplishments you have done so far to get you where you are right now!

Start knowing you are amazing for yourself and others.

Start loving yourself and every portion of yourself unconditionally!

Start allowing the experiences that the universe has been presenting to you to take affect and finally learn from them.

Start living in the Now!

I Love You!

10-21-14

I was guided by a voice to begin experiencing a water fast. So I obliged…

Day 1 of my first Water Fast for 5 days.

Beautiful sun as it rises fill me with light.

Sun give me your warmth and sustenance and love.
Sun How I love you for keeping me alive.

1st Distraction during meditation.
It was a park ranger as I laid on the grass on a blanket
he drove up on a cart and said to me no sleeping in the
park. I was not sleeping but I was in meditation. I
broke my vow of silence the very first
day....Unconsciously. I need to work on this Back to
the vow of silence.

2nd Distraction. Caterpillars Upon analyzing the
caterpillars it showed up 3 times this day once when I
was riding with Kevin and Zen to the sunrise
meditation and twice during my meditations at the
park. It crawled on me till it reached my neck and i
snapped out of my meditation and I realized it was a
hairy caterpillar. I moved it away into the grass and
thought nothing of it... 30minutes later or so it came
back to me and crawled again on my neck. It was the
same one I feel, trying to give me a message that I am
still in a larva phase of my growth and I will emerge
something much more beautiful then before. I played
with him for several moments moving him to different
parts of the blanket and it would keep crawling back
on top of me. I even moved it to the grass, on top of
my water bottle, on top of a book. It still wanted to be
with me.

The thought of food came up a few times this first
day. The stomach made some motion but I was in a
meditative state and I envisioned white light entering
from the top of my head down into my stomach and I
felt full. Each time a thought of food came up I did a
similar method but each was different, on some
occasions I asked Pachamama for sustenance and on

others I asked The Sun.

The reason food came up so much this day was because Mondays is a food truck invasion at the circle and I kept smelling it's delicious goodness. I reasoned with my body and told it I would reward it with a Buffalo Sloppy joe at the end of this. Which is my absolute favorite thing to eat. But I will get more on this later.

Another technique I used was to gather energy from all around into my hand and I formed little white balls in my hand and then I motioned as If I were to eat it.

It is interesting that as I read Kevin's Medicine wheel and 7 sacred directions that I was facing the North. In such I will type what it says as I was reading it.

"NORTH (White)

From the North is abundance, wisdom, wholeness, rest, and completion. We experience the element of Earth, our mother. This element is one of foundation, sustenance, wealth, and life's wisdom. We find what needs doing, the knowledge of how to do it, and we learn in giving to others we are sustaining life and contributing to its evolution, yet the giving must come from the heart without thought of reward or gain. Enlightenment here can be painful, like the harsh cold season that stings our flesh or drives us indoors, because it can hurt to leave things behind sometimes, but we understand we must often empty out to make room for new. This direction represents

Winter, the ending cycle that completes our transformation. This ending also marks new beginnings, more transformation in the cycle of life, knowing what we must do and just doing it, yet that doing comes from the heart. The gateway emotion is joy. To own our joy, is to transmute it into its more mature form, peace. Peace teaches us how to live harmoniously with others and ourselves, recognizing our individual expressions of source to exist alongside one another, applying that awareness, that playful potential, creatively and constructively. The symbolic animal is the Buffalo. This spirit keeper teaches the giving of the self from the heart, to roam freely forging our own path, with strength held in reserve until it is needed. We receive the energy, and we honor the spirit of the North, aho."

    I did not even put it together until I read that verse that the North not only represented sustenance, but it represented a lot about me, Earth since I am a Taurus which is an earth sign and the enlightenment portion hit home to me on this as I choose to feel this and feel the pain to allow room to grow and let it go to move on to the next task at hand.

    Night 1 Dreams.

I woke up within my dream (lucid dream) to find that I was in a future world where in the society everything was controlled. Everything we ate or drank. The thoughts we had were monitored by these robots which could read your mind. They would circulate the cubicles in which many of the slaves would work. I asked for water and the slaves laughed at me as if it was a joke and they showed me a commercial with what happens to those who drink water. You were jailed and beaten because they replaced water with this pink gas that you inhaled to replenish your body. I asked the other slaves that they must know this insane right? There must be others who know this is wrong. They agreed and they said yes but we cannot do anything because "They Won". I then woke up. I feel this was a glimpse into the future of what may come if our own united action against what is being done to our society is not addressed more sooner then later.

Day 2. I woke up with a huge hunger pain. Kevin came to pick me up for sunrise meditation on the way I was going into a meditative state to ease the pain in my stomach. It was at this moment I realized once this was over that Buffalo sloppy joe was mine. I also realized that I chose to no longer be vegetarian. My body tried to communicate that to me a few months back but I did not listen. The initial reason I became vegetarian was because my body asked for it. I stopped eating meat all together one day. It also was a way to discipline my body to let it know I am here and that it no longer controls my actions. Once I learned this lesson the act of being vegetarian was no longer necessary. Now I know some of you who are vegetarian may frown on this idea but it is my reality and I create it. I know I have learned what I needed by practicing that for a year. Now that my body and I are in union I can choose my diet based on feeling. I also realize that a lot of the meat people eat is not "cleansed" of all the fear during the preparation of it.

Those animals go through so much pain to be able to feed billions of people. But know that they too are making this choice, as all things are creating their reality. In turn you consume that fear into your own body. So I now know you can cleanse that fear from the meat by merely having an intention to clean it away and saying thank you for their sacrifice, when was the last time you thanked your meals? Even if you are vegetarian. Give love and respect to those that you put in your body, your body will reward you in turn with tingling chills throughout.

Day 3. This day has taught me that we are so afraid of trying and failing. I know this because of all of these thoughts of food rushing through my body, it is all I can think about. For example I love tiramisu it is my absolute favorite, but why have I not taken the time to learn how to make this delicious dessert? It was because I was afraid of failing at it. I will now take on the story that I will learn new dishes and be a master at those dishes I choose to make. I also learned it is the love it self that you put into an action that determines the end result of anything you do. If you do something half assed you will get a mediocre result. Knowing this, I will commit to being that amazing cook I envision my self to be. What comes next after I master that is limitless.

Day 4. I wanted to give up this day because the cravings are unbearable all I can think of is food and the dishes I want to make. I could not meditate to much because the stomach was uneasy and food was everywhere. I gave up my silence and the use of my phone this day.

Day 5. I am completing my fast at 12 today and am having a banana dipped in honey with bee pollen. Along with Acai juice. Later Loni is coming over to support me with Vegetable soup as I ease my self back into foods.

All in all this experience was an amazing one and it definitely was a journey of the mind and soul. It allowed me to further understand myself and see how I process information and what limits I still have that I need to overcome.

I thank you graciously for reading this and know that I do all of this out of love for my self and for you to share the experience because that is all we can do is share.

10-23-14

Just had a very intense and vivid dream...Like I literally was there and it was just awesome...
Wanted to write it down before I forgot it.

It started where Erika and I were in some sort of compound. It looked like a prison. We were able to create some sort of escape plan and managed to nearly get out just the two of us. Until we became trapped in a certain section.

In this room we were basically telling each other how we had a good run and well see each other in the next life.
Then out of no where a Blue portal gun comes through the wall and I look at it and I'm like no...that's not a....
I look through it to see a friend but I couldn't see who it was.

I told Erika Alright lets jump through. She looks at me and says what? How? I just run into it. We end up in this limbo tunnel until my friend fired another Red Portal at another end. Where we met with him, then he got shot down.

For what ever reason all of this felt and "played" liked a video game. So when he died he dropped loot and it was 2 AK47s, 1 Sniper rifle, 1 Motor cycle which had a Gatling gun on the sides and 1 crossbow.

I dashed on my side to the loot and threw Erika an AK an the Sniper rifle to cover me. As I did in came Randal from a different position with a grin saying I'm here to help get you out of here.

So I proceed to grab this motor cycle as if it weighed nothing and used its Gatling guns on all the incoming waves of Alien looking creatures , there was thousands of them. The vision of this scene is still fresh in my mind. Randall then yells "Get the fuck out of here I'll handle this" That was when Erika and I started running the opposite direction and that was when I woke up.

Oh vivid fun dreams...I love thee.

11-25-14

The idea of creating a food distributer to sell intentional food when water is used came. Just like Dr. Masaru Emoto's discovery but apply it to the intention in food to all so the world will learn their power.

12-12-14

So today Erika and I shared how we saw a blue scarab in a vision when we were intertwined in sex. I then remembered I used to own a blue scarab when I was younger. I showed her a photo of what they looked like and she said she had one too. I lost mine but I am looking for it now. She still has hers. So I began researching the meaning and it means change, cosmic teachings and astral travel. We then talked about ankhs and my wand I have. The idea of how to use them during sex for spiritual growth came. One use is to focus all attention on the wand during climax and then focus on a goal you both want to create. At the moment of orgasm you send it out through the wand to manifest. The other is to focus it on the partner and allow them to get a super charge so they can get into a deep meditation to receive a vision or writings that is to be shared. Another upon climax focus the climax on the object to super charge it to support others in the process of healing.

1-3-15

Yesterday during my yoga teacher training I was in meditation and after a very good kundalini class a new symbol came to me. This is the third symbol I have seen in a meditation now. I am not sure the meaning but I will look it up and see if I can find anything. I will be creating a seperate book on the sigils I have seen and how to use them.

4-24-15

It has been awhile since I made an entry. But I am in a day 3 of my Colombia trip. Day 1 was exciting to be able to see my godmother again after 20 years. Erika and I spent some time with her and had lunch. We then went to her apartment and she showed us some amazing crystals she had. We then went back to the meeting place and got onto the bus for a 20hr bus ride north to Sierra Nevada. Day 2 still on the bus but many pit stops. We were able see some amazing buildings and people. I have been having visions one was of the road with buildings on both sides another happened when I had a nap with Erika. It was a bunch of cars driving back and fourth. No idea the meaning to these.

I woke up at 4am to do a meditation. Then we did

a fire ceremony to cleanse the body of illness of the mind. After this, we did an amazing yoga practice. I was told I could teach ashtanga tomorrow.

4-25-15

Today we moved to a new location much more rural then the first. We had to take motorcycles up the side of a mountain and cross a river. This place is truly beautiful. We were told we could not sleep in the same tent nor to have sex or kiss. It was to respect the land. We had issues with this because Erika wanted to for my birthday.

4-26-15

Today the men went to a river that had a water fall I brought my enhydro quartz crystal from the I Love You Water crystals. There was such an amazing presence about this area where the waterfall was. Some men undressed and went in nude. I decided not to because of judgment of self and fear. I swam through the water fall and felt like almost drowning from the current. But I made it through. There was a smaller pond that I climbed and went into. After I wandered to explore up ahead more. My sandals broke on the way there. Probably because it wanted me to connect to the earth. I continued bare foot. Each time I climbed and found a small pond, I dipped my crystal in it. I went up to 7 different ponds climbing the mountain higher and higher. Each one for a specific chakra.

The last one had a rock that called to me to sit in lotus position which was in the middle of the body of water. From here I began to address my attachment with Erika. I went deep within my mind to let go of aspects of my self and cried as I went through each one. A voice came through telling me to open my crown so that I could receive a DNA upgrade as it said this I felt chills surge through out my entire body. I cried. A single tear, I felt energized. I opened my eyes and something in me told me to have my hands in prayer and to bow my head to the 7 trees in my area. I felt as though they were a council of the forest to speak with me and address me.

With each bow towards each tree, I felt chills in acknowledging them. I then stood up and I raised my hands in the air. The image of my tattoo on my back came up and I realized I was in the same position as the Y. I envisioned the 3 orbs and at the bottom of me energy rising. As I did this I cried again in gratitude for how beautiful everything was. In that moment a beautiful vibrant blue butterfly flew near by and landed and it was a very dark blue. It then flew away because I thought it was a feather at first and I walked near it. Then I grabbed my things and headed back to the rest of the group. This forest is so amazing. I love you.

5-10-15

Today I was vending at an event. I met some interesting people and connected with a young guy who offered me Rappe from Brazil. I had some and in it I felt things expand and contract. Upon analyzing this I realized it was that each of us had a sphere and when we speak to another this sphere expands its universe to all who hear it and it collides with the other spheres as well to allow them in their world.

6-7-15

I have realized the reason for my sexual dreams to be a form of teaching in the dream state to make me aware that I am in fact dreaming. A better suited way I've realized is to have a figment notify me with a trigger word. So that I can be aware of the dream training.

6-9-15
Erika and I are broken up, After a year of dating.
6-12-15
I just woke up from a very vivid and intense dream. It started with Erika and I boarded on an Airplane. We sat down and the time went by. There was a child that kept running down the middle of the plane and it stopped at me asking if I had any issues. He had the personality of an older man. After this I got in an argument with him and the scene changed to him being older. I said something and he told me I would be sorry. The scene changed and Erika told me she wanted to date me again. Scene changed again and I was now nearly naked with boxes and I was wet from water. I don't know why or how. In the dream I lost my phone and Erika is now with 4 of her exes who were on the plane with her. At this time I am angry with her because she is spending time with them.

The guy who said I would be sorry is also flirting with her. I ran off crying and sad. It appears we land on a place to buy souvenirs and a group of children see me crying and alone. They approach me and comfort me telling me everything is ok and not to worry. They breakout into a musical song and dance like a movie. I join along and begin to feel better. After this I had an insight that the man-child had my phone somehow. I go to find Erika and ask her to call my phone and the guy's pocket rings with a different ring tone. He laughs and says Oh I was holding onto it for you. Which was a lie. I grab it and take it into my hand and see a bunch of texts and photos but I don't look at them yet.

I told him I would get my revenge. At this moment Erika's ex reaches over to put his arm around her and she pushes him off telling him to stop. I run off again because I was angry she still would hang out with them and not me. I begin to look at the phone and find photos of Erika and I before I lost my phone and I didn't remember taking them. One photo was of this huge wax castle with the #31 as if it was a birthday number.

Author's Note: Which as I am transcribing this I realize now It was Fractal Beach 2016 Festival. In this festival there was a huge castle and I was 31 years old when I was there. This was a about 10 months after this dream.

7-6-15

Your words are magic, casting spells of what you believe to be true. Make sure what you say is what you truly mean.
Speak your truth from the heart, not the ego catering to someone else's story.

7-7-15

When your heart is wide open without fear of it getting hurt. Allowing your vulnerability to shine out wards for all to see. Speaking your truth, Those who seek themselves to learn how to love will find you.

What you will discover at a certain point in your life.

Is that once you surrender to the ebb and flow of what we call this reality, it begins to become seamless. Moving at a rate of which water may flow freely. But to get in the way and say to that flow, no I don't want to face it. Is to create a dam on the river of life. Eventually that water will overflow and you have to face it.

Surrender is key to being your true self.

7-10-15

The time has come and is a pivotal moment in our realities where you must make a decision.

Understand that you are all that is and will ever be. Understand that as we progress and move forward things may seem harder or more difficult because you are not allowing it flow. You may latch on to something, someone, but where we are going there is no room for attachments.

It is nearly upon us as we progress in this human consciousness.

You are loved beyond measure and know no matter what you will still be loved.

The decision is this: Fear or Love?

Do you choose to empower those around you or limit them based on your experiences and belief system that you have been indoctrinated into.

Begin to let go of all that you know to allow room for truth. We have been spoon fed lies and it is time reclaim that power within us.

Love or Fear? You Decide.

As you progress in this path of self exploration. What you will come to find is there are many ups and downs.

Even though you are aware of your self it takes time to find that balance of energies. At times it may feel overwhelming in up or down momentum.

But know that you are there and experiencing that point to better your growth. These are points of reference for your self for you to be able to reflect upon and know where you have been. To know what you are capable of. For you to strive for that balance and resonance.

Know you are infinitely supported by all. Never doubt for moment you are doing this alone.

We are one and I love you.

7-12-15

We all have wings. We all just collectively decided to hide them for a short while because the funny looks we would get and we would have to walk in sideways through doors.

I invite you to begin being aware of them and place your attention and awareness between your shoulder blades. Close your eyes and just feel. Picture them, what color are they?

Feel them move as they open wider and know they are always there. When you embrace a fellow brother or sister envision them wrapping around their body and fill them with love.

7-15-15

You will come to realize that the thing you wanted the most may not play out the same way you envisioned it. Allow your self to be ok with the outcome and move forward. Staying stuck in the past and thinking about how you could have changed something is a losing battle.

Push forward and be present. Flow like water into the next experience.

7-19-15

My second Peyote ceremony. I came with Erika to this ceremony and this was felt a lot less intense then the first one. I had two visions

One was of an older man with a huge beard. The other vision was of a huge corridor with many doors and it was of a blue energy with grids all over.

Author's Note: Which as I am typing this out from my journal. I now realize it was me.

7-26-15

Our purpose as light workers and being awakened at this time is to be the pillars of light for society when it begins to break down.
To live in a fearless state and show others to not live in fear when the time comes. We are that shining beacon of light that will pave the way to our evolutionary birth right of self awareness and understanding of who we really are.

In such remember during difficult times and fear is everywhere, maintain your focus and spiritual practices and know you are made of unconditional love and you can live without that fear.

Join with me and be that pillar of light to hold up your sector of the world. To teach others how to calm and ease their mind in hard times to come.

Repeat out loud when you read this to join with me in this cause:

I am that I am one with source I am,
Shining bright for all to see.
I am that I am.

I love you
9-4-15

When you begin to see that love within your self.
All other distractions no longer draw your attention.
The only focus now is the one going inward.
Because all those are are stories, to learn the truth you begin diving deep into the self.
As you do you begin to gain that motivation for no one other then your self.
No longer seeking validation.
No longer seeking attention.
No longer seeking another.
No longer seeking comfort in things out side of your self.
You can then begin to witness the stories and struggles of the other beautiful souls around you in this co-created world and hold space for them.
For they are only learning themselves as well.
So it is a game of being aware enough to take that step back and realize what those souls are creating are just stories so they can begin to come back to the love for self once more.

9-13-15

As you begin to let go of expectations of receiving anything in return for your deeds.
You will come to find the most beautiful abundance that will reach your door step.

When you give, do it from the heart, not for what is in it for you or what you would gain.

I speak from experience and when you begin to understand this concept, as you give things get returned to you 10 fold.

Because the simple truth of all of this is...when you give you never really lose anything, but you gain everything

9-16-15

When will the choice be made in your mind to end the repetition of old stories you have been telling your self?

Those stories of telling your self you are not worth it, you are not valued, wanted, worthy of love.

It is JUST stories! Why do you feel that way?

Dig deep into your self as you read this.

What is it that is keeping you complacent in not feeling the emotions you have been bottling up?

Those rough times in our lives we all go through and if that story keeps repeating. You never learned the lesson the first time.

So it keeps coming back over and over stronger and louder each time until you finally say OK I HAVE HAD ENOUGH!!

Why does it have to even get to that point?

Why couldn't you follow that inner voice guiding you the entire time?

Because we are stubborn, and because we feel we always know what is best for us...We have been taught for so long to not feel, don't feel that, don't cry you're a pussy, you're weak.

DON'T FEEL DON'T FEEL!!

You know what, That is my story of not feeling and it has come to a head a while back. I see so many of you struggling because you do not know how to face those feelings. Because you feel it is overwhelming. But it is only love...It is that love wanting to so badly hug you inside of your deepest wounds of the heart and mind.

It is love that wants you to face these emotions head on without projecting it out or passing it on to someone else.

Those times where you play small and act a victim because you feel you have no control over your environment is a very old story...It's beautiful....but where we are going it is no longer serving. It's time to have strength, have courage. Face your fears head on because those fears only take you back to love.

In that darkness you will discover so many treasures about your self that you thought were lost. But they were just hidden, tucked away neatly waiting for you to remember once more. We are living in a new age of remembrance. A new age of knowledge and wisdom.

This old paradigm no longer works. The new one is recognizing our truest potential that we absolutely create our reality 100% of the time.

Are you ready? I am.

Start that growth dear ones...You are not alone.

9-17-15

When you woke up today what was the first emotion you felt?

As you begin to wake up each day ask your self how you feel, that very first emotion that is felt is usually the feeling that carries throughout the whole day.

So it is essential to create a daily practice in the morning to change the way you feel so that can be the feeling to carry with you.

You are experiencing those feelings for a reason, rather then saying you dislike where you are. Accept where you are and love that feeling, then make a choice to grow from it.

Be thankful you are experiencing this life, be thankful you are able to see, taste, touch, feel.

9-24-15 *Poem/Song*

I'm free, I'm free I'm finally free
Spreading my wings baby cause I'm finally free
Going to be that person I was destined to be
The one who's soul was wanting to see
That light of day to shine so bright
for those in their darkness to see it's alright

Cause I'm free, I'm Free I'm finally free baby
Moving on up while sharing my love
Spreading my wings like a beautiful white dove
Hugging those around me with emotions so pure
Surrounding them with my wings as I embrace their soul

Oh you can see that the light surrounds me is here to stay
Cause now you're watching, and you know I'm free
Shining orbs of light surround me now
Orbs of love and peace they show me the way
Spirit Guides illuminating the path to salvation
Of the internal mind baby

Cause I'm Free, I'm free, I'm finally free.

9-30-15

Open the door to your own heart and in it you will find the key to your own greatness.

10-5-15

I challenge all of you who are reading this to right now get a pen and paper and write 10 things you are thankful for that have happened this past week.

As you write them think of how each of those moments made you feel. This is the feeling you can always be at once you become aware that you create your reality. That same feeling can be by your side at a moments notice....Just tune into it.

I love you.

10-7-15

I have a new challenge for you all...have you ever written your self a love letter? Yeah maybe to someone else...but write one and direct it to your self. You deserve it . thats your challenge for today. Write a love letter to your self. Make it as long or short as you want.

See what comes up as you do this. What judgments do you have on yourself. Does it seem silly or pointless? Be aware of all those thoughts as you are pouring your love for your self.

My challenge love letter to my self:

The time we have spent together has had so many ups and downs. It wasn't until the past 2 years where I was actually able to truly see you for how beautiful you were. I want to say I am sorry for all this time having ignored you and focusing on other people. When it was just you the entire time. It was always you. The love of my life.

These last few years we have shared together have

been such a growth for us. I see how I used to be towards you and How I now honor you as my temple. I now support all our ideas together without fear of what others may think. Because those judgments are only showing us what we have to work on.
I have cried so many nights on my own always feeling alone. But you were always there for me...Always and I never saw you. Until recently, I now know I can never be alone because I see you. I finally see me.

This being that so much wanted to give his love to others but was neglecting his own self love. I am sorry I neglected you in this way. I am sorry I made you lash out in many different emotions because you were just attempting to gain my attention. The moods of anger, jealously, insecurity. It was all you. Always showing me to focus within my self.

I love you, I thank you for being so patient with me and holding space until I was finally mature enough to see how beautiful and vibrant you have been for me. My one and only love that will always be there for me regardless of what happens out side of the self.
I Love You David.

10-11-15

There is only one place you will ever find your truth. It will not be from someone else's experience. It will ultimately be within your self. Once you find something that resonates with your own reality you just feel it in your core being as a truth. It is at this moment you begin to step forward into the path of self awareness, when those simple truths begin to come fourth into your being.

You then will use these truths to mold your reality

in any way you choose, based on those core beliefs you took on from either your parents, your churches, your religions, your mentors, your gurus, your guides and spirit guides.

It ultimately is you who decides what truth will mold your reality. With this in mind...What is the reality you wish to create?
One of lack? One of Powerlessness? One of Unworthiness? One of Insecurity?
Or one of understanding that you never lack anything, you are all powerful, you are worthy of everything in your life and more and you are perfectly imperfect.

Step into this reality with me and understand you create EVERYTHING that you experience for the sheer purpose of growth and all it takes is a simple choice to shift that into the perspective you have always wanted to live your life in.

I love you.
10-12-15
This is your new challenge:
Every day this week do 1 selfless act of kindness.
They can range from giving money to homeless, buying food for them. Giving a random stranger a hug.
Doing a pay it forward at your favorite coffee place.
Calling up a long lost friend to reconnect.

What ever it may be, but do 1 act of kindness each day this week.
Know that just like water, you are sending ripples amongst those who are receiving this act.

10-15-15
That feeling of the "ah ha moment" when you finally understand why someone was placed in your

sphere of reality was only to show how you, an aspect of your self, you disliked.

Every judgment you have on others is a judgment you have within. Every feeling of annoyance, unease, anger. It all stems from things within your self you do not want to see so badly that you decide to co create with another soul so they can then play that role out in front of you.

So that you can begin to work on that aspect of your self within your mind. No one is ever against you or out to hurt you. Nothing outside of your self can ever harm you unless you give it that permission to do so. Unless you really believed it could hurt you in the first place.

I had an aha moment last night as to why a certain person was in my sphere. Oh it feels good to see that part of me. I am eternally grateful for this life. Thank you. Time to keep on thriving!

10-17-15

Blessed ones, those of light. Yes you. The one reading this message. I know lately you may have felt a tremendous amount of stories coming to the surface. At times it may feel over powering or over bearing. But know this, you would not be feeling these things or going through what you are if you were not strong enough to heal that aspect of yourself.

The times now are accelerating in our rate of learning. Look back at your past and look at how long it took you to learn a lesson and then look at your self now. Look at how quickly you are now able to distinguish patterns of habit or "tendencies". It is beginning pachamama is awakening. You are awakening. You are only given that which you can handle. So that you can begin to be the best version of your selves in this life time.

We have chosen a very beautiful and monumental point in history to return. We are the blessed ones, the ones destined to make the impact in our sectors. We specifically came back with our soul group to key points. So that we may be that shining light for others to see and bare witness that it is ok to come out and play once more.

The time for hiding our selves is over. The time for thinking we had to lower our own selves to not make another feel bad is over. It is now. No longer feeling odd or strange in bringing up a topic other then what is on TV and the media. We chose our parents, we chose them because of the lessons they could pass on to us so that we could experience those traumas, which in turn activated portions of our compassion for the fellow human.

If it were not for that compassion you would still be in your own bubble of reality not having the awareness to understand what is written. You have all come a long way and it is time.

The time is now to reawaken that ability to control our realities 100% of the time. The time is now to no longer play the victim thinking you were any less to begin with. Know that those lessons of victim hood were only in play so you can know your true power.

You are all powerful and loved unconditionally. This message is for you. Because you are me. I am merely speaking to my other selves who have forgotten who they were. How funny it will be when we all fully remember once more so that we can create a world filled with abundance in all ways. It is coming. I can feel it.

I know you can too. Do not lose heart. Stick to that path of self love and understanding your purpose for the sectors of which you operate. You do make a difference and without you, this whole plan would cease to be.

We love you.

10-17-15

We all have wings. Do you feel them? Place your attention behind the shoulder blades and close thine eyes. Imagine them expanding out wards from the back.

Expand the wings as far as you can imagine. Use these wings to embrace one another when you hug.

Use these wings to draw in energy to your self by swaying them.

This is your divine right. Feel them.

Fly, Fly My beautiful.

10-22-15

When was the last time you dove into the desires you have? Have you ever asked....where this desire originated from? Was it a social construct based on programming of repeatedly watching a certain show , movie or other media.

Was it something that was instilled within you at a young age and now you have taken that on?

To break your self of these desires you have to begin to ask how it was even there in the first place. The same can be said with attraction. Physical attraction is all programmed. But there is another form of attraction that cannot be programmed into us.

That is the attraction to another soul that may have

the codes to share with you in some way and you find your self compelled to be a part of their sphere of reality.

Are you able to tell the difference?

I have been working within my self to break certain desires because they no longer serve the path I am walking. It has been a struggle because even in my dreams the desire comes up and at times I succeed and other times I do not. Last night I had a dream in which was a test and when I failed, the dream paused and it was a form of training ground for my self.

I then was sent back to the beginning of the dream to test my self once more. To see if that is truly what i wanted. When you begin to dive into the dream world, and astral world. You will be tested of all of your desires you have. It is in place to determine how far you truly want to go to get the information.

I distinctly remember one time I was traveling down a dirt road and the kundalini snakes were in front of me telling me to follow them. We then appeared at a cross roads one pointed left, one pointed right. They told me to choose a direction. I paused here and I said no. I kept going forward and when I did I broke the fabric of time and space in that area. When I did this they congratulated me for understanding that it was all a test.

What I am saying is make your choice as to what it is you truly desire. Because once you fixate on that, things will come in your way to truly test if that is what you want in the first place. It is just how the world works. Make a choice, and stick to it no matter what comes up. You will see it come to fruition.

You are loved.

10-25-15

I did a yoga and creative writing work shop today hosted By Sergio Mora and his Girlfriend. I went in with no expectations. I have had some what of a writers block and I know where it stems from...

So as I went through the workshop I wanted to share some of my writings with you.

--The breathe is the key to finding your peace. Being inside of this awareness you can begin to feel the subtle shifts in the body. You will discover more of your self as you are in this state.

We tend to think, as we go about our day, too much but as time goes on you will see when focusing on the breathe all ideas will begin to be pulled into you as insights and inspiration. In the insights it sometimes feels as though you are making it up but that is because you are not used to this feeling just yet. As you progress you will be more fluid with your words.

Then this next part was I was teamed up with a pregnant women and We were to send some blessings to each other. This is what I wrote to her.

--I felt the baby wanted to speak to you and tell you thank you. You are allowing space for her to be the best version of her self by clearing away your own stress from work. Putting in its place unconditional love to be within and as you give this love to your self you program the water in your body with love. So you nurture that fruit of your love and you get to share beautiful moments to come ahead. A lot of self discovery awaits you and she will be that direct mirror to you, showing you aspects of self to be healed and continue to nurture.

Some free writing what ever came to mind:
Tree standing tall shining that brightness of the sun.
Soul bearing out wards to be that light for others to see
when in their own darkness. Beacon of truth when in
this field I know those souls can feel it too.
Unwavering love for the self and others allows you to
be this reflection for those who are ready to see. Be
the true you without that voice of being better or
stronger then another. Just be you. The one so eagerly
wanting to show it's self because of how long it's been
in the shadows, worrying about how you are
perceived. When in reality it is all in your mind
anyways. Everyone is busy focusing on themselves as
well filtering the word magic we play on each other
because we fear judgment. The time is now to shed
these fears so you can be that example for others to
step into who they are. Allowing them space to
explore more of themselves.

and finally a few haikus they had us do.

1. Powerful blessing
Inner Peace be bountiful
I see within me

2. Energetic body
pulsating light of love within
holding space for you

3. Heart aching wanting
to feel that love from a soul
Never alone here

10-26-15
The battle within...The shadow begins to come
through wanting it's time in this realm.
Showing you aspects of your self you thought you

healed.

Fighting these battles in the mind, telling your self you are ok.

When in reality you have broken through but are unable to handle the energy given to you just yet. So the shadow now has its time with you. Enjoy it and be with it.

Know it is teaching you the ways back to your love for your self.

You are placing your self in this space with purpose. You may not know it, but that feeling of wanting someone out side of the self is like a drug.

You are slowly weening your self off of it and you have the repercussions of this addiction.

You are cleaning the body emotionally and energetically, so you can be the best version of your self. Know this always. Your path is already on its way to the vision you once had in that deep state of meditation.

Embrace this lack of motivation that is with you, this lack of inspiration. From it you will re emerge like a phoenix from the ashes once more.

Once again we share with you to be with this feeling you have inside. Truly feel it, do not pass it off and distract your self from it.

It only wants your love, attention, admiration, compassion.

My free writing to my self.

11-2-15

Do you know what it is you truly want?

You might say you do, but if you did and truly knew what you wanted you would have gotten it by now. Because you mold your reality based on choice. But there may be lessons that you must learn before what you truly want is even able to manifest in your reality. It could be right there in front of you, with dust on it and mud...But look at the lessons as a form of polishing the thing in front of you to see it for what it really is.

Slowly removing the dirt as you learn.

To find something under neath that is the key to what you truly wanted.

You must learn to accept where you are and accept the person you are seeking truly 100%. If what you want is truly that.

No single thing or person will ever be that "perfect" being you envision. It is something that has to be worked on through lessons of the self and understanding of the self.

So when you finally come into contact with that thing you have wanted, your own stories are cleared and you have put into perspective your own creations that you may make when that time comes. To not place the blame on the instance or person that is in front of you, and for you to take that responsibility knowing you created this because you have not learned that lesson.

So you keep polishing that thing that is there in front of you with these lessons of the heart and self. Until finally the finished product is a bright, shining ball of light and love and low and behold it was what you have always desired to receive, because you are now complete within your self from all the life lessons.

To share that space with your true desire.

That is what it means to know what you truly

want....to already have gone through all of the process
and lessons of understanding. Be honest with your
self.

What has been holding you back from attaining it?
The answer will always be your self.
You are loved , you are accepted and I see you for the
shining light you are. I am here for when you finally
see the true you and it wants to come out and play.

No more hiding.

11-3-15

I notice a lot of people seeking, always seeking
something outside of themselves.
Saying " I want a person to be this and this way and
that way"
Those qualities you are asking in a person are they
qualities that you personally posses?
If not why?
How can you begin to attract something that you are
not.
Do you think by having that thing outside of the self,
you will magically be complete because of it?
Because you wont.

You have to first exhibit those qualities within your
self to attract the mate that you are saying you desire.
The only ways this would happen is if one you are
already those qualities, or two you will find someone
of that quality only to find out that the only reason you
wanted to be with that person was to fill a void within
your self that had those qualities.

Once that becomes the focus and you begin to
understand you will no longer require that person
because they will have shown you like a mirror the
thing you have been lacking.

Yes you may possibly stay together with that person, but in order to truly understand your own self after learning the lessons space is required to utilize and process the lesson that had been learned.

Every single person you have ever disliked you only disliked because they showed you aspects of your self you didn't want to see.
Every single person you have ever liked or loved you have only loved because they showed you aspects of your self which you loved about you that you loved seeing.

Go back through out the people in your life that had given you hard ships. Truly do that and write all the qualities down. Notice those qualities are things within your self you have yet to heal.

You are loved and infinity supported because you are all God's and Goddess's. You can not make any mistake when you finally have a partner with you even if you feel the relationship ended horribly. It was all steps to get to that best version of your self you have always wanted to be.
Maybe some of you are afraid of being that best version, so you continue that endless cycle of choosing the "wrong" person.

Each time that story gets louder until you become fed up and have finally learned the lesson. It is just how it works.

So before you say you know what you want in a partner, are you that for your self first??

I love you

11-5-15
When you begin to see how beautiful the sun is.

The purest form of unconditional love and the most vibrant of it all that is visible in this realm. You can truly see the vastness of your power within your self. Because you too are made of this same unconditional love. The sun only knows one thing and that is to illuminate. It's love is so massive that it literally shines light to show its love to you.

Just like the sun, you too can shine your light for those to see how powerful and loved they are.

The waves of the ocean are like the hands of a lover gently caressing the cheeks of the shore line which are your cheeks. The ocean too knows only one way to show its love and that is to just be. Flowing the endless myriads of waves to gently love upon the cheeks of the earth. Letting the earth know it is here, always and forever.

To be that reminder for it self of how powerful it's love can extend.

Be that same love for others.

11-11-15

Letting go....What does this mean exactly...For well over the past 5 months I have had a constant battle of letting go of someone in my heart. I have been on the fence for too long and have been limiting my own self from experiencing more of my self by not allowing shared moments with others.

It is in this you can see that by holding on to something can be limiting you from experiencing more of what life has to offer. Understand that once you truly make the decision of letting go it will come back into your life for one last and final test of assurance to your own self.

This is due because you created it to be this way, you want to see where you are at. These endless nights of crying and holding on to something that is no longer the same, is holding onto a story that can be detrimental to your own growth.

They say time heals all wounds, but does it really? I think it is experience and choice that does. Once you made a decision internally it then begins to heal that aspect of the self.

Today I cried deeply and last night i had a dream in which showed me all the raw emotion I still have for someone that is very dear to me. But I understand now the ways in which our interactions have been in service to my growth.
To show me that things haven't shifted.

I am ready now to clear space in my heart to allow room for greater exploration of the self to display that love for my self. By typing this all out it is a way for me to release this and truly let go.

This choice has not come easy and at times I have said internally yeah I am fine, I can let them go. But I was never truly able to.
I held on so dearly to a story of limitation and fear with this person.
I never saw it for what it was showing me, which is the limitations I was setting on my own self.

So by truly expressing my feelings on this subject I want to say. I am letting go. I have to follow my own bliss and happiness and by holding on I wasn't doing this. It wasn't fair to my self and my own emotions.

What a huge shift this is for me. I am unable even express truly the sensations I have inside of truly making a decision.

But it is in this moment I am able to do so just internally without having someone tell me they have moved on. It is my life, my happiness.

I hope that by those of you who are having trouble letting go of something or someone. This can resonate to you. It is a very difficult thing to do. I am crying as I write this because of how deeply felt these emotions carry inside. But I know only greater things can come from it and I am excited to see what I am going to create in it's place.

You have to let go of something in order to gain something even greater!

Thank you, and I truly Love you. I am free.

11-12-15

I rise this morning a beautiful man. One that has grown after many traumas, many abuses, many past stories that were all created by me to form who I am in this exact moment. It is in this moment I feel love. Because I am that unconditional love.

Know where you came from was from a place that formed who you are now and who you are becoming. All those hard ships every single experience perfectly orchestrated to mold this beautiful being who is reading this right now.

THE WORLD IS AT YOUR FINGER TIPS!!! Prior to tonight I would say to my self I surrender to what the world wants to create...without knowing what it truly ment.

Today I know what it means based on such amazing visions and dreams I have been having the past few days. Even last night.

Surrender is fully accepting what is to come without placing a thought or feeling to what it is you may experience. Allowing the intention to be set not knowing how it will manifest and begin moving forward.

Exploring your self, exploring that inner land scape of the self. Of love, of life, IT FEELS GOOD TO FEEL!!

Allow your self to feel. I spoke my affirmations today and I felt as though I shattered walls within my apartment. I felt as though the tingling sensations were literally creating a world for me to step into once I leave this apartment today.

Set your self free to the realization that you have no control over how the creation process is. So to place judgments on something or someone while your intention is manifesting is to place a road block towards that thing you have truly wanted.

Let it flow, LET IT FLOOWWWWW Don't Hold on annyymmooorrreeeee!! *yeah I stole that from frozen*

I AM LOVE!!!

11-17-15

Amazing..I re watched Aladdin with the mind set I have now. The main thing taught is to always live in your own integrity. Live in your uncompromising truth. You do not have to shield or hide your self to present your self to be someone you are not.

It's time to shed the masks we have been wearing in society so people can see the true you. The one who has been afraid due to the judgments you have on your self about what you "think" others have on you. The constant struggle and lessons lead to this...You spend more energy making up lies and falsehoods of who you say you are rather than just being. Just be.

144

Seeing the gradual decline of Aladdin is a metaphor for yourself being gradually sucked into the story of society, not allowing the true you to shine. Not allowing your vulnerability to show. Because of all the judgments.
FREE YOUR SELF!
Speak your truth, live it, feel it.
I love you.

11-20-15

I am writing again because of a dream I had last night. I have had many insightful dreams the past 2 weeks but in last nights my mom knew about magic and had a delivery system where she received many magical items to see if she wanted to buy them and if not they would be returned. One box came in the mail and it was a wand. This was is still fresh in my mind it looks like the De Shen Den Sigil but has a terminated Pink Crystal I think it was rose quartz. Here is my attempt at the drawing of it.

SHARE WHAT YOU FEEL

It had a wooden base and a lot of copper. There was a copper spiral where all of the energy would shoot out of.

Then there was another wand I saw and it had a green crystal which was used to generate money. The copper formation was like the Kundalini snake and that snake was connected to a tiny terminated lemurian quartz. So the energy of the green crystal connected to the quartz and shot out that way. When I grabbed these wands I knew exactly how to use them and I was creating a vortex of energy that showed such beautiful colors. I feel it is a dream for me to make these two wands for my self out of copper and wood. So mote it be.

11-27-15

Today I would like to discuss Trust. What is trust....throughout my journey of this spiritual path I have heard the phrase of Trust the process but never truly understanding what it means.
I can now say that I do.

To trust the process is to get out of your own way. Meaning if you want to manifest something in your life make that declaration out loud and then simply let it go. Then continue to push forward towards that. If those voices of saying no, I don't have time, or "No I don't think I can" come into the picture, that is getting in your own way of achieving that desire.

It is a learning process to be able to truly get out of your own way in terms of your thoughts that you have. If you do get those thoughts, imagine your thoughts like a weight on a tipping scale.

Every time you think of something that you say in

your mind that makes you not move forward, you are placing more weight in the opposite side of the one that benefits you and you are getting in your way.

So what do you do ? When that thought comes up, immediately recognize it as a pattern to shift, and begin then shifting the thought and envision your self moving forward and thinking the positive outcome of that thought. For example:
I want to manifest my self $500 today. I set the intention and I move towards that throughout the day. As I am progressing possibly in the emails or calls to people because I fix computers. A voice pops in and says " Aggh I am never going to make this $500, let me just watch a show and not do anything"
I immediately would turn that around in my mind and envision my self receiving that $500 and I would allow my self to feel the emotion of happiness from receiving that $500. You just tipped the scale in your favor by shifting that thought into a positive one. Give more energy to the positive outcomes rather than the ones of laziness and lack of follow through.

This is going to push you towards the trust and process of manifesting.
So to trust the process is simply to not create scenarios in your mind that would otherwise supersede what it was you set out to achieve in the first place. Just trust that as you move forward, even if in your mind you feel like you are not making any distance. That you are still moving towards that goal and you do not allow the thoughts of negativity to cloud what it was you wanted. Once that cloudiness takes over you will have lost site of that main desire, and you will have to clear the clouds in order to see it clearly again.

I Love You

Channeling and Energy

12-1-15

As you emerge from your darkness into the light
just as the sun rises to shine its own. You begin to
shine awareness on aspects of your self you have been
hiding from. In this you will unravel the secrets of
your true self.
Are you ready?

So I made it a point today to write my self a love
letter by the end of the day. Here it is.
Dear Me,

What a time we have had this past month. We are
now coming to the final day of celibacy for us. What
have we learned in these 7 months? We learned to
harness our sexual energy and transmute it to go up
towards the upper level of the chakra system and the
self. Further empowering your will to what it is you
want to manifest. I know these stories of jealously that
have been coming up have been quite difficult for you
considering the strong attachment you have. But know
in this you are learning to further love in ways you
have not. This is a new world for you and understand
that it is with purpose.

The times you feel you have to validate your self
by seeking attention outside of us is only showing you
where you are misplacing your attention. It is within. I
see you David and I love you no matter what stories
you are telling your self in this physical world. I am
here with you until we die. The love I have for you is

unconditional because I know that you will always be by my side, always with me when I look in the mirror. The beautiful soul that so much wants to see others overcome their own fears just as you are doing the same and overcoming your own. I know you want to make huge changes in this world and I see all that you do for them, those outside of your self.

In it you will continue to see my reflection in each of them, as you grow these reflections are merely showing you further aspects of your self that you love or dislike. It is in this letter I wish to acknowledge you for how far you have come in such a short period of time. You are destined for greatness and even though you want others to see it, the only true being that matters is you.

Do you feel ready for that greatness or are you going to continue to hold your self back with things that no longer serve you.

Even up until this point you were hesitant in writing this letter, and you made up the story that you were busy with other things. But now you know as you write this you are facing that fear of uncovering more of your self. This writing is not the physical body, it is coming from a different place. A place full of understanding of all that you are going through and we only see the love in all that you do.

So as we finish our moment together know I see you and as you progress in this water fast many new codes will begin to unlock within you based on those visions you had earlier in the week. Be ready because "shift" is coming. You and many of your soul group are here to lead the way in this together. What a beautiful time will be had once it all begins to unfold truly.

I love you.

12-5-15

Greetings and salutations to all light workers,

I know many of you have had some strong battles internally coming up and it has been causing quite some uneasiness. But know that as you awaken these stories must be played out in order to attain that version of your self you see your self as.

If you have chosen to be self aware there is only one thing you can do, and that is to keep being even more aware. The amount of awareness will begin to increase as the frequency of all vibrations within us expands and multiplies. We are in a great time of change which is why you are beginning to see alot of violence arise. It is all stories playing out that have to in order to move onto the new paradigm of reality. As such some of these souls do not know how to react to the story and find themselves reacting out of violence.

It is up to us as healers, light workers, light bringers to show them the way of truth, peace, openness, vulnerability to ensure this transition is smooth. It is important to know that you are completely safe in fully expressing your self how you wish to in this time. These inclinations or notions you have of wanting to say something to someone, but in fear of what they may think about it, is your own self judgment on the idea of it. It is time to speak your truth and open your mouth and say those words you have been holding back.

The yielding of what you wish to say is only holding

and preventing the other versions of you from growing along side you, thus making it difficult. Because you are making it difficult. Once you begin to let go and flow with what the truth is without getting in the way of the information that must be spoken you will see your life shift in the most profound way.

It is time to be follow that intuition, what has it been saying to you? You have already experienced the freedom to choose. Isn't it time to choose a different story? A story where you follow that intuition that is always there maybe a subtle voice in the background noise, sometimes loud and screaming for it to be heard.

Take that time as you read this and be aware of each word that is written. Listen that voice in your head as you read this but as you do envision a second version of your self standing directly behind you. This version of your self is watching you and hearing you read this. This is the practice of being the observer. You are not that body.

We tell our selves yes, we are the body...Because it has all we have ever known so far in said experience. But let me tell you, there is so much more beyond the capacity of the mind and ego can comprehend. Allow your self to be open to receive the information your guides and ascended masters who have been tasked to support you. All you have to do is close your eyes and ask them for support.

They are listening to your every thought , But know it is just you. Other experiences of your self all infinitely supporting you.
Where ever you are based out of and where ever you

are reading this from know that your field of energy is that of a dome. Everything you feel especially love expands your field further and further. When it interacts with others fields they begin to shift because you have shifted. You then allow them that safe space to shift a story of limitation because you have paved the way for them.

So begin to face these stories that you feel limit you. Anything that comes from fear, walk towards it because it is all illusion of the mind.
The one true emotion is love, in which we were born with. Fear was something we were taught. We are not born with fear.
As I finish what I have to say to you all know that this is such a beautiful time to return to support one another, even the times I my self feel limited and at the whim of my own creations I get stuck in the story until I take that step back and practice being the observer. It is then I can realize how funny this all really is. You will too see the humor in it all. I am working towards getting and maintaining this state of awareness , I can do so in fragments and then I lose the sense and am back in a story. But in this moment I am here with you all feeling and knowing those who are going to read this because I am contracted by each of you to provide this as a reminder. I am fulfilling that contract throughout this life time, as well as many other contracts.
Know that when you begin to release, you allow space for new things to appear inside of that space, such as love and gratitude.
I love you.

12-6-15

My new power statement to say every morning to get me geared and pumped for my day!

I am The Water Magister, Flowing, Complete, Abundant, Intuitive, Insightful, Inspiring, Limitless and I travel the world while making money.
12-10-15

When you find peace within it reflects outwardly. Just as every emotion. Find your inner peace and heal the world. Still the waters within to see a beautiful world just waiting for you to recognize it.

12-12-15

The time is always now we say to our selves. But do we live in that state? Are there ever times you sit back and ask your self...Whelp...Where do I go from here?

It seems to me I have a lot of those moments and I get lost in where I want to take my day, or life and it is in those moments that you get sucked into the past or future thought rather then going off what feeling you have inside of what makes you happy.

If we took less time thinking about how an outcome would play out and create expectations we could truly enjoy how a moment would be, because it would play out like a movie and you are not influencing it based on a positive or negative belief.

So if you ever get a thought while your on your phone or on your computer like for example you get a craving for some food. But inside you say nah I'll get that tomorrow. What would happen if on that you listened. There may be someone at that location you were supposed to meet.

This has been happening an immense amount of times for me. The times I tell my self I dont want to do anything, then a thought comes in of where to go and boom I meet someone who I was supposed to and learn more about my own self. How divinely timed is it when you get out of the way of your own greatness?

The timing of things never truly matters, it just matters that you act on what the thought is rather then putting a fear of saying no, this or no that.

Step it up, the game is progressing rapidly now.

12-13-15

How do you want to be loved?
Does it have to be your way?
Does it have to be all the things you see placing expectations?
What if the one you were looking for the whole time doesn't love you the way you want it.
But instead loves you the best way he knows how.
Would that be enough for you?
Or do you have to place limitations on your ideal way.
Will it be too late to notice when they move away?
How do you want to be loved?
What would you let get in the way?
The fear and worries that it isn't your way.
Grasping to hold on to an ideal lover but casting

aside one another
because you want to be loved your way.
What if that was all they knew? Would it make you
complete?
Acceptance is the key, but would you let them love
you his way?
Or does it have to be your way?

How do you want to be loved?
Allowing space for one another to shine in your own
truth and love.
Can you feel it in your heart as its beating how they
want to so badly beat along side you.

But this love has to be the way you see it, so the
synchronistic moments of the beating lovers heart is at
a tune that you are not able to hear. Because you are
too focused on how it has to be rather than how it is
and allowing one another that love to expand.

How do I want to be loved? I know how I want to
be.
The open arms of another lover beside me seeing me
for me.
Crying there with me sharing moments of
vulnerability.
The lovers embrace and eyes locked in one another.
This is how I want my love to be.

Not placing an expectation on how the love has to
be. But just accepting and knowing we are here to
grow together and to own our power. A love that
would push me if they see me stagnant.
A love that empowers and lifts my soul to new heights
rather than placing fears and limitations on how the
way I show my love has to be.

That is my love to be, until that point arrives. The

only way I want to be loved, is the way I give love to me.

12-14-15

I learned that I can do a very old and powerful mudra that has been written in Ayurvedic texts called "Kechari Mudra". I have been able to do this since age 16. I never really knew what the meaning of it or if it had one. But I spent an entire night researching this mudra and the significance. The understanding of my role in this world is becoming stronger and stronger. Doubts are beginning to fade. Here is what I found: Kechari Mudra is considered the king among mudras. In Sanskrit, the word 'Kha' indicates Brahman or the Supreme Reality and 'Chara' means to move. Kechari Mudra helps the practitioner to move in the blissful infinite consciousness of Brahman. Kechari is an advanced practice that enables the yogi to reach higher states of consciousness. Kechari Mudra is mentioned in Gheranda Samhita, Hatha Yoga Pradeepika and various other yogic and tantric texts.

Kechari mudra is a yoga practice where the tongue is rolled up to touch the soft palate. This is an advanced practice and the yogi is said to overcome thirst, hunger, decay and death by this practice. For most people this needs prolonged effort. The tongue can be rolled up to touch the upper palate. Initially it may be able to touch only the hard palate. With practice, it can go further behind to touch the soft palate. Later it can touch the uluva at the back of the throat. With practice, the tongue can go beyond the uvula and enters the nasal cavity to stimulate certain points inside the cavity. This may take months or years of practice. Eventually the yogi is able to taste the nectar (or amrit) which flows from the roof of the nasal cavity. This nectar energizes the body and helps to overcome the need for thirst and food.

There are two ways to perform Kechari mudra, with or without cutting the frenum membrane under the tongue. In the Raja Yoga method, cutting the frenum is not advised. Instead, with certain practices, the tongue can be made long enough to enter the nasal cavity. In Hatha Yoga method, the frenum membrane below the tongue is cut bit by bit to extend the tongue. This enables the tongue to easily pass into the nasal cavity. The Hatha Yoga technique is only for advanced yogis and should be done only under the guidance of a yogi who is an expert in Kechari Mudra.

12-20-15

I feel like discussing something...
There are many of you out there that have heard the phrase you create your reality. But do you truly believe it? Not only do you truly believe it, do you believe everyone else lives this way as well, meaning the plants and the animals.

Now let's take a moment and reflect...The reason I bring it up is I see many vegetarians and vegans getting in rants about the mistreatment of the animals and to stop eating meat. I was vegetarian for a full year. Not for the reasons of "saving the animals" But because my body told me to do so, so I listened.

Do you think that those animals did not create their

reality in such a way that they were "victims" of their circumstances of mistreatment?

Do you feel their experience is invalid as to what they chose?

This applies to everything not just the "mistreated" animals. It applies to people and events we witness, do you feel those events are invalid? How can you truly say that you know exactly why things happened the way they did. Think about what happens behind the scenes, for example at an animal slaughter place.

These animals are choosing to experience this for what ever reason they are choosing, maybe they put others through suffering in concurrent lives. So now they want to feel how they treated others? Now think about all the humans that interact with this animal. The humans doing the killing. What do you think plays on in their minds?

I can only believe they have a moral story popping into their heads quite often. That animal is offering a service, a selfless act of love to be that reminder for all those humans that interact with the animal to show them there is another way. But that animal will not outright tell the human this.

It cannot effect another's free will. So it does what it can to the best of its ability to also serve what ever purpose it has to fulfill in this physical state. It, then makes contracts with other souls to support them in their growth. Not only that it then supports those who consume this meat and flesh.

Think about those who consume the meat, what stories may be going on in their heads. When they eat the fear from the animal. They too begin to absorb that fear, and then transmute that fear either back into an outward or inwardly fear or an inward or outward love through transmutation of this energy.

So then, it serves the humans consuming it as well, same goes with plants. They have consciousness, it has been proven with science that they feel. They too chose to be eaten and picked and harvested to teach us a very fundamental thing in life.

What is that fundamental thing? In my experience it is simply we always choose. We can choose to eat, to drink , to be happy, to be sad, to live off air, to live off only water. Ultimately it is always a choice.

Every single thing that happens in this world is always a choice. The victims of tragedies all chose to take part in that play on the cosmic level to teach others the way back to love. There are NO VICTIMS!

Do not invalidate another's experience because for what ever reason you "feel" bad about that experience. The question to ask yourself is why is it you are feeling "guilt". Have you personally gave love to that version of your self? Know that who ever or what ever they are going through is because it is perfectly designed for their souls growth. No matter what you judge it as.

Take ownership of your life again and understand ANYTHING outside of your self, the only thing it is showing you is your self.

So with the feeling bad about how animals are treated. Ask your self, have you been treating your self badly in some way?

Have you been ignoring aspects of your self in some way?

They are just mirrors to you, nothing outside or external of you has power over you unless you say it does.

Pay attention going forward to the feeling you have inside about situations that you witness and experience. Do not attempt to "fix" it. Because it is perfect. Just see what it is showing you about yourself and how YOU are feeling because of it.

I love you.

12-28-15

I want to share a meditation with you who have significant others and wish to connect on a whole different level.

I call it the Energy Cauldron. It came to me about a year or so ago. You will experience a lot of changes in the dynamic of the relationship utilizing this method.

1. Have you and your partner sit in easy pose, ensure your knees are touching. Have your Left Hand on top of their right, and your right hand Below their Left.
2. Begin opening your channels focus on the crown and open the connection feeling energy coming into your body, filling the entire vessel.
3. Open the root and draw in all the earths energy into your vessel.
4. Focus on the heart, then envision a ball of white light. Every inhale and exhale see it expanding and contracting.
5. Both of you envision this heart, and begin to move the ball of light through the left arm, into the palms of your hands.
6. Hover it in the palm of your hand so you can feel

each others orb.

7. Begin circulating this orb through their arm, through their heart, to the other arm.

8. Keep the circulations slow at first. and Begin speeding it up around 5-10 minutes in.

9. Begin seeing the energy mixing in the center of you.

10. Slow the orb down till it sits in the center of both of you.

11. Envision it being cut in half.

12. Pull one half into your heart, and the other pull into theirs.

13. Thank one another for the experiences you will be sharing.

14. Breathe grounding breaths.

15. GO about your day, and wait 7 days. Do this same meditation again, this time pulling that half orb you had from the heart. Back into the palm, mixing them together again.

16. Draw in only your energy from this orb and they will do the same.

You have now taken on the many emotions and experiences your partner has during these 7 days. So you can better relate to one another.

Do this practice on a regular basis and the relationship will blossom.

Take note of times you both decide you do not want to. Ask each other why?

Enjoy that tantric exercise. I love you.

New Insights

1-3-16

This is.

This is the day I tell that voice of " I'll do it tomorrow" NO! I'll do it TODAY. Right now!

This is the day I commit to finishing an unfinished project.

This is the day I live in my truth.

This is the day I honor my self.

This is the day I give the love to my body, my temple.

This is the day I finish what I start.

This is the day I push my self past the limits of my own mind.

This is the day I express my love.

This is YOUR DAY TO CREATE WHAT EVER YOU WANT!

Get up off your bum and do all those fun things you have been telling your self you want to do and just do it.

No excuses.

This is the day you don't give excuses of not having time,

because you know damn well if you truly wanted to do it time would miraculously appear.

This is the day you meet a new friend.

This is the day you tell someone their beautiful without fear of rejection.

This is the day you spend with someone you care about.

This is THAT DAY. And every day after wards.

It is Your day.

What will you make of it after you read this?
1-3-16
Remember who you are.

Your existence here is but a blink of an eye. This illusion, Although persistent, is just that, an illusion.
There is no evil.
There is no good.
There is just you, not your chemical body, but you your consciousness, your mind. Everything and Everyone, it's just you. Made by you, for you.

You are the creator, the only creator and you can do no wrong.
So bask in your Holiness, for you are immortal. Your chemical vessel, that thing you call a body may and will die.
But you are immortal, eternal.
So do as thine will by the whole of the law.
The law of one, that you are everything that has or will ever be,
And there will be no judgment for your deeds, except that which you give your self.
Serve your self or serve your other self, it is always your choice for you are god, and I love you, always have and always will.
1-5-16

Inspired by the beauty in todays sunrise. However the clouds covered the sun.

The love we have between us is never mistaken because every new breath is another blissful pill taken Swallowed whole it fills and fuels my beating heart.

Yearning and always wanting more of that beautiful connection
So every day I take that time to honor you

Seeing the awe inspiring moments that are shared
Wanting to be able to touch you physically in a human
form
　　To show my love to you and leave you wanting
more
This space is empty yet filled with so much potential
Waiting for you to manifest in the physical so I can
Honor you caress you, feel you to bring me closer
to my own divinity, allowing deeper connection like
never before
　　Every touch a sweet caress towards love for my
own inner self
understanding I am giving love to my own self as I
give it to you
feeling the warmth of the skins energy touching
will you feel this , the way i do?
　　Will you be the same as I see, knowing that the
love given outwardly
is just the love I have for my own self but it is
splurging over the
edge filling my own vessel past it's perceived limits,
so I call upon you to show your self so that we may
bask in this union
　　The energy combining to form that third energetic
connection
the holy trinity, in it we will discover more of our
selves
But until that point arrives I will always greet you
with my lungs,
my heart, my soul, admiring your beauty in all things
　　Waiting for the moment once more to give that
love to you in the physical, wondering who will be
sent to me to display this love that is bursting at its

seams, for when we lock our eyes upon each other
you will know it will be a love the likes of which we
have never felt

Listening to the sounds of the ocean as if whispers
of my long lost lover speaking into me, wanting me to
hear her, letting me know she is here and to never feel
alone. For the seconds turn to minutes and hours and
days. We will meet with new eyes gazing on this
uncharted land

Hoping you too will come with the openness and
vulnerability I have learned to embody so that we can
both excel from any teachings taught by gurus. We
will be our own teachers in this passion.
Pushing, striving, inspiring one another to our fullest
potential
With fires burning, raging an untamed heart that only
one another will ever understand

I will be here for you to manifest in the physical so
that we may connect once more and I can make love to
the one, the all.

I love you

1-7-16

I had inspiration to come up with a new workshop
revolving around the human connection. It involves
cuddling, energy cauldron meditation, eye gazing, eye
dancing, touched connection, heart connections.

1-10-16

Gems touching the sapphire eyes,
I see them clearly as I observe from afar

One day those eyes will be locked onto mine and
A surge of remembrance will flow like water
through our bodies

Remembering all the dream time we have shared
remembering all the time's I denied and forsaken-ed
you
because of fear
But now I know it was all a test to see if I was
ready for my next chapter in my life to
leave space for you to manifest into reality
Can you hear me? Are you out there Sapphire
Goddess?
I feel you nearing, closing in, the frequency is almost
right
Right for both to cross one another and share
The memories of past experiences
I want to hear your troubles, I want to see you cry
I want to feel your pain of the past, so I can share
mine
and you can know you are not alone
I desire to feel your soul and you to feel mine
We will share these stories and as we speak them
realize we both have gone through similar stories
in order for our frequencies to be able to match
Until then I will continue to bask in the love of my
own self
For I know I require nothing outside of the self
But I do yearn for another to share experiences with
I love you
1-11-16
This breath
This breath I take in allows me to remember my
divinity
When I breathe normally I take in the normal amount
of source energy
When I breathe faster than normal I begin to feel

tingling sensations because I am breathing in more of this source energy
The way I like to look at breath is it is data coming into your computer
Normally this data travels at a steady rate
The in flow sends you information from source
The out flow sends information back to source

When you begin to do breath work you send this signal a lot quicker back and fourth so source understands what feelings and sensations to feel, and you also begin to feel more of source energy running through your body.

The communication is much more rapid allowing for a beautiful connection.

It is amazing to think that this air you breath is the same air your ancestors have breathed as well as your future lovers you have yet to meet.

Know they are out there always connected to you, you just are not at the vibration to be in their presence just yet.

But once you begin to learn lessons and grow within the heart you begin to leave open space for them to appear in your reality.

Stop seeking and be when the time arises synchronicity always plays in your favor. Always the perfect time, always.

Have no fear that you are never alone because all things are connected via this breath. It flows in us all and then flows out to the next.

I love you.

1-17-16 *Free Writing*

The Release

This release reminiscing of past times, feeling that

connection
Every time when in each others space it comes back
over and over
Why does it hurt so much
I just want someone to take this pain away
I cry and release, release, release
Not even wanting someone to make it go away but
someone to share it with, to tell me they can feel it too.
Someone to understand where I am and where I want
to be
So I turn to the only true love that has always been
there for me, my self.
I stare at my self in that mirror and I ask Why do
you keep doing this to your self?
That feeling that comes up is just showing you the
love within your self.
And then it comes again, the tears of release, release,
release
Wanting a beloved to see me for who I am and still
want to stand there beside me no matter what
Wanting to support me with picking up these pieces of
this broken heart that is piece by piece being taped
together
and then I remember again, and Release, Release,
Release
Looking back up at my self after my head was
hanging down now shifting to anger and yelling What
the fuck David?
Let it go! LET IT GO LET IT FUCKING GO!
Wanting to just throw everything away and leave
yoga, meditation supporting others, because whats the
fucking point the Ego says.
Then I cry and Release, Release, Release

Remembering I am doing this because it makes me happy,
seeing tears fall down peoples faces as they too heal their stories because in truth....it is healing mine when I support others. and again,......sweet....release, release, release

Now I lay to prepare for sleep, feeling this ache in the heart that can only be healed by accepting where I am .... and that is...

The Release.

1-19-16

I am Love.
I am Light.
I am Peace.
I am Joy.
I am Abundance.
I am Abundant.
I am Worthy.
I am Truth.
I am Free.

I have been receiving so many positive affirmations from not only my self but reflections from people the past few days and just in general. But I never really acknowledge them because I think to my self....Nah That isn't me.

We truly do not honor our selves enough for the tasks we have taken on in this life time. The deeds we do simply by writing or by a smile, by a hug , by listening to another.

Acknowledge your self for something right now after you read this!
What is something you have done that made you feel amazing for your self or another person?

You are so incredibly loved, even in my times of my "shit" where I feel I don't want to come out of my fox hole. I still understand I am creating it all for my self, but the nature of things is that I have to truly dive into that emotion to feel its vast oceans. After I realize I can simply swim or float in this sea, I quickly swim back ashore to start the next roller coaster of emotions or stories to explore.

And thus is the cycle of truly figuring out who you are and that you are loved no matter what you do.

1-20-16

I want to speak on a subject that came up earlier this morning.

Tattoos.

What are they really? To put it simply they are amplifiers of intentions when applied on your body.

If we think about the work Dr. Masaru Emoto did. He proved that by intention you change the molecular structure of water. He applied labels on containers of water with different intentions to amplify the water.

Your body is a vessel for the water within it. The same principle applies. Any tattoo you have on your body the moment you received it and the intention you had when receiving it is what it is doing to the body.

So make sure you go over the intentions of the tattoos on your body to see if the intention you got when receiving it still aligns with what you wish to create in this life. If they do not, then re purpose the intention simply by making a choice as to what it is from this point forward.

In short...tattoos amplify your intentions. :)

Which is why I have tattooed the sigil of Cho Go Pal on my back. It is my sigil of remembrance to share with everyone.

When I then speak with others or am in others presence I embody that for them.

Ancient tribes knew this knowledge which is why they applied them on their body to embody that within the water and soul.

1-27-16

Lately I have had very little drive in waking up in the morning. I am lacking inspiration and motivation. I am still exploring the concept of this and why it has manifested. It started a week and a half ago.

I have no issues inspiring others. But when it comes to my self. I could lay in bed until 12 or 1pm. What I usually do in my mind is I say when someone calls or texts me, that is when I will get up. It leads me to ask the question....where does drive, motivation, inspiration even come from?

It is something that I am being taught, because I used to have inspiration big time. Just hitting a dry spell of it. I think it comes from making a choice and seeing it through until that choice is then manifested.

Not allowing anything else to get in the way of this choice.

Yes you will be tempted, but that is where discipline comes into play. Maybe my inspiration and motivation is inspiring others?

I have slacked a bit this month in terms of my goal of gaining the weight I wanted. Ahh these stories that pop up always at the right time to ensure what is we set our minds and hearts on is what we truly want.

So Its time I dive back into that goal of mine and don't look back. Because where I am going is a place I have never been.

Conquering that fear of the unknown.

Step up your game David.

Stop slacking David.

Break this cycle David.

Time to move forward!!

1-27-16

Free writing to let out some of this thing I am feeling.

Raining outside as time transcends
emotions flowing feeling as if I am controlling this
based on what I am feeling right now
So much emotion wants to break free, finding outlets
letting it out little by little, but when will it be enough
enough to clear that space of the heart to allow room
for another
always thinking of a past lover and what could have
been
its only as difficult as I make it, i say to my self
but I am still living in this state of uncertainty

Wanting another to come on through to take me out
of these murky waters as I sink deeper and deeper into
the emotions
I keep giving my self the love I would but it seems
my soul aches for companionship to share emotions
to bounce ideas with, to share workshops with
to co create a world together with

Every morning I wake up I remember what could
have been and I start my day with affirmations to set
the day
I look through my news feed and see similar souls
experiencing the same so i create workshops revolving
around this
to fill in that gap of emotion that I feel I lack

but is it truly lack? Or is it just a story I tell my self

I have this set story in my mind of someone who constantly visited my dreams and then the other half that tears at the heart is the past

Wanting these attachments to completely fade away so I can be that version of my self I was prior. But do I really want to go back to that version? The one that was still inexperienced in certain areas?

No, I don't think I would want that. So I am back to where I am feeling this emptiness inside. But what is really interesting is I feel complete some days and others it creeps up on me. Not wanting anyone to be around just to be on my own. Then the days when It is the true longing, i slip back into those stories of lack.

Finding that balance that medium ground. So I can gain my footing and begin climbing again to the higher realms.

What is it that is holding you back? I ask my self. I have this story in my mind of creating a romance that transcends time.

But each time I get in my own way when that time comes. Because relationships and lovers are only mirrors to your soul.

To show you what you have to dive into, or what you haven't been paying attention to.

In such I am familiar with what was shown to me last.

This is my medicine letting it all out for all to see. I feel pressure subsiding within me as each word flows without the thought of what the next word will be. As if my fingers do the typing for me.

Getting lost in these written words I clear space of my mind, the chatter that lately has been getting the best of me.

I thought I had it in proper perspective, but I am shown I have more to learn. How beautiful is that.

The moment you surrender to the fact that you know nothing, more flows inside of you.

The moment you admit your faults, you begin to create space to heal them.

The moment you are vulnerable, it allows others to see it is safe to come out and express your self.

Be free with how you feel in this moment.

It is funny to say...but I am enjoying this sadness, anger, melancholy. Because it reminds me of where I started from.

You can only know your truth by living in the falsehood.

You can only experience the light by experiencing your darkest hour.

I love the fact that I can feel what I am feeling.

It's not always gumdrops and unicorns on this path to understanding the self.

What a beautiful life it is that I chose to be able to go through the myriad of emotions that is openly available to the human experience.

I love you.

1-31-16

Inspired by The Avatar Quote and reworked.

Let go of your earthly tether, enter the void, empty and become wind.

Flow like the internal cosmos of the mind, embody no form, endless and become water.

Ground your self to the present moment, dig deep, solidify and become earth.

Ignite the passion with in, unwavering embers of love,

spark and become fire.

2-2-16

Every breath I take is a remembrance of the love I have for you.

The one who will always be with me by my side no matter what.

The self. As I connect with this luminous sun it shows me I am never alone.

I feel the warm touch of its rays hitting my skin like a lover gently caressing me to comfort me.
Relishing in the moments of bliss. As the sun emerges I feel a sense of awe, The universe's eyes first opening to gaze upon my soul.

I imagine a beautiful smile once it's eyes opening. Knowing I am doing amazing things in this realm. I feel it's love trans-versing the cosmos to fill my vessel up with radiance and understanding.
These cosmic rays of light shining codes of knowledge into this physical vessel I chose.

To later be deciphered and decrypted into wisdom. Utilizing this wisdom to be the best version of my self I can be with the tools I have. I am here basking in your light, which essentially is my own light.

Thank you and I Love You.

2-4-16

Will you be there for me like the morning sun? Always shining the truth in my presence even when I am in my darkest hour?

Will you be the one who holds space for me when I am in my shit, knowing to not take what I say personal, to not judge and just be with what I am saying.

As I heal past traumas, past life traumas, karmic blood

line traumas for the world.

Will you still be there standing strong?

As I do the same for you, knowing to never take it personal.

To know all things said in the moment are things that have to be said to trigger these aspects of our selves so we can heal.

Will your love stand strong through all of it?

Will you own your own shit as I do the same? Understanding anything you direct outside of the self is merely a reflection of what you are battling inside. To never be the victim.

Or will you run at the bumps in the road because you are afraid of what it could be, what true unconditional love can be.

I will find you some day this one I describe the one who will never take things personal and the one who calls me out on my own things.

Because as I progress on this path, I realize I am that for my self.

I love you.

2-5-16

Ahh a new subject came into my reality today.

The subject is proclaiming you are bored.

Every time i hear the phrase my ears are stung by a sharp piercing sound.

Boredom comes from the idea of having to constantly distract yourself from the silence which in turn is listening to your heart.

To say you are bored is to say you do not admire the beauty that is literally happening all around you at all moments.

To say you are bored is to forget that you are creating

all that you see and in that seeing how powerful all
moments are.
To say you are bored is to proclaim i do not enjoy the
silence in all things and thus dislike feeling.
To say you are bored is to turn off all of your feelings
and numbing your self to the divine.
You are never bored.
Your ego is.
I love you.
2-7-16
Serendipity filling the vessel of my self
Cold hands and feet as I stare along that open sea
Feeling the warmth and radiance of another soul
shining the expansive light they hold.
As we share in the moment of creation we both
created.
What a wondrous thing to know that all moments you
are in are moments you personally created for your
self based on wanting to feel something and
experience something.
At times things that feel brand new but is the same,
with different souls, but different perspectives to give
greater expansion of the self.
Grateful we cherish this day and the air around us
never forgetting that it can be all gone once we have
served the souls purpose. So I bask in every moment
now in true awe.
Loving this life, even with the downfalls, even
with the sadness I've endured, even with the anger that
has been felt from the past. I would never trade any of
it for another.
Thank you , I love you.
2-10-16

Expressions of creativity
I for a long time used to believe that I was not a
creative person.
I associated creativity to painting. It wasn't until
recently I truly understood what it means to be
creative.

You create every moment of every day, you
literally are the creator. You create based on feeling.
It goes to show how powerful these stories are that we
tell our selves.

People who say they are not worthy of affection,
People who say they do not deserve to be loved,
People who say they do not deserve the abundance in
their life,
People who say they will never accomplish anything.

It's all bullshit stories we tell our selves due to past
traumas and experiences that has become solidified
into the subconscious. You ARE worthy, You ARE
loved, You ARE Abundant, You CAN Accomplish
anything!

Shed these limitations you placed on your self
because a parent told you something when you were
younger,
Shed these limitations you placed on your self because
a past lover scolded you and you chose to feel a
certain emotion.

I realize now I am amazing at creating things.
Because I believe it now. I have created such amazing
things because I let go of that block that I am not
creative.
FUCK yes I am creative! Just as you are!
Step into this new version of your self with gusto.

Say it with me I am a Powerful source creator sent

here to be that shining pillar of light for the masses so they can too see they have that same light within them.

Be the example, You want to make a difference in the world?
Do it by displaying your practice, do it by being the best version of you , you can possibly be.

Do not do it by thinking you have to change the outside world. Because that fight is futile. Do the things you love FOR YOU!
Everything else will fall into place. Trust me!

I am going to continue creating beautiful expressions of my self ranging from workshops, meditations, art pieces, water art(which is in the works). Because I can, Because I believe, and most importantly because I am a Creator!

YOU ARE TOO! Stop playing small!
RISE!!
2-11-16
Feeling of not being seen or acknowledged came up a few moments ago.
It is something that has been in my reality lately.

I find my self at times wanting to "prove" my self to certain people. It reminds me of wanting to prove to a parent something. Bringing that awareness to it and understanding why I am feeling this way is essential in actually overcoming and accepting this aspect of my self.

Awareness is key when you feel a certain way on what comes up in your reality. Then vocalizing it and acknowledging that it is there.
This reflection is showing me that I do not acknowledge my self enough in the things that I do.

I feel I do things that support others, but I get to

take time to truly appreciate what I have been doing for others and my self.

Thank you for this reflection.

2-16-16

Oh Fear...How I have grown to love you.
Every time I am with someone who presents this emotion I notice it so well.
I notice the hesitation because in truth it is only the fear of what is beyond that limitation the mind had created, the fear of the unknown. We grow to be so comfortable with this fear that it is scary to move past it.

Due to a past trauma in life. We like to think it is something we can never overcome.
But when I push those beautiful souls past that fear, what they discover is beauty, limitlessness.
The way I feel when I support another past a fear makes me feel as if I am healing aspects of my self because in truth I am. As I support the healing process in another I am actually just healing my self.

There are days that I do not do this and I feel as if I have not accomplished much. But the days where I support another I feel alive...moving past these traumas together.

An amazing teacher named Kevin A. Walton told me the only thing fear is doing is showing us the way back to love. I understand what he means by this.

To me the funniest thing about fear is how we rationalize it in our mind to stay at this point, at this limitation, these chains we allowed to be placed around our hearts.

It is the fear that is in our life as hurdles to overcome to be the next version of ourselves. It is our fear that allows us to truly attain what we want in life. When you notice a fear know that is the way to go to get to the next step in your evolution.

Because we are not alone in this, we are family just providing safe space for one another to remember it's ok to come out of that shell, that wall.

You are Safe.

You are Loved.

You are FREE!

2-17-16

Dreams

Last nights dream brought some clarity as to where I am in a story that has taken me quite some time to accept.

It was a repetition of a scenario that has played out and I found my self still lost in the story of it again.

When I awoke I was angry at my self for still falling into the same cycle of what has always been. I stayed laying in my bed for 2 hours contemplating why I am still in this loop.

I realize it is because I do not want to accept truly where I was at. I keep telling my self no, no I am good. But Obviously if the scenario keeps repeating, even in my dream and I fall into the same cycle it isn't quite over.

I love my dream time because it allows me to relive certain instances but not exactly the same. I am able to recreate an environment to see if I have truly healed a story without actually being there.

I even go into other peoples dreams to support them with their stories. But this one really has got me thinking things. I am still seeking something outside of the self and I get angry when I am not able to attain it.

In this dream I specifically remember going out of my way to see something. Always seeking....In it I had to remind my self to go and do the things I want to do that would make me happy without giving my power away to someone.

The attachment strings are quite strong when it comes to things like this. I am just using this to release my thoughts because otherwise I would be in it for quite awhile. So I think I am still giving my power away to an outside force. Which in reality makes me feel weak because I do not feel whole.

The jist of this is....do things in your life that make you feel powerful, whole and complete. All things will fall into place. At times you will require reminders of this because the mind will constantly want to ask, well I wonder about...Just keep moving forward in your own growth.

My rambling is done. Thank you and I love you.
2-19-16
What troubles your mind dear ones?
What is it you are keeping bottled up, afraid to speak into words so that others can feel and understand you?

Know that when you speak those things into reality you free yourself from the imprisonment of what is holding you back from being the best version of your self. In your vulnerability you will discover others can too relate to you and thus you allow others to heal these aspects of the self.

Ahhh, the release of being the true you, the authentic you of speaking what is on your mind freely, without the judgments we give our selves.
Inhale......Exhale.....remember who you are and what

you chose to come here to do...

Freeing our selves from these shackles little by little, the veil of disillusion is lifted. You will begin to see the beautiful world that is all around.
The absolute freedom of expression to speak that truth.
Know you are loved, you are safe.

Speak your truth today!
Open your eyes to the possibility of what truly is.

I Love You.

2-19-16

Know that this is all with purpose.
It is driving us to understanding how powerful water will become in this Age of Aquarius.

The age of enlightenment and knowledge of water.
Be ok with how it is occurring because it is divine.
Accept what is. This is the process of awakening the masses. Once we are all awake to the power of water these disasters will cease to occur.
But it has to for now to bring awareness to our water, to our bodies.

Just as you must accept the emotions you have within you, they are valid. This too is valid in the nature of what is happening on the earth.
The earth has emotions and feelings, chakras too. It is living.
She knows what she is allowing. If she didn't want this to occur, it would not.

Learn to accept, validate and understand the process and your emotions.
They are always speaking something to you.

2-20-16

I just want to be seen said the ego.
I just want to be love said the heart.
I awake each day with a new version of love i never
thought possible.
My heart grows as my awareness grows.
In this i accept all reflections.
I am free.
One day someone will see you for who you are.
One day they will look into your bodies eyes, through
the doorway to your soul.
They will see the sheer absolute beauty and warm
filled love you have.
They will acknowledge and truly see the real you,
without these masks we wear for others to see.
The facade of society that we show to some, and not
others.
One day you will have a relationship with someone
not based out of fear or ownership of someone.
One day they will inspire you because they are aspects
of you that you wish to attain, so it becomes an
exchange of realities.
To show each other how to be the best version of each
other. While still being the whole perfect person you
are.
Without losing the integrity of who you were before
you went into it.
Without feeling the cage surrounding you, without the
feelings of your wings being clipped.
Without the worry of what that other person is doing
when not in your presence.
One day you will feel safe, whole. But not because of
this other person. Because you have found it within
your self first.

One day you will have moments set aside for each
other to truly express open and honest communication
with safe space for each other to be.
One day you will have truly cosmic sex the likes of
which you are not even able to fathom.
One day that connection will drive you to the divine
understanding that we truly are one.
One day that feeling of oneness will carry into your
every day actions and you can share that love with
others.
One day that love for others will turn into that
knowing, and understanding that they are where they
are to be at every moment of every day.
One day....That one day.....is Now.

2-21-16
When you truly surrender to the moment you allow
your self the vulnerable space to be the true you.
It is in this moment connection is built and a new love
can be formed.
Not the sexual love, but a love that transcends all that
is, that love and understanding that we are in this
together.
Not against each other, but here to support,
acknowledge, listen, to the best of our ability.
I allowed this to happen last night, and the comfort
felt from it was exhilarating. Just allow and everything
will fall into place.
You are loved.
2-22-16
If you are going to love, love with every fiber of
your being.
Do not hold back because of fear.

Do not hold back because of the past experience.
Love and open your heart, surrender to that feeling
without
judging it.
Be the true you, the one you want the other to see. No
walls, no hesitation. Just pure love.

Be the love you want in return. Give as much as
you want to get in return.

I love you.

2-23-16

Thinking about what your hands will feel like upon
my skin...
Feeling the energetic bonds we would create

The touching of our lips combining to form
the first explosion of passion for the entire cosmos to
ripple outward.

The love shared would be matching of the love I
have for my self.
This new lover knowing and understanding we do not
have to take ownership of each other.
To continue to live our own lives in the pursuit of
serving and assisting others growth in all ways.

The understanding that when we share our time
with each other, it is the only true currency we have in
this world. So we cherish and value it when in each
others field.
Feeling my finger tips on your back as you enjoy the
expression of the love I have for my self.

As I honor your body and understand as I give this
love , I am giving it to my self and it is a form of
healing.
A form of knowing our divinity.

These are all just fantasies I have in my mind of

when that lover will cross my path, and allow her self to be as vulnerable as I am.

To hear her stories of the past traumas.

To allow me to dive deep into her past so that I may support her as she supports me with mine.

We will cry together, we will laugh together because of how beautiful of a life it was we chose to live up until that moment of connection.

To see it all had to play out this way to bring us to the same vibration of love in order for us to be able to touch each other physically.

For if we did not experience those moments, we would never cross paths or see each other in the visible spectrum of reality because we would not be able to relate and thus our energies would repel one another.

How beautiful is it to understand what was just said to know every experience brings you closer to your mirror, closer to your self, closer....to the creator.

In this I call out to my lover where ever she is. To step fourth into reality. Allow your self to shed your layers, your baggage to meet me. Because when you do, the ripples of this love will effect the masses.

I sit here waiting patiently for you.

I Love You.

2-29-16

May you find your voice in the moment.

May you learn your power through experience.

May you take ownership of your life again.

May you learn you are never alone.

May you find your inner peace.

May you learn it is ok to be afraid of facing an emotion.

May you know this life is a playground for our soul.
May you live in your authenticity.
May you learn your purpose.

Fly, Fly. Spread your wings and fly.

Love = 50% vulnerability + 50% willingness to surrender to the moment.

Surrender and allow your words to be as true as you are.
Allowing it flow out without filtering because of the fear you hold.
Time to come out and play.

Have you ever truly shared every single skeleton in your closet with someone?

Allowed someone to truly see the deepest darkest hour of your being, and know they would hold you high still without judgment?

I am in this exploration and it will be glorious. Share your deepest memory with someone and watch as your reality shifts because that no longer has power over you.

There is nothing that will harm you, allow your self that freedom.

3-1-16

You do not heal others, you are only shining your light so the other can recognize their own, and then heal themselves if they choose it.

3-8-16

So over the weekend I had a woman place the sigil of Cho Go Pal Tattooed on her shoulder.

If you do not know what a sigil is. It is a symbol

that when given attention or seen feeds it further power to the intention that it has. In this case it is " The remembrance of who we are before we chose this physical body" To allow the shedding of the stories of limitation we hold.

By her getting this tattooed she is allowing others to see this sigil and further feeding it. Thus the people who use this sigil can use it on water and vessels that hold water.

So I thank you and honor you for taking that step and supporting this sigils growth. As I am by having it on my back.

She went even deeper and mentioned something profound about this sigil. That when seen in the 3D it is a pyramid and a sphere in the middle of the pyramid. The blue Y is a human that has 3 orbs. The Snake spiral is the kundalini energy, or DNA energy being completed within that human.

I think I may commission an artist eventually to turn that into a painting for me.

This is just showing me how powerful this sigil is becoming. That another soul sees it and is inspired to do so. The places we will go in this life.

Thank you Reflection!

3-9-16

Rise a new version of your self in the remembrance of your power.

The power to declare what it is you want to experience in your life.

I have a home work assignment for you today.

I call it the Manifesting game. I played it over the festival with a Beautiful Goddess and the results were epic...

Here is how you play:

1. Decide something random you want to see someone wear or an object you want to see on a person or sign or anything in your life. Example: I would like to see someone wearing a teenage mutant ninja turtle teeshirt.

2. Next Visualize this in your mind someone wearing it or where the object would be on a person or building. Note: That when you see this object or thing it may not be exactly how you envisioned it. That is because when you let go of the outcome it will appear how it is ment to appear in your life. Do not have a fixed way of how you will experience it.

3. Let go of the expectation of seeing it today or any other day. Completely forget about it.

4. Wait to see how long it takes to show up in your reality.

After the first one, kick it up a notch and get bigger and bolder with your manifesting. Until the point you truly create the reality of your choosing.

Game on My Loves.

I Love You.

3-10-16

The Game You play

This game you play pretending to not feel, running from the emotion

When will you learn that the more you run the deeper the emotion gets stored

In that the deeper the pain will be felt

Bursting from the pressure at it's seems

Projecting the emotions onto others, like projectile emotional vomit

Own the feeling, it is time, stop running

You have my support in this, but you never reach out
You say you are ok, but I see through the mask that is
duct taped to your raw face, I see the light
It is piercing through wanting to be heard but, it keeps
getting buried

This game you play you think no one else can see
it?
Those who have already gone through the struggle,
the emotional pain of it can see through it perfectly.

I know it is rough, it is a birthing process of the
new version you are ment to be. It is the next version
of who you see your self to be but you do not put in
the work, so it just keeps getting buried.

I want you to feel, to see, to touch, and experience
what you are. Inside I know you are not wanting to
feel because subconsciously I understand...you want to
dive deep into this emotion to see if you can make it
out. But without the breathes of air, without the
admittance that you are in pain. You dive deeper.

Like the scene from What Dreams may come when
she is deep inside her mind and No one could get her
out of it or else they too would lose them selves.

I know you like to pretend you are stronger then
you are. You care what people think of you. But know
I love you and I want you to feel. Rise up, shine your
light. Feel the pain, It's all part of the process.

The game you play, is the one I played and I beat
that game and graduated to a new one. Will you join
me in it?

I Love You.

3-11-16

Those who say they "can't" never will.
Those who say they can will push fourth.

193

Waiting for the souls who are limited by their own fears.
The doers pave the road ahead to shine the light ahead.
Like a lantern on the road to the unknown.
Once they show the way, the can't suddenly turns to "That seems easy".

Thus the cycle continues while the leaders forge their way through the unknown, conquering their fear of what is in front.
The truth is we fear the unknown.
Look at it like once you take your foot off the ground, that step disappears....the step in front of you will only emerge once you trust and allow that foot to fall.

So just keep trekking. The road ahead is only as easy as you want to make it for your self. Know that your light shines bright.

I Love You.

3-14-16

Embracement of Healing

Spinning in my own universe guided by the compass of the heart
Seeing all that is from a perspective that was never witnessed
Seeing things as fast forwarded videos as I sat down in amazement at the world we create.

I stared out at the ocean to an island ahead able to place my consciousness on the shoreline witnessing others play and embrace one another.

I felt their joy, their love, their fears and worries.
After reuniting with a soul that was as bright as the sun.
Feeling grounded by their field surrounding me.
Warm embraces over the ocean.

Feeling one another's soul in a divine connection.
All the dreams and feelings returning.

Felt the heart burn with a new yearning
One of love for my self shinning onto another
feeling like foxes cuddling in their warm den
listening to the noises of wind chimes and oceans

Life was felt perfectly in this moment, realizing
once I let go
a new space opened to allow this moment to be created
attachment is what holds the bind,
the space in the mind that limits the self
Seeing the images of galactic foxes in my mind eye
I felt your soul and you felt mine

Living in the moment in the cool wind,
warm embraces to enable connection
this embracement of healing was what we both desired
no words had to truly be spoken, it was all felt within

But words wanted to come through to see if you
felt it,
the ego checking in its little voice

Moon over head smiling at us, like the chests-hire
cat grinning with happiness, that two souls shared that
embracement of healing.

Co creating worlds together to move forward.
A feeling I will always cherish as I dive deeper into
my own love for my self, it emanates outward to give
space for you.

You will discover your power, as the walls you
have up
begin to break down, with each embrace chipping
away
the pain and fear.

Waiting for the next, embracement of healing...

3-15-16

Little by little these emotions you have buried will resurface....maybe at times you least expect it.

Which is why its best to truly feel them at the time they are created, or go back to the moments when they were and confront them.

They only want your love and attention and they will be free.

Look into a mirror and confront those versions of your self.

They deserve that much.

When that voice pops in "this is too good to be true".

Know that it is fear showing its face to check in with you to see if you truly want it.

If you make the choice out of fear you will begin to manifest everything in your reality to make you believe you are not worthy enough to receive it.

Even though you may have asked for it, we create these check points to gauge where our attention goes.

Fear will limit you, Love will empower you.

Ask your self before a decision, will this make me feel limited or empowered?

Based on the answer you will know if the choice is coming from the heart or from the ego.

I Love You

3-16-16

Take ownership and responsibility of your world.

All the things that anger you that someone else is "doing to you".

Is simply you creating the reality to show you your own anger that you have not been wanting to feel.

All the things that make you sad, unworthy, not

heard, not valid.

All the same. Take ownership and transmute it within your self first before pointing the finger and projecting it onto someone else.

It is one of the 4 agreements. Never take anything personal.

Every single person is fighting a battle you know nothing about.

The trick is to determine when they are projecting, and for you to understand and hold that space for them to truly express them selves. Then once completed hold them in your loving arms and just be there for them.

This fear of not wanting to get close to anyone is just the fear of you not wanting to get close to your self.

The fear of not wanting to uncover things about your self so you place walls and blocks up for others to see where your own limits are.

But what I have learned from a beautiful and powerful soul.....If you are going to be in my sphere of reality.

You will either face your demons, just as I will, or you will be pushed away energetically to allow room for those who wish to face these things with me.

In such, I know I am always where I am supposed to be. To allow space for anyone to come close to me, to allow my own self to be vulnerable so it creates a connection with those who have not been vulnerable.

I love you.

3-17-16

I rise to this wonderful sun this morning and I had some interesting thoughts.

The Sun

The Sun never dims its light so that it can make you feel special.

The Sun always shines to illuminate your path through the darkness.

The Sun is so loving it knows one thing and that is to shine, Always.

The Sun I feel is an evolved soul that asked to be where it is so that it can be that guiding light for us all to be able to feel that warmth of love within us and around us.

The Sun as an evolved soul never worries if someone doesn't love it.

The Sun as an evolved soul never thinks "I wonder what this person thinks of me"

The Sun has but one thing on its mind and that is love, the same love you can feel as it rises each day to spread the warmth upon your skin.

The similar feeling of a lover being held close to you feeling their warmth upon your own skin, you feel that connection to the sun and it is ever lasting. A long lost friend that has nothing but your best interest in mind.

So if you ever feel lonely simply look at the sun and know it is there sending you love at all times. You just have to be open to receive it's loving gaze.

I Love You.

3-17-16

When things seem crazy and falling out of place. Just take a step back and observe it instead of reacting to it.

What you will notice is that from the observer you can now respond to it.

Rather than allow the sudden emotion to take over.

Be the observer.

3-18-16

Love Letter to my self time.

I invite you all to write a love letter to your self. Instead of writing it to your lover, direct this one to your self.

Dear David,

The past few months have been an interesting time getting over a special person in your life. But know I have always been here by your side supporting you every step of the way.

I thank you for allowing your self to become open again to begin receiving love once more instead of just giving it.

This receiving will allow you to go more in depth within your self and understand how deep your love can go. Each heart ache we have experienced together has been just but a stepping stone in unlocking these new versions of our selves. I couldn't be more happy then to share it with you. The one who for sometime I never truly saw. I was constantly wanting to find this love outside of my self and gave it away to others without seeing you first.

As each day passes a better understanding comes and better communication and respect of our intuition is made. To follow that voice that guides us to where we have to go. It is a beautiful thing to finally be heard and acknowledged by you.

As we continue to dive deeper into our vulnerability we are shining our light out wards for others to do the same. Little by little igniting the passion in others simply by just being us.

So I thank you for taking the time out of our day to

write this to ourselves.

I love you, I always have, and I always will.

Thank you.

3-19-16

Transformation

Transformation is not always the easiest to experience, it comes into our reality in form of difficult news at times. It is up to us to recognize these points as Kevin Walton says to me they are "Acceleration points" to push us even further than where we have been before.

If you think about how a bow and arrow works. In order for the arrow to shoot far into the distance it must first be pulled back and at the moment of surrender, the release of the arrow you are launched forward to uncharted areas in your life that allow you further insight.

These rough patches we go through are important to be the observer in and understand you MUST experience this to be that new version of your self that this no longer happens to. Because that new version does not experience those same stories of limitations that your current one does. So naturally you must face things that bring those emotions up.

I like to be very observant of my reality in such that when I notice butterflies or I have dreams of which my teeth fall out I know huge shifts are coming in my space. Because these are symbolic gestures that my higher self sends to me in code for me to decipher. Every day I begin to understand more how I speak to my self in symbols and every day life.

It is up to you to do the same, to find these subtle messages for you in your life. They are literally everywhere, but know that in these transformational moments of your life, you would not experience them if you were not strong enough to over come them. We always experience the things we are ready to face and heal.

We are always given opportunity for this. If we fail, it will just come back around until we finally succeed in moving past it and progressing forward.

So acknowledge your self in this moment for how far you have come, the moments you have experienced where you said to your self....FUCKKKK I am never going to make it past this....Look where you are right now....you are still alive, you still have food, you still have that love for your self, and most of all you are still serving your purpose in this world.

I love you.

3-21-16

Discouragement

There will be times when you wake up in the morning and you do not have the motivation to push forward. I experience it. It is in these times it is necessary to remember what you are.

A divine spark, a spark that has the ability to manifest at will what they desire. The spark of god is within you, and it is you. Remember you are the physical representation of such.

So to say to your self, I have no motivation to get out of bed. Remember that you exist here on this plane. And if you exist there was some motivational factor that you decided to fragment your essence into who you are right now reading this message.

There is your motivation. The one that you chose to exist at this time to place all of your focus and attention in this physical body that you created to be that representation of your divinity and love for others to see.

There are days still like this morning where I was just like...ahhh I just want to keep sleeping in. But I have to pull my self out of that bed and remember that simple fact. I even went as far as creating further tools for me to get my lazy butt out of bed like my pets. My little foxy Lily I feel is another representation of my love and divinity that she is my alarm clock at times.

She will continue to pounce on me until she completely wakes me up and I love her for that. I feel that was one of her missions in this life was to wake me up from my slumber and provide that unconditional love to me, same goes with my kitty Zoey. We always create things for our own growth.

So as you start your day this morning, bring your awareness to the fact that you chose to exist in such an amazing and monumental point in human society where we are now starting to realize how powerful we are. This is the true baby steps of our inner minds. This is where we decide what direction and at what pace we want to move at.

I love you.

3-21-16

Homework Assignment for today.

If you choose to accept it be prepared to face emotions that may arise or judgments on what you will be doing.

Begin writing down what you deserve in your life. Whether it be from a partner, job, the income level you want.

Everything within reason of what you base your

reality on. Do not shoot for making 1 Million dollars an hour as you will not even believe it for your self to be true.

Make things simple and within your reach, and go a little further even beyond that. If you make $15 an hour double it.

After you create a list of things you deserve.
Then create a column on that same list and write down a quick reason as to why you don't have that yet.

Example: First column will be : I will make $75 an hour
Second Column would be: Feeling of Unworthiness of this amount.

Short answers for why you do not have what you want in your life.

Once completed. Review it and read over it 3 times. Then Burn it.

As you burn it know that your desires is now in the ether and sent to manifest into your reality.

Do this. Get to it! I am working on mine.
3-23-16
Today has definitely been a day of testing my patience and feeling my anger.
I know Kevin is there as well.
After my phone call with him I have been experiencing some fun things entering into my reality.

One of the things I have learned that while being in the Computer field. You have to have a lot of patience when dealing with customers. Over the years I have developed this more and more. I feel that is one of the reason I chose that profession is to mainly teach me patience. My entire life has been revolving around patience as well.

From having someone ask the same question over and over, to not understanding what I am saying. It all points to the same thing, communication issues. Once you begin to have an open dialog and communication with your self you can begin to bridge those bridges with others and be open with your communication on what you mean and what you feel.

The only thing the anger was showing me today was that it has been awhile since I felt it, I would feel it subtly in annoyance, but never full on. I allowed my self a rage fit today as well. After being inspired by Kevin on his.

Little by little things are falling into place and as such these emotions have to surface for you to keep pushing forward to be that version of your self that you see your self to be.

Do not fear your emotions, they do not rule over you.

That is the work, allowing your self to truly feel the emotion acknowledge it and let it know that you love it and see it.

Then move on. Otherwise you will continue to harbor and bottle these emotions in and will explode on someone for getting your order wrong for coffee or someone cutting you off.

As I have personally witnessed. Which reminds me I just now recognized a pattern. About 4 days ago I was driving and a woman was swerving into my lane, I beeped at her. 20 seconds pass and she zooms next to me and rolls her window down and gives me a snare and puts her fist up at me as if I offended her. I simply looked at her a smiled and laughed. As I recognized the reflection of that inner anger with me that I had not acknowledged in some time. Which I see why today played out the way it did.

It is similar to a pressure valve that has to relieve the pressure otherwise the gasket will explode. In short increments allow your self to feel the emotion until it no longer rules over you. Or you can just allow your self to truly feel the emotion and surrender to it and trust it will not take over.

These little bits of anger are just minor pressure released within me. So that I can truly be that version of my self that is there to inspire the world.

You will know that you have move passed the things that anger you, when those same things now make you laugh and smile.

Just some insight and ramblings.

I Love You

3-26-16

I love the reflections and reminders I create for my self.

The times I have self doubts, I quickly create a reflection that reminds me of my worth and to continue pushing forward in what I am creating with my life.

I know the things I am doing have impact. I may not see it a lot of the times, but I know it is changing lives. Like a rock being thrown into a pool of water each bounce a new perception of awareness unlocked for the world and as they skim the surface those ripples flow outward to effect all those in its wake.

I am this rock casted into the water, it is what I chose to embody in this life time. It has been a great honor and responsibility to be that for others and my self. Because the truth of it all is when I allow my self this role, I learn more then those I am shining on to. I see the reflections and smiles, tears that get released from each interaction. It is showing me that I am healing my self more and more every day.

As each soul that enters into my sphere of reality becomes self-healed they are allowing me to heal as well. I thank all if you who have ever been in my presence for being that reflection for me.

I love you, and honor each and every one of you. I see you and acknowledge you all.

Keep thriving.

3-28-17

I rise this morning with a sense that things are about to rapidly change once more.

I will get into that in a moment.

Last night I was at an open mic night which I didn't even know until I was there. I was inclined to speak. Prior to speaking I began to feel the nervousness. But when we begin to understand certain things you will realize this nervousness is simply an immense amount of energy you are feeling to be directed in some way so the body shakes.

As I finally allowed the energy to flow out of my face portal...The energy escaped the mouth and words hit the ear drums of all those who were there to hear it. What was said? I simply had them all take a moment of silence and close there eyes and breathe for a minute, then after spoke about letting them know it is time to start feeling their emotions and to stop hiding.

These emotions are little children versions of us who demand acknowledgment. All of what I spoke flowed from the heart.

After I said thank you and I got off the stage....not

soon after, I had a good friend of mine come and hug me and as she did my legs felt shaky still vibrating from all of the energy. She was my grounding rod to relieve a bit of the remnants. After that another girl whom I didn't know came to give me a hug telling me she had to hear that. Not soon after that, a guy came and did the same and thanked me.

The reason I am writing this is to remind each of you to take the opportunities when you have them to remind your soul family how powerful they are. Because in turn they will shine their light onto others. Thus allowing you to grow further.

Last night I had a dream of my teeth falling out again. Which every time this has happened a major shift in reality occurs in the waking life. I am eager to confront what this shift entails and I thank you for allowing me so many opportunities to remind our brothers and sisters it is time to start feeling again.

3-29-16 *Poem*

I'll be your shining ray of light
I'll be that pillar of truth to illuminate your way
If only you truly allow your eyes to see me for who I am

Will you then appreciate the beauty that is within ?
I'll be that gentle hand to comfort your pain
I'll be the ocean that cleanses your soul
If only you allowed your self the vulnerability to express it

Will you then understand the power you possess by opening up?
I'll be that everlasting love
I'll be that burning desire of passion that accelerates us to union

If only you see that I am but a mere reflection of the love within

Will you then learn no one will ever complete you but yourself?

I'll be that constant reminder
I'll be that reflection of your own emotions
If only you promise to be that for me when my light dims

Will you then learn the dance of facing our fears?

I'll always be here in reflection to our love
Waiting....For when you have the courage to stand up and show your self
I'll still be here just shining moving forward.
Waiting ..... for you to walk beside me and take my hand as we move into the direction of ascension.
Understanding that there is no ownership or attachment to one another.

Just a sheer acceptance that we are on this same road to be reflections of emotions.
Taking ownership of the world we create and not projecting onto one another.

I'll be your shining ray of light, until you make your way to me, and continue on even when you do.

3-31-16

Here you are again. Even after I block you in my life for feeling unappreciated by checking up on you and wanting you to face your fears. But instead you hide and say it isn't welcome. So I shut you out. But you keep showing up in my dreams wanting to see me. I know your hurting but are afraid of saying it because of the guilt you hold. We had a good thing but fear won in the end. I still hold space for you when you want to truly be a friend in my life. One where we can share our experiences. You don't always have to think there is a hidden agenda. But I get it. You are in constant pain.

I often wonder if you ever took time for yourself to process the breakup rather then just jump into a new relationship. But you were never truly honest with me. You taught me to be honest with my self. Because it was something you couldn't do. I have been growing. I know you have too at your own pace. You can always reach out to me, because this time I won't. I love you, I wish you well my beloved.

Stop hiding your feelings.
Take a chance. Jump in. The water is fine.
Believe me. I used to run as well. You will never grow in comfortable settings. Time to change your pattern.

4-5-16
Every day is an opportunity to follow through with your word on a choice. Meaning to set your mind on something you want to manifest and to keep following through until you make it a reality.

What is stopping you? What are you afraid of? Know that if a fear comes up you are on the right path. Begin looking at fears as way points towards your success if you ever forget which way to go, follow the fear. It will show you the way.

Fear only leads you back to your own divine beauty and love.

I Love You.

4-6-16 *Free Writing*

Does it hurt

Does it hurt to run from the pain of your past? Always looking over your shoulder because of the big bad emotion slowly creeping up on you.

How does it feel to constantly run? Do you ever get so tired of it all and say to your self Enough is enough, I am facing this emotion NOW.

At what point does this happen? When will you make that choice to stop living in fear To stop running from an emotion that is running at you full speed, slowly at first. Tip toeing possibly because it does
not want to startle you.
But when you notice it coming, you begin to place walls around it.
This emotion is crafty because it wants to be seen and felt and acknowledged. Just as a child wants your attention.
So it begins running after you faster and faster. Tearing down these imaginary walls you place around it.

You are still running at the same pace. Not knowing that this emotion has been growing older and older. Progressing from a baby to an adult now running full speed towards you.

Until the point you make that choice. To stop running and turn around and to face it or to keep running until it catches you.

Which of the two would you prefer? To be surprised randomly by an emotion that you have been bottling in for so long, or truly seeing it hurling towards you with arms wide open, crying and desperately wanting you to tell it you love it?

It's always a choice...You use so much more energy in running from an emotion and pretending it isn't there, then you would if you just said Hello to it and embraced it fully to allow it to truly be felt.

It will not over power you. It just wants that warm embrace from you. Just like how when you are in those lonely nights and you want to be felt, to be touched. These emotions wants to be touched and felt. But you touch and feel them by facing them.
By telling them you love them, by saying Thank you for allowing you to see these aspects of your self you have been denying because of a past experience that seemed so hurtful that it has put you running and constantly looking back.

You know there are times where you remember a certain experience. But instead of facing it, you pass it off as if it didn't exist, as if it wasn't a valid experience, as if you were a victim in that situation.

But there is a secret....You created it....You created it all.
Why? Simply because you can, because you wanted that lesson in this life time to be the strong person you see your self to be.

In order to be that person these emotions have to be held, and nurtured and seen and most importantly loved.

Are you ready to turn around for just a moment and acknowledge these little children versions of you embodying different emotions you have been neglecting?
They only want your love and attention.

If not when? Tomorrow? The next day? When you have a little bit more free time? When you are less busy?

Make the choice. Release. Release Release.

At a certain point you will realize all of this perceived pain is simply your energetic body healing. It is all love.

4-7-16

Spread your wings and fly, now is always the time. Remember how powerful you are to be able to create such a beautiful reality filled with what ever purpose you decide.

No one else can choose that for you.

It is always YOUR choice to make meaning from anything you experience in this life.

Stop waiting on someone else to move forward.

They can catch up when they are ready, they have to make the choice for themselves.

No longer choosing to listen to the negative dialog that may be said to you.

No longer taking it personal.

Reclaim it your power. Now!

4-9-16

Hesitation

The game is hesitation. Do you play it? I am sure some of you do, if not all of you.

It is when you have that sudden impulse from the heart or intuition to act on but yet you still say no to it completely because it couldn't possibly be that easy. I witnessed a very beautiful moment that stood out today more so than any other. It was when I went to get some food.

I was on the highway and noticed a person driving in front of me had their blinker on. But for the life of him he wouldn't commit to changing lanes. So other cars began to honk at him and swerve and nearly hit him. He blocked the flow of traffic.

That is the game of hesitation. When you kind have one foot in the door but you refuse to commit to the choice. Because once you fully make a choice in your mind you will get it and that frightens you. So we put up all these fears and expectations on things so we get mad at our selves when things don't turn out that way and we hold on to a past moment that keeps cycling.

Which makes sense as to why some of us refuse to commit 100% to a choice. Because then who are we without what we have been experiencing? We are so used to the things in our life that doesn't benefit us, that we feel we are unworthy to receive something more that actually would.

For example when you fully commit to a choice you no longer hold back the flow of abundance, flow of energy that flows in and out of you. You no longer put a wall up on the intuition. You begin to allow all that is to flow in and out because you are living in your authentic self. The self who lives with no limit. The self who commits to what they believe in because they know it will work out.

There is something very interesting that happens once you commit to a choice and truly believe in it. You will create a scenario that truly tests you to see if that is the choice you really want in life. It is that fear, that little road block just checking in with your free will. I call these free will check points. But if you really made your choice this scenario that is created will not falter your decision on continuing forward to getting what you want.

That in it self is so powerful to know. That we created a check in system with our free will to ask our selves since we are the divine creators. Hey, I know you said you wanted this thing you say you do, so I am just checking in. That is what the fear is.
That is what the hesitation is.

Those check in points are markers for you to to know to keep moving forward.

Follow your fears and you will never be lost in a dark room.
For they will always illuminate your way back to divine creator.

4-12-16

As you become more comfortable with your self.
Your desires of having to be with someone else diminishes.
Because you are now supplying all the love to your self from your self. You require nothing outside of the self.

Things then become bonuses to your life. Rather then completions to you.
This is where you begin to recognize attachments.

4-13-16

What do you want to create today?
Ask your self this question when you wake up.
Find out what is blocking you from getting it.
Then face it and keep moving forward.
We are in the home stretch.

4-14-16

Be truthful with how you feel about those who are in your sphere.

Living life with regret is one of the top three things
that people deal with on their death beds.
Just let it flow, regardless of how it is taken.
It feels amazing.

4-15-16
They say it takes 10,000 hours to be a master at
something. Considering the amount of times we have
chosen to come back to this place. I would say a lot of
us are masters of a number of things and we don't even
realize it.

I want to whisper sweet universal wisdom to
accelerate your growth nothings into your ear.
I want to tell you how beautiful of a reflection of
the universe you are and for you to truly receive and
believe it.
I want to caress your energetic body with mine so
that we can feel that there is never any separation from
one another regardless of distance.
I want you to see you are me and I am you, always
and forever.
I want you to be as emotionally available as I am
so that we can dive deep into the oceans of our hearts
and discover what treasures we have yet to find.
I love you.
4-17-16
Another beautiful workshop is completed. It is
such an inspiring thing to see people share emotion
and experiences in a room. To see the shift from the
beginning to the end and truly see how much they
grow from such a short time.
It just shows that our life is just a choice away from

happiness.

I cried last night from seeing the beauty in the moment that was being shared. It felt amazing, It felt as though a huge release was given from me in that as well.

These workshops are not only healing others, but it is allowing my self to heal as well.

Many more to come. This is just the beginning of a spark of transformational workshops!

Love you all.

4-18-16

She saw my heart and ran because of the depth and unknown.

I cried because I knew she was just afraid of the love it showed her she was capable of.

4-19-16

....And when she finally sets both feet within my sphere of reality. I will know that she has faced the same demons that I too have faced.

To be at the equal of my self.

Knowing she too can now bask in the same light that I have been basking in.

Knowing that she can pull that energy from all around her and not depending on each other for that feeling.

Understanding that we do not own each other and are free to come and go as we please.

For if we were to place ownership, this would signify we have attachment to one another. In such we can begin to step back and address these cords of attachment to move further on the same path together.

It is then we shall be the pillars of light for others to see that they too can do the same.

4-20-16

And I know as your eyes begin to open to the sheer beauty of what this world has to offer. You will break down and cry tears of joy because you are finally seeing through the eyes of the heart and not the mind.

This is where you will find me and this is where you will discover your true worth.

4-21-16

Time is the only real currency we have in this life. So instead of being attached to how things are supposed to be or go because of expectation.
Be present and aware of the moments that are passing you by or the moments that you have already shared with that special someone. Because regardless of how things ended or are, nothing can ever take back those experiences.

If a person decides to spend their "time" with you truly honor that person and value those precious moments as they are fleeting.

I Love You.

4-24-16

Peace is the natural state of our being in that it shows us nothing in this life truly matters and it is hilarious. You give it all the meaning you want. You have the power of choice to decide to feel angry, annoyed, afraid, peaceful, scared etc etc. It is all a choice that you wanted to make because you felt it suited you in that instance.

Understanding this when you begin to see it all as a choice those fears you had about letting go of someone or starting something new and the perceived "risks" involved fade away. Because it is all illusion and choice on that emotion of fear.

The only true state is the peace, the feeling of knowing everything is perfect the way it is and it is ok. You begin to laugh at how funny the world is and how you have lived your life by certain emotions as if you were that emotion or experience.

You begin to see the earth does not "need" your help to protect her, she will be fine. It is your sense of significance that you get from supporting her that is the choice and drive for you. All these tragedies, the shootings, the wars, the racism, all of it is beautiful and perfect because it is allowing us to remember who we truly are and showing us certain emotions and reflections of ourselves.

I used to fight certain things and want to protect people and the world. But now I realize I was only doing that because it made me feel like I was doing something. When the whole time the only thing you have to do is love your self.

Be that peace, there nothing you must do outside of your self.
It is all inside of you and the more you fight the things out side of your self, the more you perpetuate the story and it continues the cycle, there is no fighting necessary. Just love and heal those aspects within your self and what emotions surface and you will see how beautiful your reality outside of the self begins to shift into that same state of being that you now represent.

You will see it to all be choices.
I Love You
4-25-16
What do you want to create in your life?
I asked this to a friend and they said it was a rather huge question to ask.

Why is it? It isn't a huge question. It is a necessary question so that you can begin to analyze your life and see how your current actions are doing and seeing if they align with what you want to create in your life.

Notice the fears that surface of I don't have the money for it, or I don't have the time for it, or no one will like it.

Who cares about any of that, once you step your feet towards it all of those fade away and fall into place.

Declare what you want to create in your life right NOW!

If you fall on the way towards it, which you will. Get right back up. Set up reminders for what it was you wanted in your life like post it notes or other things. Work towards that goal until you make it a reality.

Take your life back. You deserve it.

I love you.

4-28-16

Remember to be present in your actions.
Instead of reacting to certain situations and living in the ego and fear.

Take a moment to observe the feeling that is coming up and choose to respond. In this you begin to take your power back rather then being a victim to your emotions.

You begin to take ownership and responsibility of your emotions and that is a beautiful feeling.

Every situation and experience is showing you how to be more of your self.

I Love You

Only water is able to absorb the entire range of

frequencies that exist in nature.

Think of all the information that you can store in a single droplet of water....Oh the beautiful things that will be done with you water.

4-29-16

You will be tested and asked things that if and when you speak the truth it may hurt the other person. So I in the past have lied to not hurt the other person or to spare them from that or to avoid an argument. But by living in your integrity and authenticity you allow the other person to grow, as well as your self, rather than cater to their stories they have been telling.

You can then be that authentic true version of your self without fears of judgment and keep walking forward to your destination where ever it may be. But knowing you spoke your truth, in that is where you feel free.

The DMT Experience

5-2-16

Last night I faced a version of my self that I felt was like that of a final boss of a video game...It was a portion of my self i have not been loving because of the strong judgment I had on it of what I have done in the past.

I felt crippled at the sight of the memory, like seeing a huge dragon before me and not knowing what to do. Words eluded me and did not want to come out, actions froze and did not want to move. This crippling sensation was followed by a deep resonance of crying to release. Each tear as it hit my cheek releasing the chains that binded my soul into a reality of limitation.

I feel a spell has been lifted upon my soul by acknowledging this version of my self...There is still much work to be done in this area but it has allowed me to uncover stories of limitation that I have been deceiving my self on. That I have been playing the role of in my present life because I have been defining who I am based on what happened in the past.

This is a call out to all of you who have that final boss within your self that you have yet to face...that you are afraid of facing because you feel the emotion may over power you.

The moment I faced it I felt a purge, I literally threw up from it and I felt like an ayahausca ceremony where that perceived demon was casted out of my body because it no longer had power over me. I am that representation of all of you to remind you, it is safe to face this. You are strong enough to. In its place you can place more love and acceptance within your self to fill that spot.

Yes I may still cry the next few days, but I know in my reality I had the courage to finally face this dragon in the closet. Because I have the tools to succeed in it, but the truth of it all is that you don't have to fight it. Just provide love to your self in that area and acknowledge it had to be that way to be who you are today. No matter what it was that was done in the past.

If I can face this, you can too.

You are supported and loved.

I Love You.

I Love all versions of my self, this showed me that I have not been giving my attention to portions of myself.

Thank you.

5-3-16

Pain, Guilt, Shame

All emotions and chains to my heart whom is crying

Crying because the chains and bondage of these emotions are being activated and ripped out of me.

They dug deep into my heart, burrowing and sinking their thorns within.

Growing roots, like that of weeds that dig deeper the longer you go without addressing them.

I am the gardener of my emotions, to allow the garden of my heart to flourish and be free of the chains and vines.

I have pulled out the weeds, I had to use two hands this time and in so the wounds are bleeding, because there is now empty space to fill it with the love that I have been neglecting.

Every space the weeds grew are now all burning and

bleeding.

What did I expect when I dove deep into an emotion I have not been wanting to feel? The soil and dirt are now overturned.

It is prime and ready to plant new seeds for the garden of my heart. The soil is tilled and fertilized with the blood and tears of myself. To foster a new beginning within the self.

I know this will lead to forgiveness because every moment was created by me and for me. In that forgiveness of self my love will expand greater. Because I deserve that love.
I am learning every day how to receive, because for me it has always been easier to give.

From this healing a new sense of self worth will take its place as well. Because I denied who I was, my inheritance of the divine creator of my reality. How could I have defined my self in this way. To think no one would love me because of what I did in the past.

It matters not as the only person that ever matters is yourself and the forgiveness of yourself. So as I free flow the inner workings of my thoughts, I am able to better process what the next course of action is.

I thank my self for the ramblings and vulnerability. I honor my self by allowing others to connect.
I forgive my self.
I love you David.

5-4-16

I keep putting off writing to you. I miss the way the pen feels on the paper. Today as I thought of wanting my logo or sigil in better quality I let go and a friend randomly asked if I wanted a higher quality sigil logo. Life is funny that way when you begin to create and manifest. It is raining outside and I decided to run out in the rain and declare my power statement and my worth. That I am now choosing to live without fears and limitations of money. I declared what I am here to do with the water. And that is to create awareness of intention. So mote it be.

I love this feeling of bliss that is created in the body after a healing or attunement session with someone. How can i describe this...
It feels like light headedness but it is not disorienting. It is the opposite. It is a realignment of who I am. I feel high.
A feeling of surging inspiration and remembrance that I can truly create and do anything I want.
If you have ever felt this bliss, I would like for you to describe it in your own words to the best of your ability.
Let us share with others how it feels to us and remember we can always tune into this feeling if we so choose.

5-7-16
I have created a new workshop called Art of Intention. A student gave me an invocation spell.

LIGHT LIGHT LIGHT

I invoke the light to activate and to complete a divine search and my divine mind to restore.
The triangular configuration of my sacred heart, My divinity, divine mind, all seeing, all knowing, The

LIGHT and LOVE of my sacred heart.

My higher selves and THE LIGHT of the lineage that I am connected to, all states of existence of my being from the beginning of creation. And all of my

Incarnations in all dimensions and realms. And the communication between my body and my soul.

5-6-16

I wanted to take some time and express how truly grateful I am for you being my master teacher.
For teaching me true surrender and letting go of an outcome.
I remember I created such a beautiful reality in my mind on how things ought to be and these expectations on how it would all go down.

But you were there as my reminder to let me know to release expectation, release future projections, simply have an end goal. You were that master teacher for me.
As each month passed by, the realization began to set in to let me know things don't always go the way we want them to in our minds. We have to just truly surrender the control we think we have.

The memory of you still lingers because I feel connection to you, I feel you as I breathe, I feel you as I look at the sky, I feel you as I touch the grass, I feel you as my feet touch the sand.
Remembering all the moments that have been shared to even make me create those realities in my mind.

What a beautiful reality it was, at some level of existence we are there living in it. How amazing and poetic it is. But this was all necessary to teach me that everything is simply a story and we have no control as to how it will play out, we are just along for the ride and the true choice we have is the one of how are we choosing to feel in the moment as it is happening.

Again, thank you for being that master teacher for me. A reflection into the depths of my soul, to unlock new versions of my self I never knew were possible until you appeared, and how beautiful you are.

I Love You, Always and Forever.

5-8-16

I received more information on the metatrons cube meditation. It was spoken to me that it will create a 3 mile sphere in the surrounding perimeter. All those inside this would experience immediate self awareness.

Our wings that we all have... What if these wings are the bellows for our body to utilize and push the love from our hearts forward at a more rapid rate, raising the vibration in our area and within us.

5-10-16

Today I did a session on a system called Pandora star. It Is a system that uses LED light in a certain order to stimulate the pineal gland so that you can go into deeper mediations and visualizations. It creates natural DMT in the body. I was also hooked up to a machine called the Heart quest system. Which showed me my percentage rate of my chakras and other physical body statistics. I received all 100%'s and the operator said she had never seen this before on someone. Here is a link to my pdf file I received:
http://www.thewatermagister.com/wp-

content/uploads/2018/02/David-R-min.pdf

I chose the sequence for the pandora star of astral travel. I closed my eyes and began the internal journey. The brightly closed lights began hitting the back of my eyelides and it made me flinch numerous times. I began to find peace in it and my face then became relaxes.

Once relaxed I began to see certain sacred geometry patterns and eventually made my way into a space where I saw an energetic hand beginning to reach out to me. As it came towards my face I felt it perfectly as if you were to caress my face. I began having conversations with what ever this was. It said it was performing an energetic upgrade of some sort on me. I then saw a bright white light that felt very warming and the physical sensation felt as if I was doing a back flip out of the body to see this light. Once I saw this the session was over and the hour had passed. I felt like only 10 minutes had passed. But the information I received was for me to keep pushing forward in the many projects I am working on that I have not yet unveiled because I am waiting for a few last pieces to be put in place. But once set, the ball will be in motion to create a beautiful new technology that will support in the transition of the old paradigm.

Poem
I let you go tonight through ash and smoke
Into the ether the memories of past loves flow.
The left over tears letting me know
that I am releasing the control.

True surrender leaving room to grow
Another new love which I have yet to explore.
Opening new space, so that it can show.
One of which will bring me closer
to the truth, that it was me,
I fell in love with, the whole time.
Always me. Just a different skin.
I love you, Always and forever within.

5-11-16

This life man...you never know how much you
truly impact another soul. Even just by sharing space
with them. Years down the road you may run into
them again and they will stop you and say how much
of a light you have been for them.
I love all of my reflections and it is my honor to be
that reminder of the light within each of you whom i
have had the pleasure of interacting with and sharing
my time with.
Which is the only true currency in this physical world.
Time.
I love you.

5-12-16

I went to Kevin's meeting today and a beetle hit
my face. Yay for me. After this a man gifted me a
peacock ore crystal.
People often ask how I receive information or
channel when I write at times. My answer is to read
"Conversations with God". Then you will know.

Feeling the necessity to release about romance.
In your space I feel as the energies of our souls

228

intertwine
To form a union of which I have yet to experience
Ecstatic every time our eyes lock and we both grin
because we know each other feels the same.
We give off the same love and it is easy to feel it
But we hold back because we want it to build
Building up to a boiling point until the moment arrives
Where we connect in a divine embrace

It always feels right to build up the romance
I enjoy the sensation it creates within me
While at the same time understanding we place no
ownership on one another, we are free to explore
connections that arise
I love this exploration of my self because I see it from
a higher awareness then other moments in my life
I recognize if I begin to place attachments and I
quickly address those portions of my self that believe I
require anything outside of the self.

It begins to turn into a game for my mind and I
love this challenge it brings because it places me in
uncomfortability, because I am so used to approaching
things from a different way. I greatly enjoy the
reflection of love that is emitted because it shows me
my own power within.

It is a constant reminder for me as I explore my
self deeper then I have gone, with every moment that
is shared a deeper connection is built. A foundation is
being built and once solidified a new reality emerges,
one of which I am not able to fathom because I have
never experienced it.

I see another reflection as well, one of whom wants
to own their power and step up to the plate of
understanding just how much of a vital role to the

process of integration is. This was the initial reflection I studied. It is an amazing thing to be able to bare witness to reflections in others and loved ones when you become present to it.

A simple remembrance of the touch of skin elates me into the feeling of radiance within my heart, because it is a book mark for my self. So that I can always tune to it, and you were simply there to show me it was always there to begin with as there are never any separations whether you know you are showing me or not.

I love these feelings as I begin to further understand who I am.

My intuition is on point. I allow my vessel to be open to receive wisdom all around from entities whom wish to speak through me. Not caring about what their names are because it is irrelevant in the grand scheme of things. In such those who are physically around me hear these words and it inspires them to speak out further because now the space is open.

For others to know it is safe to speak on it, There have been many times lately I have spoken words that just flow out without thought, and after these words are spoken because of what was said it inspired others to speak up without holding back.

I smile internally because I know I am allowing my own self to become vulnerable and open and by doing so this space magnifies for others to be free.

I am this open because I trust. I allow, I surrender. I am Free.

Thank you.

5-13-16

I am more then the fucking stories I tell my self.

I am a powerful creative being and everything I do turns to success.

I am financially independent and create a steady stream of income to support all of my ideas and inventions.

I am vulnerable, honest and open in every instance of my life.

I am POWER, I am STRENGTH, I am COURAGE.

I DECIDE, I fucking DECIDE! POWER!!

I am the FUCKING LIGHT!!

I AM MOTIVATED, I AM INSPIRED.

PUSH PAST THE BLOCKS DAVID!!!!

YES!

GO!

5-15-16

The eye gazing last night was phenomenal. I want to give some back story to a few things.

On my drive there I like to play manifesting games with my self to see what I can create in my reality and then I let go of the thought to see if it comes up. So on the drive I thought it would be awesome if someone gave me food or bought me food. I left it at that and kept on, found my parking spot.

I arrived around 8pm, I wanted to sit where I normally do which was under the Here sign but they took that sign down.

Also there was a guy who was selling paintings there. I walked up to him and I asked her would you mind if I sat down near you I am doing an eye gazing thing where people could interact, it may bring you more people as well. He said ok, then once i sat down, he changed his mind and is like No you going to ruin my business.

I said alright, I walked away and found a different spot nearby. I had 4 people sit down to do a 2minute eye gazing each. Then a friend of mine arrived and we decided to look for a different spot.

It then began drizzling rain...I laughed internally because...well, Water. As we were walking around looking for a better spot. I noticed the guy with the paintings his things were getting wet and he decided to start packing up. When he was making a big deal about me sitting at that spot.

He ended up leaving and I got the spot I normally sit at. I laughed again because of how funny it was that either way I got what I wanted. We had a few people roll in and sit down in front of me about 6 more. Then in between people a beautiful women walked up to us and offered my friend food because she didn't want it anymore. He said nah not really, She then looked at me and I said I am vegetarian I don't think I can have it. She said oh no its vegetarian tacos. I again...laughed in my mind. I said Ok Sure!

So I manifested the spot I wanted, I manifested food for my self.

In total I had about 20 people sit with me and share beautiful moments. About 15 of them for the first time in their lives experienced no thought. They were all shocked and amazed that it was possible and I let them know they essentially just meditated. I gave them a business card and a flyer for the #thelightbeingscommunity. www.thelightbeingscommunity.com. You could see that a light bulb began to turn on in their field. It is such a beautiful feeling to be able to ignite the flame in another with a simple 2 minutes out of my day per person. I gladly give that to them as a gift.

Overall I love this work, I love the smiles and laughter, I love the emotions of those who cried because they never felt it before.
I am blessed, I love this life. I am a master manifestor!!

I love you. I am grateful, I am thankful.
5-17-16
This movie I call my life gets more and more hilarious the more aware I become. The people I cast and the events that follow are some of the most ironically funny moments. My movie is a box office hit and I'm the only one watching it.

5-18-16
My dream last night was rather interesting. I made it a point to eat blue cheese...quite a bit of it as it allows your dreams to become much more vivid and lucid while also making a mugwort tea.

I was in this class room and we were all discussing ways to better the civilization we were ment to go visit. My task was water and they asked me what I would do and it switched to a scene in a lunch room area where I was asked to eat a tree frog, it was to be used as a medicine. It kept slipping away and eventually I caught it and swallowed it whole.

The dream then transitioned again to another class room and the class was in a state of shock and in a way shouting who woke up the spirit of the water? I stood up and spoke and stated that it was me, and I will be embodying it. Everyone was proud that I would do this and then I woke up.

5-19-16

Last night I went to another sweat lodge to dextox the body. It was a beautiful group. I went rather spontaneously because a friend of mine visited to drop off money and he said he was going to one. So I joined in. Prior to the sweat I saw a blue jay above in the trees. Inside the tepee I saw a fox face within the rocks. The second round when new rocks were placed took shape of a snakes head. My dreams last night were rather profound as it showed me an aspect of my self that I have not been noticing. The dream was of me driving in a van with about 4 friends and there was an intersection with stop lights it just turned red and I decided to go for it anyways. The van was then side swiped by another card and we tumbled into the woods then ended up in a car dealer ship.

My friends were angry and asked why I did that. In my mind I thought I could make it but instead what came out of my mouth was that the brakes didn't work. I had lied to not get in trouble. This is something I will have to address within my self as I had the feeling of wanting to protect my self is still lingering. The funny thing I hit a bunch of cars in the dealership and they didn't call the cops, infact they liked that I did that because they said they can just get insurance money without getting police involved. Also the van was back to normal and no scratches or marks were on it. Showing me that regardless everything was ok.

"Obstacles are there to signify how bad you want something.

Failure is a passageway to success, its how you respond to failures or obstacles that will ultimately determine your results."
-Anonymous

But once you understand the only obstacles created are in your mind and are simply illusion...Well... You can guess what comes next.... is FUCKING GREATNESS in the making!

GO GET IT!!

5-20-16

Here's to all the beautiful wild Goddesses out there that truly honor themselves and their bodies. That follow their hearts, that value their integrity and would never compromise it for someone else's bullshit ego story to feel safe and secure.

Here is to all the Goddesses who use their intuition to drill into the men knowing there is something there to dig into to allow our growth. So that we men can begin to truly own our own divinity.

Here is to the challenges they provide us and the lessons that are taught.

Keep being wild, keep being free.
Never let another soul chain you or cage your divinity.
YOU WERE BORN FREE!
Never cater to another persons insecurity.
The time is changing.

YES!!!

5-21-16

I did a DMT session and I saw a concurrent life of mine. In this DMT sessions I came out of a pool of water. There were two naked women which were blue energetic bodies, and two energetic red men outside of the pool. The women asked me if I wanted to have sex with them and I said "No, I am here because I want to discover more of who I am". They said good and waved their hands, when they did this a temple opened and the temple doors opened. I was transfered there and spoke to someone at the entrance. They escorted me to a book and in this book I saw my self as a scientist. I learned who that scientist was recently....and I am pumped to know I created some amazing fucking shit in that life time and I am going to carry on that legacy.

Author Note: It took me about 3-4 months to find out who that scientist was and It was Buckminister Fuller.

5-23-16
The Key of each other
Feeling the glance of a lost lovers embrace
Remembering the times we have done this all before
Different roles play, different planets, star systems but over all
The course stays the same
We find people in our life that is the key to the next level
Of our evolution
I am that key and you are as well.
I am unlocking your wild divine nature as you are unlocking mine
Sharing an ever lasting embrace as the skin touches one another
We pause to acknowledge the moment and bask in the light of each other
At times so bright it is blinding as if we were to

be looking at this morning sun that always graces us with it's love.

As the vulnerability continues to expand we become more open then we have allowed in the past and in so we venture into uncharted realms of reality where in it we are able to explore more of our own selves to realize the things that have been preventing us from doing so.

Similar sensations as chills run through my body because I remember the truth, that you are me in a different perspective.
Choosing to experience life from different realities to learn different sides of things.

It can be easy getting lost in the beautiful organized chaos of the divine union of realities. But to remember that we still have choice places a huge role to not get lost.
But then again if we get lost, we are simply learning another way. So we never truly get lost.

I think to my self it's been awhile since I have allowed my wild divine masculine to shine outwards without fear of what others think or say. Because I used to care what others thought of me.
But ultimately you are your own judge. So I embrace who I am. I embrace my expression of sexuality and the ways it manifests out of this vessel.

It is me, It is my authenticity. These looks that we continue to share will continue to send shivers and chills through my body because I feel the vulnerability as we each begin to truly understand one another and the overall goal of our purpose together.

But remembering we place no ownership on one another's actions or placing restrictions on how we can express our loves to one another or others as connections arise in our reality to evolve and grow.

One day though you will shine your light out wards as I do with my open communication and the fear of what others may think will melt away. For if they do not, you simply will make a different choice as to what serves you in your growth and we will go our own ways back to source. But ultimately we are already there.

One way or another love is the driving force and will always be that, as I continue to shine my divinity for those to witness their own reflection of love.

Once you make the choice to embody certain aspects of your self that you feel you are not yet. You will then create outside experiences that allow you to heal and bring things up to be that version of your self you see your self to be. Because that version of you does not experience what you currently are.

In such, you will begin to become aware of automatic usage of words or automatic usages of actions because you are learning how to become fully aware 100% of the time, in every instance and experience that happens.

So truly honor your growth once you face these aspects and speak your truth. It is a process of acceptance for your self and learning your self worth. Because as you do this you allow others around you to grow as well, as it then reflects things to them based on the experience to learn and grow from.

We are all serving each others highest good to be that divine radiance of love.

I Love You
5-24-16

Good Morning You Balls of Radiance Shining In and Out of Reality every Second to Human Form.

Honor this day for every moment is truly a blessing, The courage we took coming to this place Class room Earth.

Honor the breathe you inhale and exhale for it is the same breathe our ancestors inhaled in this human form. We are always connected.

Honor where you are at today and the actions that it took for you to be here reading this message.

Honor the times you speak your truth.

Honor the times you face a fear to bring you back to love.

Honor the love for your self you have.

Honor the other beautiful reflections on this reality to shine back to you and let you know what you get to work on.

You are seen, You are Acknowledged, You are Loved.

5-25-16

On the topic of Ideal Relationships.

Our society has a common misconception from all the programming of romance tv shows, novels, and movies that we must find a partner. That we must not only find a partner but find one that doesn't give us any trouble so that can be comfortable and mundane. It teaches women to look for that knight in shining armor.

Do you know why that knight has armor? Because he is afraid. Because he has placed walls on him self from feeling due to past experiences. He is in fear and he thinks he has to protect him self. A real knight takes off his armor, or has many battle wounds on him.

Because he knows the truth. He knows that by shining his heart and allowing himself to be vulnerable he allows true intimacy and connection to his partner.

I feel that is entirely to unrealistic to seek the romantic novel type that media suggests to find.

Throughout my life I have been guilty of not being open, honest, and vulnerable. But as times progress I have learned that vulnerability is not a weakness like most of the society suggests. It is your biggest strength. Why? Because not only does it create connection. There is no longer anything you have to defend your self from. What could a person possibly say to you that would hurt or offend you if you have been open and honest about every instance of your life?

You would simply look at them and giggle because you see what they are attempting to do.

-A real relationship to me is one that is raw and open, You share all of your hidden past secrets. Ones that you have been ashamed of so that you can heal together from. Ones that you have been guilty of doing so that you can heal together from.

But regardless of what you have done your partner still loves and accepts who you are without judgment. But then again even if they have judgment if they are strong enough to heal their own judgment to move forward from. Because they realize that you had to go through all of that to be the person you are today. To be that big ball of love you are in this very moment and they can see past all of the things you may still be holding on to.

-A real relationship to me is one where you understand situations will come up that you may perceive as mistakes, but in actuality had to play out the way it did so that you can continue to grow together. But you still decide to stick it through because you are both growing.

We are like children still learning how to walk, and then run.

-A real relationship to me is having no attachment on one another and not being in fear if that person is no longer going to be in our lives. Because we understand that person was not the cause for our greatness, our happiness, our peace, our bliss. It was simply that they were a mirror to this reflecting the potential of what you are and you decided to walk through the door to then experience it your self.

-A real relationship to me is one where the sexual expression is not limited by fear. It is raw, dirty, sexy, sensual, slow, fast, hard, soft. But yet you still take time to honor one another during the act and you take time and pause to look into each others eyes because you realize something very profound...that this body you are holding, kissing, touching, is another expression of your own divinity. That you are never separate from each other and in essence you are simply making love to your self.

-A real relationship to me understands that limitations that are placed on how each other can express their love to them or others that will come into their lives is placing a block on your unconditional love to be that shining radiance for all to witness. To allow the freedom to explore and truly give your self to who ever you feel requires your connection. But still you return to one another. Because you are each others foundation, you are each others rock. We place no ownership on each other.

-A real relationship to me is simply being and deciding to truly walk the path together. Taking ownership for all of your outside creations and not placing blame on one another no matter what it is because everything was created by you for you, to reflect an emotion you have yet to be addressing. Calling each other out and not catering to any bullshit stories of limitations and fears that each other may exhibit. So we can continuously grow together. Because the moment we become comfortable is the moment we begin to stop growing.

So kick that shit up, stop catering to another persons story of fear and limitation.

And lastly...

-A real relationship to me is one where you truly drop all walls, all armors, all barriers and expose your heart and give your all without fear of getting heart broken. Because heart break only comes when you place attachment on what you want.

Yes you can have goals together, but be ok if it doesn't play out the way you envision it.

I love you.

5-26-16

Space Flight

Flying through this spaceship shaped as a ball
In the center, the core was where the inhabitants resided

There was a space from the core to the shell that no one ventured but you could see the stars so bright.

I had a power that everyone was amazed by,
I had the power of flight.

Every day in this dream I flew off the core into the

space
between it and the shell as we traveled through the
cosmos.

I saw the eyes and bewilderment of everyone
around
familiar faces as they saw me flying wondering how.

They wanted to learn how I did it
I taught some but they never understood it.

I sometimes in the dream was able to create
a lasso around someone and take them into flight.

I loved this dream
and I loved that night.

I Love you.

5-28-16

May this be the day you finally face a fear you
have been running from to discover the love within
your self that has always existed.
It is time, it is always time...
Are you ready?

5-29-16

For some time I used to think intimidating others
or making them feel uncomfortable was a bad thing.

I realize now why it is I do this or have this effect
on people.
It is the love within my self, that puts the ego in fear.
It knows if it sets foot in my sphere of reality. It has to
then face shit it has been running from.

I am Intimidating
I am Fierce
I am the Water Magister
I will make you feel uncomfortable
I am passionate in my love and expressions and refuse

to dim that
I refuse to not display my love and hold my self low to
make others feel comfortable
I am sensual
I am sexually powerful in all of my actions as this
energy is my driving force in my creativity
When the ego sees me it will run and want to hide
Because that is what I embody, Divine love and
acceptance.

If you set foot in my sphere and it intimidates you.
Good.
It is a compliment and I relish in it, This is my
resolution to no longer feel bad or insecure that I bring
this up in people.
I deserve better, I deserve my love in all areas, I give
my love to my side of self in which I intimidate.

I desire the same in my lovers. I want you to make
me feel intimidated, uncomfortable. It allows me to
grow continuously.

I want you to be open and expressive in all
instances.
I am open, honest and vulnerable in every instance of
my life.
I embody that which I want to attract.
You want to know something? Ask. Do not be afraid.

I choose to live this life that I preach because to
not do so is being a false teacher.

I DECIDE, I DECIDE. POWER!
I am The Water Magister, Open, Honest, Vulnerable,
Fierce, Intimidating, Inspiring, Intuitive, Insightful,
Abundant, Free flowing, Victorious, Limitless and I
am that beacon of light that when you step in my
sphere all of your walls comes down to begin to face

who you are.

This is my fierce fox face.

5-30-16

Subject: Lying

For a good majority of my life I have learned the ability to lie. Why? Because it was a way for me to get out of situations in which I felt uncomfortable with.

I developed it since I was a child, mostly in middle school and high school. It allowed me to avoid bullies and to manipulate my environment in my favor. It was quite an amazing tool in my tool belt.

However as I progressed into adult hood. I began realizing I no longer required this tool because it was hindering my growth spiritually. It was not until my most recent break up that I had a total glimpse into it and what it showed me. I lied to cater to a persons insecurity because if I told the truth in my mind would have hurt them. But the truth of this is when you speak your truth, you allow the other to grow.

I realize now that this is a gift. It is a gift to tell the truth. I slowly started being truthful in areas because I realized now that everything outside of my self was but a mere reflection of an emotion within my self. So who am I to deny my self that emotion and growth?

I now live in my authenticity in all instances to the best of my ability. Yes I have caught my self in automatic lies because the ego is still wanting to defend it self, or protect it self from addressing an issue. But I am at a state of awareness that I catch it rather quickly and address it and reclaim my authenticity.

In such I recognize others very easily in their lies or half truths.

I know why you each do it and how you feel about doing it. It is a fear of wanting to address aspects of your self you have been hiding from. But know when you withhold information this is a form of a lie and manipulating a situation in your favor to not address an emotion that has been crying out to you to feel. The ego justifies it any way it can because it does not want to address a fear just yet. Simply catch it and be present.

It is ok, You each have your process. But know you are safe in speaking your truth. I was afraid for so long as well. But I recognized my power in my truth and authenticity. It allows me now to truly face aspects and emotions of my self that I have been burying inside because I felt It would over take me or overwhelm me.

It doesn't. The moment you disallow the ego to justify to speak a half truth or withholding of information. Is the moment you become liberated in your reality and it allows you to feel. Truly feel and begin to master your emotions. I have been a pathological liar because I cared about how people perceived me. I wanted to present my self a certain way, I wanted to get out of a conversation, I wanted to get out of an argument, I wanted to not make a person feel hurt or bad.

I know the stories the ego tells. But it is safe, It is safe to come out and play with the emotions again. Know if you ever set foot in my space or reality, I can detect it and I know it very well. I will probe it, but I will not push any further then that as it has to ultimately be your choice to step foot into the reality of love with me. The reality of which all truth is spoken and I choose to embody this because it is a step in to the direction of what I aim to be for others.

Speak your truth, open your heart and know what is going to occur after your truth is spoken is going to be because you now are living in authenticity and there is not a damn thing anyone can say to you to hurt you anymore because you are living in that state of pure vulnerability.

I love you. Come out and play.

5-30-16

He loved himself the way no one could. He was always seeking outside of himself and realized that when he turned that love in wards. He was complete. No one could ever love him the way he wanted. In so, he found himself.

5-31-16

Understanding the difference between your mind justifying a fear and what actual boundaries and preferences are will be a huge challenge for some of us. Why? Because the ego will constantly want to cloud and place the energy to something else instead of truly facing and realizing how an experience is showing up for you.

So instead you might say well it is my preference to not do that. Or it is my choice to place a boundary on something.
Yes ultimately everything is your choice because you are the ultimate creator in your reality.

But know when you use this as a cope out to not feel an emotion or run from a fear, instead of facing it. You are justifying a fear of self and you are slowing down your spiritual growth.

A real boundary or preference is something that you may have already experienced and you said well I have done that already and I learned the lesson of what was shown. So I prefer to go down this path now.

The opposite would be, well I do not like what is down that other path. So I prefer to go down this other one because I am not sure what is there.

I used to cater to peoples insecurities and uncomfortabilities. Because that was when I did not realize what the difference in decisions of what was coming from fear or love.

I even allowed an ex of mine to put a choice into my sphere of not writing or withholding certain information from a book I am writing. Because of her insecurity and how it made her feel about it when I wrote it. When I did that and took on that choice I had a writers block for 6-7 months. It felt like I was in a cage. Because I did not want her to feel uncomfortable for me writing about sex dreams I would have in my book.

I am in a much different place in my life now. Understand this.
If you are in my life whether it be romantically, friendship, or a stranger. If you ignite my passion of writing. I will write about you.

If you are in my space you have given me permission to write about my experiences. Keyword is My, My purpose for writing is to allow others to connect in ways they may have never connected to another writer or poet. All of my writings come from true experience. They come from the love and passion within my self that I feel for others.

I will never allow another person to dim my light

248

and my freedom to express openly and honestly in every instance of my life. This is one of my affirmations every day. "I am open , honest, and vulnerable in every instance of my life".

So if you do not like that about me. All you have to do is make a different choice.

My words flow, I cater to no one but my self. But I love dearly all of my reflections equally and I honor the lessons learned. It has given me a much wanted overview of how far I have progressed in my life since an ex.

I Love Each of You.

The 100th Monkey Rule

6-1-16

Today is a beautiful new moment. In it I rise and realize that I am not bound and limited by fear of my mind in areas that I used to be. I acknowledge my self and honor the moments in which I reclaim the divinity of who I am. Understanding that at any moment I have the ability to make a choice.

A choice in which empowers who I am rather than limits me because of a fear I may have had of how powerful beyond measure we are. That I may misuse this power in a way.

But I know now it is impossible to misuse something because all the moments in every experience are perfect. All perfect to allow you further opportunities for growth of the soul level. So who am I to deny that divinity and unlimited creative potential because of a fear of misuse of power?

I decide and my choice is that of breaking the chains of my mind every moment of every day. I honor the reflections that show up in my reality to give me that opportunity to do so. Otherwise I would not have known the chains were there.

Little by little we are reflecting to one another so that we can push each other to grow out of the same mundane comfortable environments we have created to push the narrative forward in this story of the human experience. So as I rise, I thank my self for allowing me another beautiful day to experience and to take hold. I am honored at the choices I have had to make to be who I am in this moment.

I Love You.

6-1-16

When you feel you want to change something, it ceases to be that thing in which you loved in the first place. So to allow that thing to be without placing a condition is unconditional love.

Love is not conditional, love is unconditional and it will always love regardless. But the funny thing about all of this is...Deep down inside, we are only made of love. We are only playing out a story in which we place conditions to bring us back to unconditional love.

6-2-16

In this moment as I sit and look at the horizon. The clouds hiding the suns light from my face. But I know it is still there because I have seen it previous sunrises. I notice the clouds represent my sadness in which I feel this morning.

I used to run from my emotions because they would seem to be so unbearable. But now I relish in the fact that I can feel. I choose to feel this sadness and what it conveys to me.

I realize that emotions are like different spices of life. So that your life can be even more delicious of an experience. Without certain spices the dish would seem mundane and the same. So I as spirit choose to create these emotions to make life more interesting. To bring zest to the day, It is not something to be afraid of.

By diving into specific emotions you can begin to uncover aspects of your self you never knew were there until the feeling or emotion surfaced. I love my sadness and I honor it, thus transmuting it to it's more mature form, Gratitude. Being thankful just as I am for even feeling and what the emotion is showing me.

Thank you sadness. I used to run from you, now I run to you with open arms because you deserve my love and attention just as much as any other emotion.

I Love You

6-3-16 *Poem*

Heart is beating faster, living in my truth.
Every choice brings me closer, feeling the heat rising
Chills now fill the body as I draw in close to you
Feeling the touch of the energetic love
Rising higher, up into the crown
Pressure kickin in, ready to explode
Sensory over load as the beat begins to kick
Kundalini Rising, as the two become one
Here we are again, time and time again
But will you run or stick around for fun?
Fear poppin up showing you the truth
The way in which to go, its always with the flow
The choice is becoming clearer
Listening to the tune
The walls are caving in
No more room to run
It is time.

6-3-16

Creative overflow .... So much wants to come out right now.

1. You want to feel my love, face your self and you can feel the same love within your self.

2. The love within me can be felt if you only look inwards.

3. Some say they want to walk the path with me but the first sign of fear shows up and they crumble.

Not allowing themselves to bask in the inner fire as I
have basked in mine.
I have forged my self through the experiences of life to
be where I am, with the heat of pain, passion, trauma,
heartache.
You want to truly walk with me? Face these within
and take my hand.
I can be your guiding light if you only allow me to.
But it is you who will always choose what suits and
benefits you.

    4. De ja vu over and over again. Every time I am in
moments I know I am to be, to replay instances to
make a different choice. To see how the new choice
plays out in the reality of the illusion of the mind.
I feel it so deeply knowing I have done this all before.
I feel it is a check point like a video game that allows
you to go back to a specific area and go a different
path to experience something new because you wanted
to explore that other choice now that you saw what the
former choice was.

    5. Surging sensations through this vessel I chose.
My focal point to experience the love of which I have
never dove so deep into.
Thanking my teachers for they teach without them
knowing the truth of the lessons they show.
Going within to see portions of my self I have been
neglecting. Only surfacing like a newly forming island
as the volcano explodes.
Spewing the liquid lava of my soul out because the
pressure has built up for so long.
Little by little surging out so that I can face the
demons in my mind I have been ashamed of, guilty
of, afraid of. So I placed them in the depths of my

heart to be a timed release the deeper I felt love.

6. Walking the road to the understanding of my true potential with many souls. Some vier off the path to experience something like that of an attraction. This virtual reality world we created is for the use of play. To be playful with what we create and it brings us back to the understanding of who we were before we chose this experience.

At times a lonely road because of the perceived isolation from others. Some understand the struggle, But it is the significance in this struggle in which we enjoy. We like a good challenge.

7. Walk with me I say. You witness the path ahead but there is a fog you are not able to see past.
I walk through because I know it is more of who I am on the other side. You stay behind because you do not see past the fog. Going in circles until you want to face the fear.
I yell from the other side. It is safe, it is clear.
But your ears are bonded to the sound of the ego swaying you filling you with static noise and distractions.
If you could only turn on the intuitive function. You would hear me.
Come fourth and keep moving forward.

8. I've held my self small, unworthy of love for far to long. Discovering that this whole time it was my self. The creation of all has been a figment of what I choose to believe and see. Why is it then, I ask....That I create figments outside of my self that do not see the same as I do.
The other part of me says, because then you just wouldn't be unique. Your perspective is that of a

higher presence for others to witness. There are not many like you. I question this voice further and it explains that I am a baby just now opening my eyes and learning to walk, and talk, and run. So that I can show the others how to do the same.

9. Free writing answering a question of mine: Why is it I keep creating women in which say they want to own their power but when the time comes they run and hide?

My child, this is because it is you who is running from your true essence of what you are to do for humanity. Your light, your essence sends chills, sends fear, sends the ego into a state of shock and panic. When those souls look at you the intimidation takes hold and they feel all of the essence of the universe you have chosen to embody. Not everyone has the ability to be ok with that much at a time.

They must take breaks, but know it is depicting something within your self as well. You are still afraid of your power and it gets reflected in those around you and will continue to be so because of this.

You are providing a service to those women who state this initially but one day, one will truly claim her power and be able to stand in that light, that vibration you hold because then it will be perfect.

As are all things, But continue giving love to your self as you have been and continue being ok with your reflections that run from you after sharing space because this is also teaching you to be ok with the fear of your self.

You are powerful beyond measure, the moment you truly acknowledge this worlds will shatter in those that you are near.

Even more so, there will no longer be any room to hide from the dark when they stand in your light. There will come a time in your current souls existence that when they step foot into your sphere. An immediate shift in every other soul that decides to see you or feel you. Will be instantly transformed. That is why the ideology you seek about the water is such a huge task and purpose for you. You will eventually realize it is simply a catalyst for growth. But it is always you who has been the source of the catalyst. It is simply you expanding your love out wards of that which you embody within that will shake the fabric of your sector in which you chose to support with the ascension.

Keep in mind you will begin to travel and expand your vibration out to other sectors, further activating others in the wake. You are that stone in the still water to create a disturbance. A ripple for those to feel within. Your task is a big one but you know very well this isn't the first time you have done this. We are actually laughing quite a bit at your struggle because by now we would have thought this would have been easy for you. But I guess the personality in which you chose to embody this life time, along with the karmic lineage has been an interesting one for your human experience.

But just know we are always by your side, watching and listening. You are never alone as you have felt many times we have reached out and touched you physically and energetically.

So the final words before this question is completed. Honor your self for how far you have come. Continue to bring your attention and awareness back to your self. The teachers outside of you, your reflections, are of the highest quality that you have personally hand picked to give you the challenge. Because of the mission you chose to take on this in this current human experience.

And what a beautiful job they are doing for you as we can see. They are great actors in this drama of life in the 3d world. You keep getting pulled into it. But as time goes on....your awareness and skill and emotional mastery as you may have already noticed is becoming stronger every day. Your will power stronger every day. The signs and signals stronger every day, your ability to manifest on a quicker scale stronger every day.

Keep going dear one. You have many miracles to perform.
You are loved and we see all that you do from here.

Everything outside of your self is an illusion, all created to bring you back to the understanding of attention. Teaching you to always bring it back to your self.
The illusions although as real as they may seem, will always do their best to seduce you to misplace your attention because that is their role.

They are the animatrons that do not know that they them selfs are experiencing the same thing.

Everything outside of them is illusion, all co creating a reality of illusion. The universe is mental, held in the mind of The All.
A paradox.

The one thing that will ever be real, is what you create within your self, how you feel about yourself, realizing that you in essence are an incarnate of divine love learning that through acts of self love draws you near to this understanding.

Thus at a certain tipping point all of your actions will be drawn inward towards you , no longer misplacing your attention to your illusions, as beautiful, as perfect, as magnificent as they may seem.

I am breaking the code of disillusion, I choose to see what is before me.

There is only you, and it always has been this way.

Break the code.

Affirmation Challenge:

Every day I wake up I recite the following phrases for my self. Because once you understand that our bodies are 70%+ water. You can understand that your intention molds your reality and your body. Just as Dr. Masaru Emoto states.

You literally can mold who you are simply by stating affirmations and reprogramming your DNA.

If you want to create your own go to this website and pick positive adjectives and do it in a similar format.

http://systemagicmotives.com/positiveadjectiveglossary.htm

I challenge you to begin this practice.

EMPOWER YOUR SELF. No one else can do it for you. Take that step! Say your affirmations every day. ESPECIALLY when you do not feel like it. Stare into a mirror and face your self when you state them. Feel that surge of power coarse through your body.

Here is mine:

I am The Water Magister, flowing, limitless, intuitive, insightful, frees spirited, tactical, transparent, zealous and i travel the world while making money.

Abundance:
I experience my abundance in a limitless fashion.
I am successful, strategic, innovative in all of my
actions.
I bring in over $15,000 every month and every month
it increases.
I always have a minimum of $100,000 in my bank
account.
I always have more than enough money to act on my
next idea and invention.

Motivation:
I am inspired, motivated, goal driven every day the
moment I wake up.
I feel alert, awake, dynamic, energized when I start my
day.
I always have a goal in my mind to work towards.
I love the feeling of having a lot of time to work on
my next big thing.

Water Business:
I am always flowing and pushing my self to make a
business out of water.
I am influential, well reknowned and powerful when I
speak.
I love seeing my sigil of Cho go pal on each bottle of
water.
I love seeing all of the colors of the chakras as the
water flows through each one.

Add Ons:
I am open , honest, and vulnerable in every
instance of my life.
I feel accomplished, grateful, powerful and limitless.

I love seeing all of my workshops sold out.

I am the Source Commander, motivated, energetic, bold, adaptive, courageous, fortuitous, grateful, imaginative, impeccable, legendary, triumphant, and everything I do is driven by unconditional love.

Remember who you are.

Remember your strength is in your vulnerability.

Remember to continually face your fears.

Remember to stop projecting your emotions onto others.

Remember to not change your outside world, but rather your inside world.

Remember you are unconditional divine love.

Remember to own your power every day.

Remember your dreams and never let another take them away.

Remember your drive.

Remember why it is you wake up each day.

Remember to give thanks to waking up.

Remember to be in a constant state of gratitude.

Remember to honor your reflections.

Remember to thank them for showing you more of yourself.

6-4-16

I must share this amazing dream I had...

In the dream I was driving to get some where. I do not know where. But I had to do a U turn and when I did that a group of people wanted to get my attention. I got out of my car and went up to them and the leader gave me Peruvian money.

I was like wow why are you giving this to me, he said because you will need it soon. So I followed them for a bit and they were talking about philosophy. He was essentially a guru with his followers with him. I was just there observing. At some point I ended up getting in their car and driving with him and his girlfriend to his apartment complex to get something. They left me in the car.

This is where it gets interesting. A group of people approached to the right. The complex was in a very poverty stricken area. One of the people in the group, it was about 8 of them. Opened the car door, looked at me and grabbed the purse in the front seat. I looked at her like what...

So she quickly shut the door, but I had grabbed a portion of her hand or skin and wouldn't let go. She was in pain and screaming to let go. I was wanting to reason with her to put it back. Then her group members began to surround the car. One began to open the left side back door. And she was bout to spray hair spray with a lighter on me.

I applied more pressure to the womens arm and they placed the purse half way back in, knowing the moment I let go she would just take it again.
The women with the hair spray began to light her lighter, and I said...do not do that. I will reach behind me and grab my gun. I did not have a gun, I was bluffing but said it in a very stern way.
She then backed off. Then I began to reason with the women. I began to ask her why she is doing this and saying I know times are hard for all of them but to please let go of the purse and place it back. This was slightly working. I began to tell her about my sexual abuse, my getting picked on. I hit a string because she began to tear up.

Which then I began to cry. Then I was saying how much I love her for wanting to look after her family and her friends the way they did but it doesn't have to be this way.

I let go of her arm because I was now instead of fear, pain, guilt, I was coming from love. I surrendered. When I surrendered she opened my door and gave me a big hug and said thank you. She told the rest of the group to place the purse back into the car and she went on her way.

The moral of this dream: Always come from love in any situation. Share your heart, share your inner self with everyone at all times. Love truly conquers all.

What an amazing fucking dream. I woke up so happy.

The most difficult thing in the world for me is to see someone

do something in which you already know the outcome.

To allow them to learn from the experience and still be there at the other end and still not hold resentment. With open arms and unconditional love because you knew they would eventually find their way.

6-5-16

Our consciousness is like that of elasticity and force. We are pulled to the far out reaches of one side of the spectrum. To experience the darkest moments our unlimited creative potential can create. As we do, we influence others sphere of realities in the process.

Then we get flung back in the opposite direction to experience the holiest of moments our unlimited creative potential can create.

Your sphere of reality continues to go back and fourth until it stabilizes at an equilibrium in the center. In this moment we are complete and we have been both the light and the dark. Thus completing our incarnations.

This happens in the course of a souls incarnation upon many and many life times. And mini cycles of this happens within one human experience life span as well.

6-6-16

What is an emotion that you have not been allowing your self to feel lately?
You know it very well as your outside world has been continuing to bring it up within you because of the amount of times you have been suppressing it.

Why will you not allow your self to feel it? Do you think it is not ok to feel it? Do you think the emotion will overwhelm you?

Know it is a valid emotion and it is showing up because you are ready to face it. You are never given anything in which you are not strong enough to face.

Don't you think this emotion deserves your love and attention? Emotions are like children versions of your self whom cry and scream for your attention because they want to be seen and heard.

Today is the day in which you allow your self to face that one emotion you haven't been wanting to feel. You are safe to feel it.

Go to a mirror and look into it and speak to it as you would a child, what would you say to it to stop it from crying? What are the things you have been wanting to say to your self but have been afraid of it?

I promise you on the other end of it will just be

love.

Once the emotion feels acknowledged it will no longer continue to be shown to you in outside experiences. Because now you have given it love and attention.

Do this with every emotion that surfaces, whether it is from annoyance, fear, impatience, sadness etc.

You are loved.

6-7-16

We create constant experiences to test our selves. To see what we are ok with, what we are not ok with. So that we can grow from.

Every single experience is a creation to own your power, to show you how amazing you are. I sat here today and I looked at my bills and I realized how silly it all is. That I stress over if I am late or behind something. Why?

The worse that would happen is I get a bad credit score.

A fictitious thing that tells you your worth in society?

In this moment as I looked at the bills I realized I am more then a credit score. I let go of the fear of not being able to pay certain things. It is very similar experiences all over the place not just with bills. It could be people pushing you, because they are the reflections in which you contracted to see if you could own your power.

Dreams constantly test you as they are the battle grounds of the mind to see if what you are in the waking life carries over into the dream life.

If you have ever done DMT, in that space you are constantly tested to see what is your true drive to even experience it. Always testing ourselves so we can become better versions of ourselves.

I know I am abundant, in all areas of my life. Even when the outside world seems to reflect otherwise. I know it is just showing up to test me to still see if I believe I am abundant even when these things show up, and you know what? I do , I feel I always have what I require to serve my purpose. My outside world does not impact me as it once did. I am whole and complete within, and I know this test was put there to show me how far I have come.

I decide, I DECIDE!

Observe your world and see what lessons are to be learned because once you receive the message it no longer will occur.

You are loved.

6-8-16

I embody the stillness and tranquility
of water as it flows through and over me.

I am that energetic bond to allow the flow of emotions to surge through this vessel and to command my emotions at will without fear of it overwhelming me.

In such I am able to go in and out of realities and mold what I wish to experience because I let go of the fear.

Water when pushed against a wall finds a way to make it through, I am that driving force that will always find a way to expand my self to higher realms of knowledge.

I submerge my self in the ebb and flow of life allowing the stream of love and consciousness to continue forward.

Paving the pathway for the remaining water

droplets so they too can flow through because they now see there was always another way through the illusion.

Never realizing the entire time we were all one in a giant myriad of life force. But there are always those that lead the way, to do what others said was silly, ridiculous, impossible, unfathomable.

The new way is found, I along with many others see the way, soon you too will see it because it is the way we are flowing.

There is a reason water is within us and around us at all times.

It is teaching us how to flow without blocks, obstacles, fears and limitations.

Flow like the water that you are and never hold your self small.

6-8-16 *Poem*

You can be my Acolyte,
and you can tuck me in a night.

I can be your Wizard casting spells,
to show you magic has been real to remove your shell.

Knowing it is now safe to come out again.
You will then unlock your hidden divine nature,
the truth of what was once was before the rule of the masculine.

We can learn from each other the hidden knowledge of the universe.
As we both own our power together, while we own our stories.
No longer being a victim to circumstance, we can now act
and make a pact.

One that we will never again allow ourselves to

feel small.

We will be each others muse, each others inspiration
in the still of the night as our skin makes contact to the
other side.

As we set intentions in what to build and what to
create,
to bring it to life in this moment of reality.

Through energetic bonds, energetic ties,
at the moment of glory our words speak aloud
bringing the thought into action and giving it form.

Each moment basking in bliss of the union
as we both learn to speak our truth.

We are both the light, a giant beacon, a dignified
flame
A Pillar for others to spring up upon, to realize we are
all the same.

That they too can cast these spells, by simply
feeling
once more and becoming the master of their emotions.

Only by the mastery of the emotion will this be
possible,
and baby with you as my reflection emotional mastery
is
where we are bound to go.

6-9-16

I've given some thought to the 100th monkey rule.
If you don't know what that is please read this:
https://en.wikipedia.org/wiki/Hundredth_monkey_effe
ct

If we understand that everything is a replica in the
microcosm and the macrocosm. We can understand
that on a cellular level everything is water. When you
realize each human is a walking water droplet in the

ocean of life.

We can then see that we as a race are just a giant ocean of souls. In so, when you begin to introduce humans with consciousness whose are far outreaching and a guiding factor.

It is a ripple effect out wards to all the other droplets that are nearby that human droplet.

Then it continues to spread, the wisdom and ideas continue to spread so that eventually the entirety of the human ocean is at the same level of understanding. But this can only happen when a critical mass is made, a tipping point. Because otherwise the individual human water drops are diluted and reintegrated back into the human ocean.

But when enough of these drops organize they then become the way in which the entire ocean of humans will be. Because their vibration is raising and bringing others with it.

Those of you who work with water have heard, that if you introduce a water of higher vibration into other water. It will raise the waters vibration to that of the higher one. This same principle plays true in the human water droplets we each are. Simply by being you and being around other human droplets. Your frequency is changing others.

It is allowing others to unravel, it is allowing others to begin to feel again. There literally is nothing you have to do, aside from doing what you love. Always understand that this water is designed to show you that you operate in the same fashion as long as you simply let your self be and flow.

Nature is always showing us how the macrocosm is, we just have to pay attention.

Each of you who understand what I am writing are that unique human water droplet sent here to raise the vibration of all the others around you. Take pride in that, it hasn't been an easy task. But you are not alone. We are everywhere.

And mostly importantly...

You are FUCKING LOVED!!!

6-10-16

Passion fills this vessel like an overflowing infinite source of water. Brimming to the point of radiance so others can feel my own passion simply by being around me.

Constantly wanting to express my self, through word, through sexual desires, through creativity.

Every moment of every day I feel this passion within my self, at times so much I am overwhelmed at which direction to even take it.

It is in the moments of clarity such as writing or love making that I can harness it and direct it to an outcome and intention.

True magick via directing of ones sexual energy, much of which our regular society hasn't even begun to play with. This is our true source of creativity.

I want to experience so much of my self and I am in a state of motivation that is fueling this passion even further.

I have yet to meet a reflection that can keep up with this passion within and has that same yearning and desire to create infinitely without fear and attachment to one another.

The projections of fear and understanding when it is a limitation or an empowerment.

Yes there are days I have to create a push for my

self. But it is because of the fear of the sensation that is throughout my body at all times. At times feeling so much I think Is this real life?

I want to meet my reflection that can show me their own passion, their own desires so that our lights can continue to reflect to one another how far we are willing to take it. I am so done with the holding my self back because it makes people feel uncomfortable. This light is beginning to shine so bright to create a beacon for others to witness.

How deep are we willing to go. To bring up those fears of connection, of vulnerability. I know you are out there, because I am here.

Come out and play.

6-11-16

Last night was a most memorable night for my self and a few others. It is a was moment I will always remember because I shed a limitation I held on my self for a long time.

It started out at my Art of Human Connection workshop. I had 2 beautiful goddesses show up and it was a small and intimate class.
We all then decided to head over to Vibe Tribe together.
On the way we were talking about how freeing it would be to go in the ocean in the nude.
When we got there I followed my intuition and just let my self be free.

I shed all the layers of clothing and ran straight in after I saw the facilitator of the Vibe tribe do it.
This is something big for me because I never shared my body to others in that way aside from lovers, It was something I truly wanted to experience. The other

270

girl from my workshop was already in and also nude, then the last girl went in after I went in.

I felt so free nude in the ocean with a bunch of others also being nude. There was 5 of us.

This was a first time for one of the girls as well but it was something she had always wanted to do. To feel free and liberated.

The two other guys went back in and we three were still out in the ocean.

I decided to empower them by having them yell affirmations out loud to the ocean. This fueled me even further to feeling how truly free I was felt.

I had them state: I am, Love, I am light, I am peace, I am Joy, I am abundance, I am abundant, I am truth, I am worthy, I am free.

We even had the other beach goers yelling back with us.

After words the fire was going and we all got out, it was just us 3...nude standing by the fire, while the others were clothed. And I still felt liberated. No feeling of shame, no feeling of guilt.

I even hugged one of the goddesses fully nude which was amazing in it self to be able to hug someone and not make it a sexual thing while fully nude.

Some of the people even said wow they wish they had the confidence to do that. Last night I truly liberated my self from a big limitation I had always placed on my self. There is no going back now. The ball has been rolling, little by little unlocking further versions of my self on the path to freedom and self discovery.

I received a massage as well, I love this life. I

absolutely love what I am creating. I love the moments where I feel sad and angry. I love the moments that I feel are overwhelming.

Thank you Mama Oshun for supporting me last night in liberating my self. It may not seem like much by simply just going nude, but energetically I lifted a lot off of me last night.

So grateful, thank you Goddesses for providing that safe space to experience that.

6-12-16

I am in love with being in love. And I am in love with who I decided to finally be.

I want you to understand what a false flag is.
It is something created purposely to create an end goal, It could be separation, it could be to cause hatred to a certain faction of people, it could be to remove something and control by fear.

What ever it may be, understand if you feel fear, hatred, anger or sadness. It is all showing you where you have not been giving your love to.
Hate will never heal hate. Anger never will heal anger.

This thing that happened in Orlando is a clear case of creating separation. Come with love and understand all parties involved, if it even really did happen. Since the media is easily faked these days. Crisis actors and what not.

Go within your self and see what you get to love. I personally see this just as people creating a beautiful opportunity for one another to connect and learn. We each create our own reality, even the "victims", the "shooters", and the family's who are affected.

Each having chosen this experience to bring up

certain emotions that they haven't been facing and they decided to kick that up a notch. All moments are perfect regardless of the judgments you have on it.

Come at it with love, because that is all we ever are.

6-13-16

What I crave is a passionate, powerful lioness who wants to walk beside me.
Both of us pushing forward past the barriers we create in our minds.
Both of us utilizing each other as motivation, inspiration, a muse.
Both of us having given permission to continue to push each other beyond our own limits because in truth we have no limits.

To know what we are all doing it for. To remember consistently to know it is all choice.

Reaching these higher realms we will learn and grow with each other, and if one falters they are pushed to keep going. Otherwise they will drift apart while the other continues forward.
Each choice is valid in the nature of this love that we have.

But to truly find a lioness powerful enough, fearless enough to keep pushing forward.

I know you are all out there.

Let me hear your Roar!
Embrace your divinity, embrace your passion, embrace your POWER!

6-27-16

I learned a valuable lesson that day, that I was in love of a vision of what I created her to be and not the person she really was.

I learned that actions truly speak louder then what comes out of their mouth.

This hurt so much to detach from that vision, that fantasy I wanted to create. But It was a beautiful lesson to know and let people be who they want to be. It doesn't mean you have to be with them, it can mean you can now love them from a distance and keep moving forward along your path.

6-28-16

If you have to chase or seek someone. It isn't worth it. The right person will want to be in your space without you even asking. It will happen naturally. Keep moving along your path until you find that one who wants to walk beside you. Not in front or behind you or in the shadows.

6-29-16

Always find ways to test your limits, your will power.

When you do this you expand your mind. You allow your self to choose a target goal and keep at it. When your will power expands you can begin to manifest things at a greater capacity because all of your focus goes into one single thing.

Here are some ways to build that will power, all of which I have done so far:

1. Be vegetarian for a set amount of time and stay at that time unless your body wants something else. I was never vegetarian to protect the animals. They do not require saving. I did it for my own exploration of self.

2. Do a water fast for 3-5 days. Boy this one was a

true test of my will.

3. Do a sweat lodge.

4. Become celibate for a set period of time. This means no sex, no masturbation. This one was an amazing tool for me to see the difference between true attraction and sexual attraction.

5. Quit a habit or quit eating one thing for a certain period of time.

6. Do a juice cleanse for 3 days or more.

7. Create a morning routine or a workout routine.

8. Give up porn!

Remember that each of these tools are designed to test your limits. When you truly challenge your self you can see what you are capable of and if you fail it just means the next time you attempt it again you know where and when to push your self.
When you want to quit....push a little bit harder.

These tests of the will, you will notice a huge difference in the rest of your daily life.

Much love.

Crystals are only to be used as a tool or placeholder of an intention, until you solidify the belief in your mind of what it represents. So that you no longer require it. Remember to let go of the belief that you require something out side of your self to make you feel whole. They are all tools of remembrance.

6-30-16

It is both a curse and a blessing to be able to see straight through into a persons soul and see past all the stories they tell them selves. To hold back certain information because you know inside they would not be ready to hear it yet and they would defend themselves. Until after the lesson has been learned is when you can speak up on what was felt, but even then it would just be a "told you so" type of thing.

I experience this nearly every day. Where I have insights on many people I come across. But I never speak out because they never ask me a direct question to that specific action.

Because I feel it would interrupt their karmic lesson if I interfere too soon.

But I love the exploration of holding space to see if my intuition was wrong...but guess what...It's always right.

Thus is the life of The Hermit Archetype. To have thousands of teachers in your ear but to have the wisdom to speak only when necessary.

The Protection Realization

7-2-16

I am in love with all of my reflections and what they show me about my self.

I am in love with exploration of my divinity.

I am in love with the emotions that are deep within me even when I feel anger, sadness and any other perceived negative emotions.

I am in love with the reflections that bring out the best in me.

I am in love with the reflections that bring out the worst in me.

I am in love with my shadow self.

I am in love with my light self.

I am in love with seeing the interactions of my reflections with one another.

I am in love with seeing all of these actors and how they each represent different aspects of my self at all times.

I am in love with knowing this is just the beginning.

I am in love with supporting others in their growth.

I am in love with being in control of nothing, but in command of everything.

I am in love with no longer being a victim of my circumstances.

I am in love with knowing I am you and you are me.

I am in love with being free.

7-3-16

She shined as bright as the sun.

That was how I knew she was just my reflection.

The only thing I chase these days are my dreams and ideas.
Everything else is a bonus when it wants to materialize in my reality.

7-5-16

One by one the strings of fear begin to be cut. Knowing that on the other side of this is just love. As each string is cut and each fear and limitation is faced. It allows for the soul to float higher, to receive more wisdom of the universe. "How many more strings are left to go" the self asks. I do not know...but I am excited to find out.

Because now the universe knows you know. It will then conspire to support you in your expansion of the self. Giving you subtle realizations that you can then practice and use in the daily life. To teach to others, if they are willing.

The secrets of the universe that are held within this mind and in this body will be shared as long as the proper questions are asked. I know as these fears are faced the illusion, the smoke and mirrors dissipates and it was just me behind it all grinning, smiling and laughing because of how fun it was to play the part of fear. To continuously bring me back to love.

In this moment I am grateful for the fears that show up, because I know I am going in the right direction. The thoughts of "going crazy" have no bearing when you truly have seen the things I have witnessed with this physical human eyes, what I have seen beyond the darkness of my eyes. All things that stories in books would talk about. You too would

never believe it unless you experienced it. But one day, you will and you too will
begin to know as you cut those strings that weigh you down, as you face the smokey mirror of fear and the self.

It was all a fun game of the mind to bring you to where you are right now.

You are loved so much.

7-6-16

Subject: Protection

The feeling of having to protect our selves from outside forces has always been a common story in the human existence. For my self when I was on the brink of my depression I was in a heavy fear state. I would read about conspiracy theories about the government and the illumanti.

I felt I had to protect my self, fear , fear , fear. All of these stories are purposely created to generate more fear. Once you awaken the first thing may be you study is conspiracy theories.
This same concept plays true to having to protect ourselves from demons, negative entities, negative energies. The more you play into the story of fear, the more fear you generate.

I spent a good majority of my money on guns and things to protect myself from governments, and the "bad guys". But today is the day where I have shed that layer of feeling I have to protect my self using force. When I began this, I had purchased 3 guns.

I had an AR-15, a Bolt action rifle, and a pistol. Today I finally sold the last gun, the pistol. I sold them all because I realized when I purchased them all they were all bought in a state of fear and panic. When you have something in your reality that is based on fear that space it holds is the fear within you. When you walk into a persons home every single object in their home is a direct correlation to what is going on with that person.

Depending on the intention and emotion they were in when they bought that item for their home. So when you begin to shed these layers of fear. The objects are a representation and once dealt with there is open and free space to then begin to place love back into its space.

When you understand that you are the literal creator of your reality 100% of the time. You can then truly know that you never have to protect your self from anything. Because everything outside of you is of your creation, allow it to come to you with open arms and with unconditional love. I used to feel I had to always protect my heart, my self.

But now I allow my open heart, my self to love everyone without holding back. It is usually the other parties outside of my self that will feel odd because whoa why is this person loving me this way.

That is one of the two things that will happen, you will create a space in which the person will be pushed away because they are not able to meet you at the level of love you are, or they will join you and step up to that space with you.

Allowing you true vulnerability of the self, without fear of how someone is going to take your words a sense of liberation is acquired. You no longer have to protect your self, because you are now open, honest and vulnerable with everything that surrounds your life. There are no secrets, no lies. There is nothing then that anyone can say that would hurt you, make you feel bad. Because you are your true authentic self.

I have rid my self of this symbol of having to protect my being, and In so I now trust in the process of how my life will reveal it self knowing, I am the creator in my reality. For how I feel inside of my self will dictate what I will experience outside of my self.

In this, so much freedom of self is established. There is a saying "Live by the sword, die by the sword". I now understand what this means. It means when you live in a reality of which you feel you have to protect your self through violence, you are perpetuating this same violence and in such you then have taken that story on in your reality to experience violence.

But when you instead come at things with love and understanding you do not create that story with in you and you are transferred into a different reality where this violence will simply flow under you as you witness it from the observer and how beautiful the experience can be. You then know you will not have to experience this because you have risen above it.

There is nothing we must fix, we must save, or we must do outside of selves but simply be and take ownership of our lives by facing each emotion, each fear, each limitation. Because when you do, your outside world will reflect all of that same love.
So you do not require weapons, because there will never be an experience where a weapon would be required when you know this.

Love is the Light.

7-6-16

A transmission when ORMUS was spoken into my

life. My guides wanted me to begin work on making it.

....and upon ingesting this elixir all of your thoughts, all of the things you give energy to, whether it be negative or positive will begin to manifest at a much rapid rate. Only digest this if you have control of your thoughts. Otherwise you will begin creating all that you do not desire.

Subject: Water

I have said this before but I want to reiterate it. We will continue to see our waters polluted in many ways for the following reasons.

One, it is a direct reflection on how we are treating ourselves internally. Once we begin to treat ourselves with love and not project our emotions. We will see a direct correlation of the waters miraculously heal it self.

Two, this is a necessary experience to have. I feel the water issue will get much much worse and it is to draw awareness to water and back to the original understanding that water is the key to manifesting. People these days treat water as just another beverage. But it is so much more then this, it listens, it remembers, it gives you what you want just as long as you ask it.

I heard a friend say the following and I resonate with this so much. Jesus was the messiah of the age of Pisces. We are now in the age of Aquarius and I feel the new messiah is the water. With the knowledge of intention on water you can make beautiful break throughs.

The earth wants us to focus our gaze on the water, and how is it doing this? By allowing her own waters to be contaminated. She is doing it for us. It has to get much worse for more to wake up to the potential of water.

All the efforts being done to suppress this is futile until the set number of people are aware of the potential of water.

That is my feedback... I have been working with this element for the past 3 years. Let me tell you, I have seen some miraculous things with something that people pass off as none important.

Much Love.

There comes a point in everyone awakening process where you have the choice of going back to the mundane life style or to keep pushing your limits and boundaries.

The ego will say " Well you are surely going crazy".

But the heart will say " Yes, Finally, Lets keep moving forward!"

Embrace your crazy, the things you will create from this are limitless.

Haha, Hehe, Fly. Fly.

7-7-16

You can find me in the stillness.
When the wind caresses your skin to let you know it loves you.
When the ocean waves sing beautiful melodies of life to fill your ear with peace.
Where the birds fly together to remind you of the connection to one another.

This is how you will recognize I am near and always by your side. You can catch me under the tones of light emanating from the sun off the clouds.

The light a form of my love reaching out so that you can feel the warmth upon your skin.

All you have to do is listen. I will be there, always and forever.

I Love You.

7-8-16 *Poem*

If I kiss you would you pull away?

If I kiss you would you feel the love wanting to exude out from my being into you?

If I kiss you would you feel the experiences of my past transfer to your vessel so that you can feel what I have gone through and for my self to feel the same from you?

If I kiss you would you be in bliss?

If I kiss you would you appreciate my affection?

If I kiss you would you kiss me back and bite my lip?

If I kiss you would you open your heart to the possibilities of what is to come?

If I kiss you would you feel my soul, my spirit, my essence?

If I kiss you would you connect with source, the universe?

If I kiss you would you get aroused?

If I kiss you would you feel it is just the universe kissing you?

If I kiss you what would say after?

If I kiss you would you allow our passion to intertwine?

If I kiss you would you feel the intention behind my kiss, every area being charmed by my love?

If I kissed you....

7-8-16

I wanna be loved by you father sky

I wanna be loved by you mother earth
I wanna be that shining star for all to see
I want to be loved by you....
    I love the silly games that our mind plays
I love the way the wind brushes my hair
I love the way the clouds form animals in the sky
I love the way mother earth feels under neath my feet
    I am that open circuit from above and below
I grow, they grow, we grow together.
Thank you for giving me the love.
Thank you for the angels wings to pass their feathers
on my cheeks.
Thank you for the kisses of my lost lover reminding
me who I am.
Thank you for the reminders of owning my power.
    Each day a new lesson, class room earth.
Each day we reappear inside these vessels of light to
shine.
Each day we grow in our awareness.
Each day we understand our ability to affect the
illusion by changing what we feel within.
    I feel the love by you father sky
I feel the love by you mother earth...
I feel the love by you baby....
    We are the children of the sky. Spread our wings
because we are the pillars for others, the foundation of
which will be seen very shortly.
    Take heed and not give into the illusion of fear that
will surface. Ground yourself and remind yourself that
in these moments, what you feel inside is what will be
outside.
    Remember, Remember.
    You are Divine.

Have you ever read a book or watched a movie where you could choose what outcome would happen by turning to a certain page or vote on the outcome?

This is exactly what is happening in real life. What ever we focus our attention on in terms of disasters, riots, race wars, violence. You are choosing what reality in which you want to live in.

That is why news comes out with such violence and negative outcomes. It feeds the illusion of violence.

Instead when you witness this, feed the wolf that you see beautiful communities coming together. Growing food together. This is what we must focus our energies on.

Not the violence, feed the wolf that you want to live.

I ask that if you have read this that you do the following tonight.

Sit and meditate and create a reality in your mind using your imagination. See your self walking through the community that is self sustaining, growing foods. Beautiful lectures on life, meditation. Peace. Visualize all of this! But see it as you are living there as if it was happening right now. Do this for 15 minutes. Set a timer.

I am going to do mine now.

No longer feeding the wolf of fear.

"An old Cherokee is teaching his grandson about life. "A fight is going on inside me," he said to the boy.

"It is a terrible fight and it is between two wolves. One is evil - he is anger, envy, sorrow, regret, greed, arrogance, self-pity, guilt, resentment, inferiority, lies, false pride, superiority, and ego." He continued, "The other is good - he is joy, peace, love, hope, serenity, humility, kindness, benevolence, empathy, generosity, truth, compassion, and faith. The same fight is going on inside you - and inside every other person, too."

The grandson thought about it for a minute and then asked his grandfather, "Which wolf will win?"

The old Cherokee simply replied, "The one you feed.""

Yes you do have the power to mold your reality. You just don't believe it fully yet.

These things we see on tv and movies are designed to program you to choose a scenario that leads in devastation. Is that what you want?

Just decide look within.

Either way, its going to be a fun ride.

7-9-16

Invisible Love

I feel you when I go to the beach sitting by my side
I hear you whispering into my ear as we watch the sun rise
I feel the gentle kisses on my skin as I watch the full moon doing my rituals

I sometimes get lost in others thinking it is you, but I know they show up to teach me to be more of my self until I am divine within my self.

So that we can both meet as equals in the world of earth. I call out to you every now and then. Hoping that you can hear my call...
Wanting for you to feel my beating heart against yours.
I know that seeking outside is simply seeking within.
But it is just a beautiful longing of true intimacy to

dive into the emotions of self with out fear.

I know my reflection is out there thinking this same thing.

I know I am molding a version of myself to meet me at a pre decided meeting place where we will once glance eyes and instantly know.

The Divine Goddess that has a similar mission as I do. To be able to teach side by side and travel to different places together as we teach and spread our love amongst them all.

By being the shining example of what can be attained if you simply begin to face your emotions, your fears.

One day under a full moon perhaps you will reveal your self to me. But for now I write poetry to bring you into reality. So one day I can show you what I have written and it can inspire the passion inside of you to know that there was someone waiting.

But you had to experience all the past moments to truly understand one another. To know we no longer have to project our emotions onto one another. To take ownership and responsibility of ourselves. To be truthful and authentic in all areas without holding back secrets.

It was all a preparation for us to meet. I know I breathe in the same air you are breathing and in it i know we are always connected....my beloved. One day. One day soon. It will come to pass.

I Love you for what you will reflect to me.

7-10-16

Today for the first time in my life I saw the sun wink at me with a green flash of light as it rose.

It is a rare occurrence that happens right when the sun rises on the horizon.

Green as we know is the heart chakra. I feel I was gifted the love of the sun today. In it I feel blessed to have witnessed something many have not.
Wow what a beautiful occurrence.

Right before that in the other photo a Cardinal was signing to me and my friend as we were witnessing how beautiful she was.

Fucking love this life.

Green flash shining onto my skin
Gifting me the power to love unconditionally.
I am Free.

I feel therefor I am.

7-11-16

The pineal gland is the collector of light.
It is the temple inside the head.
Like a pyramid absorbing energy/light from the outside sun.
To then funnel this light and energy to be shined on the shadow of the self.

Only by means of your words, do you solidify a belief.
To say to one self " No, I can't do that" or "I can never remember" or "I always do this".

You then solidify the belief because you are declaring that which you speak. You words are magic, but only to yourself. Words can carry other means to others outside of your self due to the meaning they give certain words based on their experiences.

So do not fret when someone misunderstands you or dislikes a word you say, because that is their story. You only have to be mindful of that which you speak out loud because it holds a very special frequency to your own self.

Do you really want to solidify a belief that of which you say "You can't" do something?

Something to ponder.

Everything begins to fall into place if you just clear the way and remove attachments, strings of limitations and fears. One by one the space will be clear for your wildest desires to begin to appear where those once were.

What a beautiful freeing feeling it is.

7-12-16

From the dream state I witnessed the central hub. Where our soul/awareness goes and we each hold a key, a phrase we can say if we know the correct herb sequence to get there.

There was also a special pressure point each unique to the body that can be utilized as well. This was shown to me on my own body.

Each body holding a different key in order to view this portal, each phrase different based on the path you chose. But none the less it is a phrase we can say in our minds to release our selves from the physical much easily then visualizing.

I had a dialog with 2 people in this space where they asked why do we not just create in this space? They stated because it would just disappear once our awareness is not placed on it.

As well as the space that is in this zone is a shared zone. A resting place for creation.

We like to think that people are not reading us. Especially in the spiritual community. There are a lot out there that act a certain way but you can feel their energies very well what is behind the mask.

You do not ever hide anything of your self in this

community. We see through it. I have times where I put a mask on but I am learning to dismantle it completely. I know what its like to present your way in a certain light because you do not want others to judge you.

I know this VERY well. If we could sit and talk about my experiences you would understand why. But just know if you are not being authentic, people can notice it. They feel it.

Intuition never lies.

You are loved though regardless in which manner you wish to present your self. Because love has no conditions.

They spoke to me to notify me of my phrase and herb combination. So I can use this as an access point until I no longer require it. A much easier way then I have been using to have astral travel experiences.

When you don't let fear take hold of you, there is nothing the illusion has over you anymore.

7-13-16

Arise this morning and know all things are possible. Just make a choice. This choice will mold your reality and the universe will always conspire to give that which you desire.

Making love

I want to make love to you under the moon light sky, starry night shining bright
As we look back to the clouds in the night sky seeing if we can make animals with our minds as the passion rises higher and higher.
Feeling connections rise as we turn back and face one

another and gaze into each others eyes so we can have a glimpse at how deep the rabbit hole goes.

I want to make love to you as the air cools our sweat down as the heat rises from the yearning of the desire we have been longing for, life time after life time we continue finding one another.

And when we do we always greet each other in a dance of union of two different perspectives to have them transferred genetically via DNA to one another.

It allows our souls growth as we connect deeper and release stories of fear, allowing our selves to be vulnerable bearing our hearts wide open for all to see.

I want to make love to you as we listen to the oceans waves hitting the sand, a soothing music for our bodies as the chemical romance continues to stir inside one another.

Creating an alchemical concoction of unconditional love and ecstasy as we both create sounds that brings a rise to one another.

I want to make love to my mirror, my reflections to show them who they truly are and hold space for their growth regardless of if they are with me in this moment or the next. So that as we make love the ecstasy can ripple through all time and space so others can feel that same love within their own bodies.

Knowing the moments shared were perfect and complete without the attachment of wanting something more, but being complete with that one moment in time, like a grain of sand in the hourglass. More moments will come....

I want to make love to you.

Because as I do, I know I am merely loving my self.

I love you.

7-14-16

Can you feel me when you dream
Tossing, turning endless nights when you appear in mine.

Do you wake up thinking of me, wondering if you want to say hello.

Can you feel me in your dreams when I have full conversations with you in mine.

Teaching you, getting to know you on deeper levels than you allow me in this place we call reality.

Waiting for that moment when you just pick up the phone to say Hello.

Can you feel me in the dreams, when you tell me about your life and how you are afraid to tell me in this one.

I feel you, know I am keeping open space for you to simply say Hello....

Hello. Unconditional Love is Calling.

To say that you are alone is to live in the reality of the monkey mind, the ego.

Know this, the same air you breathe out is the same air another breathes in. In this know physically we are all connected.

Many ways we are connected but the eyes does not perceive it.

So we forget and require reminders, hints for us because other wise the monkey mind drowns out that knowledge with subterfuge garbled beliefs that it was taught.

Remind your self. Place post it notes, wear something with intention.

Remember who you are and why you chose to return at this time.

Place your headlights on high beam, It is time, now more then ever.

7-15-16

Will you take my hand and dive deep into the unknown with me?
But I have a secret....it is no longer the unknown because I have seen the light behind the veil.
In this perceived unknown is simply more of ourselves. But we are afraid, afraid of taking true ownership of our reality to know that you are the creator.

Will you dive deep into the depths of my heart with me?
Coming up for air only when the shadow has surfaced to allow us time to heal that aspect, then we shall dive again.
Each time discovering hidden treasures of who we really are little by little.

Will you let go of your fears and let go with me?
To know that we are always supported and safe, never having to protect our selves because it is simply ourselves writing the play of our lives. We are the actor, writer, producer, director. To know this is to truly trust in the process.

Will you explore the darkness in the depths of my heart with me?
To support one another in the stories we tell our selves in the mind. So that when we emerge we are a shining light house for others to see because from the depths of the perceived unknown is more of our own light that we are rediscovering.

Will you be true and speak your mind when we are in that unknown with me?

No longer hiding because of fear of judgment from the outside world and perceptions. It is all your creation anyways.

This is what I desire, This is what I will manifest. A reflection that will dive deep with me because I want to see any remnants of fear to surface so that I can look at it in the eye and tell that portion of my self how much it is loved. How safe it is , how acknowledged it is.

I open my heart for you to step into it if you so desire.
Together we do not have to be afraid because we are both exploring things we have neither experienced. It is a beautiful feeling, like that of an explorer.

We have explored many caves, oceans, countries. But the true explorations are still within , the furthest recesses of our minds and heart. Feeling like an adrenaline junky for what other fears come up. Because I have yet to discover them.

I am ready, I am willing. If you are in my space....you are ready too.
But do you know it yet?

7-16-16

My heart is inside a labyrinth going towards connection.
I don't have the map to show me the way, so I use the guidance.
The inner voice that has gotten me this far.

So many turns, left, right, zig zaging to find the exit.
"I am worried" the ego says. "That we are lost and no longer know where we are going". The heart replies "It's okay, I am the light, just surrender".

So I do, I surrender to an unending maze of wanting to know more. But I keep navigating using my heart, because it always know the way. I continue to step forward into discovering my self.

Deeper, further into the maze. Maybe at a certain point the path will cross again and we will walk side by side as equals because she may see what I can bring to the table. But again it is the mind wanting her to see. The heart just wants to love. Give love, receive love. In all aspects. It wants to guide her as she guides me back to my self.

This is a labyrinth that many travel in, some go mad from being inside to long. Because they don't know the way out. But I see the light coming up around the corner.

That is my queue, exit stage left. I keep diving into my divinity. Leaving room for her to learn and grow in her own way by holding space. Knowing I am safe and secure within my self to know life will play out the way it is to be.

Signs, omens, confirmations, synchronicity will begin to show up guiding the way. But I know within my self I have seen them all. I know what is being guided within. It feels as though I give more then I receive. But it is because I have so much of this passion within me that I have to share it regardless of what is returned.

"I just want to be loved" The heart begins to speak softly...wondering if it is heard.

One day, she will take ownership of the creations and realize it was all an illusion. Just as I am learning my self.

What a beautiful day it will be, if I am there still or

not.

You are loved.

I am a powerful Water Alchemical Magi, reawakening my divine nature.

Learning my spells from the grimoire of the heart. Each time the heart begins to hurt and expand a new spell is unlocked within my self.

But only if I transmute this hurt , sadness, sorrow into love.

A continuous process of learning about who I am. There is a saying live each day as if it were your last. I see many do not live this way.

Wanting to so desperately create stories in their minds of what they want and they forget to see what is truly in front of them.

I've learned to wear my heart on my sleeve to be authentic with how I feel. How it is received is not up to me. I can never make a person feel the love I want to share with them.

I feel as though I want a Powerful Sorceress in my life so we can truly share our knowledge with each other. But in every fairy tale or story I've read, it normally is just one or the other. Never seeing them truly unite in this way.

Wanting to read from each others book of spells from the heart. Sharing our journey by speaking our truths. No longer living in the fear of things outside our selves.

I have shed my layers of having to protect my self. By letting go of my outside weapons. I want a powerful sorceress who knows her outside world is generated from what is within.

When it comes to matters of the heart, mine has

always wanted to challenge me to see how deeply I can love without truly receiving it fully in return.

Where art thou Goddess, Witch, Sorceress.
Let us cast spells with our words together and be that light for the world to know what is possible if we only allow our true selves to shine.
If we allow all walls to crumble without the fear of being hurt.
This could be us creating the story in our minds see how far we can take it. Because our beliefs create our reality.

7-17-16

I Love You Sun, For you are the inner Fire, The light that guides me.
You show me that it is okay to love someone unconditionally from a distance by simply holding space.

I Love You Ocean Mist, For you are the Water, The liquid of life that flows through my veins.
You show me that it is okay to feel your emotions and for it to expand the unconditional love out wards once the emotion is felt.

I Love You Wind, For you are the Air, The gentle and subtle pushes towards my divinity.
You show me that with ease as you caress my face it is okay to face my fears which can then allow me to love unconditionally.

I Love You Sand, For you are the Earth, The solid foundation of which I can build my love upon.
You show me that when grounded there is nothing that can ever detour me from sharing my unconditional love to someone.

The heart simply wants to love, regardless of what

the outside reflection shows.

It is then that our mind begins to speak and gets in the way because if it is not returned in a way we want it, then what is the purpose of going further down that path?

Instead just start a new path the mind says... But the heart knows that is fear and that these fears are simply book marks or place holders to show us the true way back to love. We purposely place these blocks to see if we want to go further or not.

So as we have this understanding, the moments where you feel the most pain and heart ache and say no this is too much to feel because of so and so.

What you are feeling is your power at that moment, it hurts because there is no measurement in the mind just yet on how to identify this feeling. So it interprets it as pain.

When you dive deeper into the feeling, the body begins to become acclimated in a way and it then identifies it as a surging remembrance of the unconditional love that we posses.

It is the love that was long before, and the love that will remain long after. Regardless of what ever stories we like to tell in between.

Subject: Sexual Energy / Creativity.

When you begin to understand everything is energy and begin learning the chakras.

The sacral chakra is the source of sexual energy and creativity.

For those who have high sex drives it is an indication that you are a extremely creative person if that energy is focused on a goal.

If you cut out masturbation and become celibate

like I did for 7 months. You then learn how to channel this energy into creation of ideas that come to you. Sometimes we look at people and ask wow, how did they come up with that, or create that.

They simply focused their sexual energy on a creative output.

It does not have to be solely on sex and passion. But if you have a high sex drive, the best way to alleviate this is to direct it into new arts and crafts or goals you want to manifest.

If you do not direct the energy towards something creative, you will become lustful for physical connection. Because that is your driving force now. Learn to focus and be deliberate.

I my self have always had a strong sex drive and I was very promiscuous when I was younger. This was until I realized how valuable the sexual energy truly is, and to be mindful with whom I share this with. As I began my practice of self discovery, I learned how to retain the seed of creation. To then utilize it for what I want in my life to become a reality.

For men, I strongly recommend you do a vow of celibacy for a minimum of 1 month. This means no sex, no masturbation, no porn. Watch how quickly you become motivated in life to do the passions and dreams you wanted. But you have been slacking and telling your self you'll do it tomorrow.

But be warned on this...The moment you make the choice, a test will appear to see if that is the choice you really want. It is simply your self checking in to see how dedicated to your will power you are. I had it happen with me. You can then see how the structure of existence works when you make a choice. To see things come up once you made a choice to detour you from that choice to see if you truly want it.

Be strong and commit to something. Direct that energy to something you have been wanting to explore.

Masturbation is not a bad thing though, But once you learn you can utilize this energy for manifesting...The game changes.

You are the game changer, you are the molder of your reality. Now team this up with a Divine Female who knows this same concept....You can then team up your sexual energies towards a goal together.

Instead of masturbating or having carnal primal sex. You can then set intention into the release or injaculation. When you do this, all the energy of your self and your partner goes towards the intended purpose.

Of course you can do this on your own and learn to channel your own energy first before you share this with a partner. But once your partner learns the technique to manifesting.

You can both choose things you wish to experience in this physical world. You then channel the Divine Masculine, and Divine Feminine Energy towards that and watch how fast it appears in your reality.

Now on that note, my sexual energy has to go create some shit otherwise I am going to go crazy. It's another reason I feel I must write so much. My creative energy has to flow out somewhere.

Time to make some more Sirian Head Bands. I have some orders to fulfill on.

7-18-16

Where ever you are, There I am.

No matter what time, There I am.
No matter the distance, There I am.
You can catch me in the rays of sunshine shining on
your face.
You can feel me when you walk as the wind meets
your face.
There I am.

When you look into another souls eyes, There I
am.
When you think of how alone you are, There I am.
When you want so badly to have someone hold you,
There I am.

We are never separate. Always in this exploration
together.
In this know that together we can mold a reality of our
choosing.

Start this morning off with 10 grounding breathes.
Inhale through the nose, out the mouth. On the final
breathe, hold for 10 seconds.

You will feel me in the essence of it.
I Love You, Always and Forever. Because I know you
do everything in love regardless of the outside story.

7-19-16

Yeah my creative juices are flowing because my
emotions are stirring.

You think of your self as an enigma, like no one
can see you.
I see through it all, I see the person you present your
self to be.
I see you so desperately wanting to be significant and
valid in your story. I know I can see it because you
showed up as that reflection in me. I too wanted to be
valid and significant. But the difference is throughout

this entire process. I found out I am , because I am alive.

I am significant because I exist. Regardless of what I do with this life I will still be valid. Just as you are. The not wanting those to judge you shows the image you have to uphold, I was there too.

I see the pain inside that you refuse to face because you are afraid. I too experienced this, it is a difficult process detaching from an illusion that was created.

I love you even when you are inauthentic with me. I love you even when you are aloof with me.

But you present your self to not be this. Which in turns makes it that much more obvious when someone gets close.

It all makes sense now that I have heard from different sides of things.

I had to get the 3rd point of view. the holy trinity of information.

The triskelion , the balance of knowledge.

Remember this phrase

"How you are with one thing, is how you are with all things."

What a powerful fucking phrase.

Pay attention to the little details and you can see a person.

In this I am grateful because I have no anger show up.

I feel the self opening wide for something greater. What a true blessing it will be to see the next marvel of the universe to enter into my reality.

I await that experience with open arms bigger, stronger, more courageous than my previous version.

Because I know I can see beyond the veil of

secrecy.

Thank you Universe for showing up in this way as my reflection.

So grateful, so thankful, now with this I am to make a mindful action on where to take this life next.

It is the feeling like that of a dagger into the skin, when the way you perceived an illusion is shattered by the words of another who speaks their truth always.

7-19-16

She came as whirlwind and it shook the walls and foundation of my once shattered heart.

Next a new marvel of nature came as a flash flood that brushed away the things in life that no longer mattered and polished the heart. So that it could truly shine and be pieced together from the wind.

Leaving it better then it once was because now I have room to work with.

When it comes to matters of the heart, all bets are off.

The heart does what it does to get the job done.

The heart knows 100% what it wants.

What fear are you willing to face to get it though?

I began my Sunrise 40 day Challenge 5 days ago. This is my entry for day 5.

Day 5 of 40

I cry tears of sadness and the sun catches them for me and turns them into tears of gratitude.

Myself : Why do I love so deeply Sun?

The Sun: Because you are still learning to apply that love within.

You then use these moments as a book mark or measurement to then begin loving your self in this way.

Myself: But I feel I love my self just as deep as I love my reflection.
What is the point? I ask again.
The Sun: You are learning to accept people as they are and how they present them selves regardless of what words they speak. You are learning to truly be vulnerable and trust in the process and to be okay with it all.
It is the understanding that people , just like you, want to be seen in a certain light. But you have the gift of seeing behind that mask.
That is why you are in the position of teaching as you are and will be. You can see past peoples stories regardless of what they say.
It is a beautiful gift to have.

Myself: It sometimes doesn't feel like it. Because when I call people out on their things. They deny it because they refuse to accept that about themselves. They want to shine without having polished the outer layers of the self.

The Sun: Why call them out on things? What is there to prove? You can see things beyond the veil. In so you already know what you are getting. But I see what you do for them. I see the solid foundation you provide for them. Your task is to accept them as they are. Without having to change anything about them.

Myself: But if thats the case then why are they even in my space. I grow as others heal. Because they are me. Why would I not speak my truth and How I see things?

The Sun: You can speak your truth, of course. But be okay with how ever that truth is taken once it leaves your mouth. It is not up to you for the other to take it the way you want.

The pain you feel is actually the fuel to the fire that burns inside you. The light that each time you love deeply it is a power that is emanating that others can see and will seek it out for their own illumination.

Thank you Sun.

I love you.

The rationalizing mind is a powerful one when it does not want to take ownership and responsibility for it's own actions.

Instead it justifies their outside influences and it plays the victim.

All of which are of your own creation to begin with.

7-21-16

Day 7 of 40 Sunrise Challenge

This journey of life has its ups and downs. We are still learning about ourselves even if we are teachers or students. Each moment and experience is testing your level of awareness and your capacity of maintaining your self.

Be okay with the times you are in the ego and you speak words out of anger or sadness.

The truth behind it all is the love doesn't care. It just wants to love unconditionally. It knows that beyond all the stories you tell that there is still love behind it all fueling the fire of passion within you.

The sun is a great teacher in that way as it always shines brightly for us to recognize our own power and when we fall it doesn't judge us. It just loves unconditionally.

That ray of line reaching out towards me is my reminder and an arm caressing my body because it just wants me to feel love. It wants me to find that love within my self.

These last 7 days have been an intense journey of the mind. I am humbled each day through all of the emotions. But I grow in awareness and my capacity to love greater extends each time I reach my critical mass where I burst open at the seams and let my raw emotions show. All to release what has always been inside of me. But wants to slowly make it self known.

I am the Light. I am the Power. I am Greatness.

7-22-16

Day 8 of 40 Sunrise/Gazing

Growth can only occur when you begin to take ownership of your experiences. Then once you have taken ownership making a choice towards being the best version of your self.

7-25-16

Day 11 of 40 Sunrise Sun gazing off Arizona St and a l a.

Each day I rise and have a date with the Sun...
I feel love ever expanding because I know it is always there.
It allows me to see my own light within as I close my eyes
I drift into the sea of my mind, colors cascading off the darkness of the eyes to create shapes that guide me for that day.

I feel my love continuing to grow and in this I know for sure I am infinite beyond measure. Because I once thought I couldn't love anymore...But this mornings sun continues to inspire me to expand my own love.

So I can be that shining light for others to see and know how possible things really are if they just let go of the fear and continue to dive into their emotions. If they just continue to let go of the limitations they place on their mind.

I will be that beacon. Because I am the Love, I am the Light.

7-26-16

Day 12 of 40 Sunrise sun gazing

It is in these moments that beautiful experiences are shared amongst brothers.

All here having chosen to rendezvous at the designated hour to view in awe the things we created behind the scenes for us to then view like a movie and wonder how it was all possible.

Literally creating, writing, producing the movie, for us to then watch it all unfold eagerly. I honor these moments because of how powerful we each are and we are still remembering how powerful we each really are.

Knowing that the one solid thing we can guarantee is the sun rising each day. The sun not caring if it doesn't look good, if its being judged. It simply rises each day to shine its light.

I aim to be that for others as do my brothers of light sitting beside me.

So we continue to reflect to one another and show that brotherhood from this lifetime until the next.

I Love You Sun.

Thank you Brothers.

7-27-16

What you have issues with outside of yourself are things you embody in some form or another and are not okay with it.
Or it brings up the emotion you have been neglecting. Think about it...

7-28-16
My Open Letter to Fear:
Dear Fear,
I used to despise how you would show up in my world to fill me with doubt and what ifs. Every time I wanted to do something to benefit my self you popped up to change my mind. You were that emotion that always kept me with my head down into the ground.

You prevented me from exploring more of who I was because you allowed me to live comfortable and complacent with life.
But now things have changed. I have seen you for what you are to me and my world. You show up every time I have a surge of inspiration towards something I truly want to live by.

I understand you now, you are the beacon of light showing me the way to my salvation. You are the invisible wall I place in front of me and the goal or experience I want to explore because you want to make sure I really want it. You are the check in point for my will power to see if its truly what I want to manifest.

But now that I know this about you, I utilize you as the tool for expansion of my divinity. You showed up recently in my finance sector. You showed up telling me I wouldn't have enough money to buy a leather whip, and then a fire whip, and then that leather mask I am going to get. You showed up through all of it because you wanted to be sure that was what my passion is.

I pushed passed the illusion, But because I took that leap, I now have sources of income coming from all different areas in my life I did not have before. All because I took that step. I pushed passed the barrier, I knew because you were the light guiding my way in the tunnel of darkness.

I now love you fear. I love everything that you stand for in my experience because I now see you never were a hindrance. You were my empowerment, you were my voice to do the opposite of and push past because on the other side of it was my salvation.

I now honor you fear because I see what you represent in others. You are simply offering them opportunities to step into their divinity little by little. By allowing them the choice to face the fear or stay comfortable and complacent.

What a beautiful emotion you have been and will continue to be for me because I now know the truth about you and because of this.

I fucking adore you.

7-29-16

Day 15 of 40 Sunrise Sun gazing

The light you seek is the light that emanates from within. The same eternal fire that fills each of us with passion. That inspires us to be the best version of ourselves we can be. This light can be ignited in others by simply allowing your self to shine in your authenticity.

Have you been authentic in all situations?

The mind will forget things to cater to the reality

that you are creating within.

So that you do not have to own up to a certain agreement with another.

It is a form of justification, rationalization and manipulation.

Just because you do not remember doesn't mean it didn't happen.

See if you can see from the other persons point of view, especially if they have been open with you since the beginning.

What use would they have in making a false reality?

I have experienced this with many friends. Things get lost in translation so that things do not get addressed. Do your best is what is asked.

Live by your words, but know your actions will always tell the truth of what you live by.

7-30-16

Day 16 of 40 Sunrise Sun gazing

You are so close, I can feel your essence surround me.

I can smell your scent getting near, the joyous bliss of love filling my vessel.

To know just how safe I am to feel, to be okay with my surroundings regardless of how it may seem.

As I gaze into this mornings sun I long for the arm to cradle this vessel and caress my hair as I go within releasing emotions.

The heart wants to be recognized by another, But it is just a deeper longing for the love of the whole.

I can feel you getting closer...Circling around my body like a moon to a planet. It wont be much longer now.

We are awakening.

I know it. I love you.

7-31-16

Day 17 of 40 Sunrise Sun gazing

You can let go of the possibilities by divorcing your self from the attachments and expectations of what you have been creating in the mind. You do not have to physically shed your self of someone in order to do so. But in most cases we do this because it gives us time to self reflect on what has been playing out with out the energy of the other.

When you begin placing expectations on how a person is to act, regardless of what comes out of their mouth on how they handle their life. You are still holding onto an idea of how a person ought to be. Rather than letting them be the way they are. In other words, when you let go of all thoughts on what a person does you can never be disappointed because then you would only be illuminated when they do things that coincide with your own path. But then we have preferences on what we prefer to surround ourselves with, is it people who are authentic to their word, people who project them selves to be a certain way they are not? Ultimately you get to decide what reflections you wish to surround your self with.

You can still walk your path and not hold onto to the story that your life would be perfect with someone else, because it already is. You do not have to place projections on how your energies will intertwine. Because the truth is we never will know. We just feel what we feel in the moments as we feel them. But to honor one another in these freedoms and express when intentions change or feelings change is the key to maintaining a healthy balance between one another. That open channel of communication must be kept otherwise that is how assumptions will be made and expectations are made. Which ultimately leads to suffering.

Come from the heart when you express and fear not how a person will take your words. Just be authentic.

7-31-16

The best way to establish a connection with anyone is just to sit back and listen. Truly listen to what they say without wanting to change the way they are feeling. Allow them to feel what they are feeling and only if they ask on how to change the emotion then offer advice. Otherwise people just want someone with no judgment to speak to and be heard.

8-1-16

Day 18 of 40 Sunrise sun gazing

Cradle me in your arms and let my shadow weep tears to release my self from the bondage of the mind.

8-2-16

Day 19 of 40 Sunrise sun gazing

I wanted passion in my life, so the sun rose to show me what unconditional love truly looks like. With it the fire rose in my heart a new day to know all things are possible.

You just have to let go and surrender to the moment.

I stared at the sun piercing the clouds and in this moment I remembered...

I already am passion.

She breathed out her pain, fear and limitations. I breathed them all in because they were reflections of my own to work through.

But in turn I transmuted it all back into love allowing

her space to over come them on her own.
The alchemy of love.

8-5-16
Day 22 of 40 Sunrise Sun gazing
It is in the moments where you lose your patience
and temperament that you gain the most wisdom.

It is those souls whom you have contracted to
support your growth to stir things up within you that
you didn't know was there.
They are the master teachers for the lesson you may
have missed in previous connections.

So to take things personal then becomes a thing
that the ego wants to attach to because it feels
threatened. We each have our own things going on in
the mind. We eventually learn that it is not what a
person is doing that we are taking offense to, it is the
way we feel about it.
And the way we feel about it is an emotion that has
always been inside of you but in this one moment the
master teacher was able to bring it up within you to
show you it has always been there.

What an awesome service this is to provide to
another soul. To simply show them what was already
there. But in order to get this understanding, we must
first take ownership of our creations.

I do not know what I don't know, until my
reflections bring things up. But when things come up
within me I apply the practices I have learned to take
me back to my peace realizing it was all my creation in
the first place. Yes, I still react to situations rather than
respond, but I am still learning. With this mindset
connections can be rebuilt, but only if the other party

didn't take what was done personally, and the service you provided was heard and their own lesson learned.

Bringing us back to the understanding we are in this together and being in service of love to one another.

You are loved.

8-10-16

I'd like to remind you that every thing is a tool of exploration to learn more of your self. Just as a hammer is used to hammer in a nail to accomplish the job. Once completed you place the hammer back into the tool box once the task is completed.

However in this essence once a lesson is learned. The same goes with crystals, numerology, sigils, symbols, medicines, zodiacs, astrology.
It is all tools to allow you to step into your divinity. But do not get stuck in the story that every single thing MUST revolve around those tools. If that is the case you have missed the point and purpose of the tool.

This goes out to all those who chase after numbers, zodiacs, crystal hunting to make you feel a certain way. You have all the power within your self to attain this without the tool once you have used the tool from the very first time.

I my self have used a tool more than once because at times it takes a few experiences to receive the lesson in the first place.
But then there were other times or medicines I only had to utilize it once to get the message and I no longer require this tool for my growth, because I now embody that energy.

This is just a gentle reminder to you to not get fixated on the tool it self. Learn to rid your self of the

315

tools. Just as a wizard knows it is not his wand that gives him power or his beard. It was simply the belief that it did. But it takes some integration to understand that.

And Yes the wizard is simply an identity for remembrance as well, as are the other archetypes. Some are more fun to play than others, just as some tools more than others. Just remind your self it wasn't the tool that gave you that power, it was always your self.

8-14-16

Day 29 of 40 Sunrise Sun gazing

It is in the moments of complete surrender where things will begin to flow effortlessly towards you. I have let go of so many things the past few weeks. Little by little the universe hears your calls and places people on your path perfectly.

8-15-16

Day 30 of 40 Sunrise Sun gazing

The journey of the soul is one of the most amazing to experience. The new found knowledge that awaits every corner can leave you at the edge of your seat. Receiving moments of epiphany that then rewires the brain to reanalyze how a previous experience was and how future ones will then play out.

If it is adventure you seek, you must only have to look within and how deep the rabbit hole truly goes. We have spent ages exploring the outside world of our creations. Now the best adventure awaits of the one within.

8-18-16

Day 32 of 40 Sunrise sun gazing

As a Master Manifestor why do you tell the story

of being in lack?

Why is it when something you truly want and is within reach do you tell your self, no that is too much money?

We are unlimited creative expression and as such we have the ability to decide how much we wish to see in our own individual expressions. We have the capability of living freely from judgment of finances just by making a choice.

But it then comes down to am I worthy enough for this said abundance? Do I feel I have "worked hard enough" to receive this abundance. Another fallacy that has been ingrained in our minds that we must work hard to attain abundance.

What would happen if we let go of that working hard story and just know you are worthy of abundance in all ways and what you say in your mind goes.

Another voice may pop in, of Oh no that means more responsibility. Do you feel you are capable of handling what is to come? For a good long while I didn't but that is shifting as well.

Any time a limiting belief comes up of money and fear pops up, challenge that fear and say to it, no I know I have enough for this.

Abundance is on the way, Abundance is here to stay.

Little by little my beliefs on money are shifting. I will see it through because I am worthy of all of it and the things I will change with this abundance will be for the benefit of the whole.

I decide, I decide, I FUCKING DECIDE! POWER!

8-22-16

I am just in a state of awe when I review my past and how far I have traveled to get to where I am today.

The lesson's I've learned, the people I've met. All
catalysts to ignite the flame within me.
Stoking the coals and embers to my heart of passion so
I can be that shining light for others to realize they too
can ignite the same passion.
They too can be the pillars of light for all to bare
witness and know it is safe to come out and play.
Letting go of the walls we place over our hearts
because we are in fear of being hurt. We fear so we
must protect ourselves.

Why??? It is just you and only you....Why would
you give your self an experience you couldn't handle?
Every moment a blessing and learning experience. But
all you have to do is take a step back and see what it
was showing you to break the cycle.
Thus a new cycle begins.

I am facing my fears much more now a days, on a
more physical level with this fire spinning. So many
time's in my mind, "Oh wow, your going to burn your
self. Oh Wow, the ropes gonna get tangled on you."

But once I do it, I am safe and no harm comes of
me. Maybe a slight burn, but the body heals. And the
body will only allow wounds to occur if you do not
handle your emotional body so it then transverses into
the physical so that you can begin paying attention to
it. But if you truly admit to your emotions and
acknowledge them. There will never be any harm that
falls upon you.

I told what I am doing to a family member and
they said wow that is dangerous...Yea to you it is. To
me it is a freeing experience to discover just how far I
can take my self through the valley of fears. To
conquer each one that arises because I do not know

what fears may come unless I take that leap.

It is never a risk, all moments you take that leap for, is a acceleration point towards your self, understanding the role of your divinity.
Taking charge of your life once more, rather then listening to what others say you have to do, or "should not do".
You are the only creator of your space, you are the only rule maker of your space.

Do you feel the change happening all around you? Because I do, and I am at the forefront. I am witnessing it all before my very eyes, when so many times I thought I was alone and isolated because I thought no one thought the same as I do.
But the secret is....many are beginning to remember. Many are beginning to become self aware once more. It isn't an instant process.

But that is why the forefront runners are taking the stand to show you it is possible, to teach you what we have learned , thus cutting the time for your acceleration in half or more. Catapulting you further then we forefront runners can go. Then you teach us and it is a cycle of growth.

I am so FUCKING ready for this new world, because I already see it. I know my role in it, and I will see this to the end.
I feel the abundance surging through my body to begin making this world a reflection of the love I have within.

Not because the world requires saving, not because the water requires saving, not because the animals require saving. Because none of it does.

But simply because the love that expands from my

heart will raise the vibration of all that set foot in my space and a new choice will be made.

I love you all dearly.

8-23-16

Day 37 of 40 Sunrise Sungazing

When two souls converge towards a common goal of self exploration, there is nothing that can stop the manifesting. As long as both continue to push forward to create the outcome. The light upon the tip of the convergence is bright enough for others to see and take note of to know they too can do the same.

8-30-16

Transformation can begin when you have the willingness to let go of old thought patterns and explore new ones that are presented from others perspectives. Then and within this exploration you surrender to the thought that things must be a certain way. You can then allow space for beautiful reflections to come through into your sphere of reality and begin to notice that the people that surround you now are all aspects of the internal dialog within your mind.

The moment this realization comes, the process of self healing can occur. Thus more space will be opened because you are clearing the shadow to allow room for more opportunities of self love and more opportunists for a Divine Opposite to be attracted to you. This is only because you know that you do not require someone outside your self, you do not require "the one" because you have already begun the union within your self. The one you have been looking for has been you all along. There is no other half, aside from the discovery and acceptance of your shadow self to transform it all back into love and acceptance.

To find another Divine Opposite though is because you can now see there are aspects of them that you wish to embody, and you possess aspects that they wish to embody. Providing incredible reflections of self growth and mastery to be those teachers to one another. Knowing you are in this same path to discover just how far you can take this human experience.

Romance is hitting me in these wee hours once more...

I want my love to be the door for you to walk through...

So you can see it has always been you on the other side looking in.

I want our love to be shared and shine as bright as the big bang and through it we can create new universes for new beings to explore.

I want you to see your worth and power beyond the vast stories of limitations we tell ourselves. But only by being the reflector to one another.

Can we begin to unlock these new potentials inside of us. Will you be that one that stays in it to grow with knowing to take full responsibility for all outcomes. Because we both know who we are and to not get lost in each others worlds.

To know and remind one another of what we wish to create but to not place attachments on how it will reveal it self.

To know if we project we take time aside and reorganize our minds to take ownership of the realities.

So that way we can continue to walk the path to divinity with each other. Not as each others half, but as our own complete selves choosing to share the walk to oneness together.

No longer craving, no longer seeking outside of selves for completion. But truly knowing the reflection walking beside us is just wanting to explore how deep their own love can go.

So we dance around one another enveloping all those who bare witness to the union to see how this template can be.

To know it is truly possible and not something that can be read in fairy tales or books.

Wanting to share a cosmic union with another complete soul who is simply wanting to see what else can be created. Thus creating the third, the trinity. The higher self and in this union of the divine.

Many teachings will inspire our onlookers, our observers, our perceiver's. This beacon of light will shine so bright because both of us are already bright stars blinding the eyes of the ones looking down. Together we will be the sun's to their U n I verses.

By simply being in our space they will instantly remember what we came here to do. This is what I will manifest, it is already in the works.

Come and walk through this door and I shall walk through yours...

Here we are go, once again and forever more.

8-31-16

Did you feel me when we shared that gaze?

Did your heart skip when our paths crossed once more in this life time?

The warming sensation in the chest a feeling of openness and vulnerability.

I stated I allow my heart to open completely to you as we were there sharing the moment.

Could you hear my thoughts as I opened my self
fully to you.
Seeing you just as a beautiful reflection and reminder
of my self knowing how far I wish to take this dream
of worlds.

I felt it in the touch, I felt it in the gaze.
I am always feeling. I remember a time I chose not to
feel as much as I do now.

Because to me it was scary, it hurt, it was painful. I
couldn't fathom the amount of love another could be
so open to give and be.

But now I know it because I allow it. I chose to be
vulnerable, I choose to be free.

Because when you close off one emotion you close
off the rest. I openly embrace all emotions that wish to
surge through me as catalysts for my own self
exploration.

The reverberation allowing safe space for others to
surf the waves of my own expansion as they begin to
discover their own.

But as I gaze into this newly found reflection I
know what it is that is felt. Whether the other knows it
or not. It makes no difference because the fire, the
passion already burns within me and when a bull fixes
its attention on something.

It continues fourth plowing until the end result.
Just to see if it could, just to see what was possible,
just to see and not to be in regret.

Thank you for the feeling that I feel in the heart
space as it begins to allow me to love even greater. It
begins to remind me that I can love so much more then
I have been. By just being in my space, you allowed
that space to expand. By sharing that gaze you have

allowed my world to reach for something greater allowing more room for new cosmos to be created. By experiencing the gentle touches you have added to the greatness of the Man I am to be.

Simply by being you.

Poem

Your skin was like touching heaven, living in the after glow.

Journeying through the electric current fields of your magnetism.

I wonder if you knew what it was you were giving off...

I wanted to flow deeper and so I knew the only way to go was through the eyes of the beholder.

I faced the fear of my self and dove into the waters of my own heart, but only because your light allowed me to do so.

I'll rise up once I must gasp up for air, but know to remain in this love I am unsure if I want to come back up.

Poem

I realize the more and more reflections of beauty that surround me and I rise in love with. The stories I create in my mind of what could be in some form or another are truly playing out in alternate universes.

Because of this each time I allow my mind to day dream of what could be with someone, I know I have already experienced it. In this knowing I also know I am complete regardless of the outcome after the day dream occurs. To not hold onto expectations of these visions.

Because I have experienced all variations, all thoughts and creations. It is an amazing feeling to allow my mind to venture into the what could's. Then acting on them until it leads you to a different path.

No longer living in the regrets, I refuse to be old and think back at what if I did that or what if this. I love that the mind has the capability of visualizing these scenarios because the feeling and expansiveness is so vast when you do not limit your self any more.

When you are truly honoring your feelings in all moments, that is when you can feel your freedom. That is when you can begin to know the only thing stopping you is your self.

So keep dreaming dreamers, but take action on the one that draws your attention and focus on that one the most. Keep on that one until your feelings changes. The moment it feels like work, or resistance to do something. Is when you must begin to withdraw and let go of the attachment of it because now you are forcing a square box into a round hole.

I call fourth all beautiful reflections to allow me to rise in my love further and further by simply being you, so that I can feel my heart expansion even more. Even if the stories I create will only ever play out in my mind, it makes no difference because it has already happened.

Love you beautiful Souls.
I can see you through the gateways and tunnels of your eye portals.

Poem

I used to look into the darkest depths of your soul,
Through the eyes of the beholder and run.

Because I was not ready yet to experience that intensity level of love.
But that was only because I was not able to love my

self to that level yet.

Now I look into your eyes and I witness what you once saw in me.

Now I hold space for you to recognize the same.

That you can love greater and when you do, you can gaze into my souls eyes and see it was always just you on the outside gazing in.

Union

9-1-16

Your emotions are delicacies and you are not appreciating those tasty morsels.

Dive in and devour these emotions for you may never know when your last meal will be.

I want to plow my self into your darkness without restraints as a bull charges towards his goal.

Go where no man has gone before, I want to see your tears.

I want to see you squirm because of how blissful it feels to allow someone into your heart and the abyssal void that may surround it.

I want your shadow to feel my gaze through your eyes.

I want to touch the inner most recesses of your mind that you hide from the normal world.

I want to fill all of your darkness with the light of love I have within me.

I want your demons, your shadows to come out and play so that they can know it is safe to frolic once more.

I want every secret, every skeleton that has been locked away to surface so we can connect on a level that you have only dreamed of.

Then and only then, do I want to feel your physical body upon mine and undress you slowly as you grin seductively gazing upon my enthralled eyes.

Knowing that we are our true selves, our authentic selves with nothing to hide or run from anymore because we accept one another as is.

So that the connection is so euphoric the simplest touch or graze of my fingers on your arms and skin sends you to an ecstatic release of pleasure and bliss.

So that the energetic bonds are so tightly woven that all it takes is a simple stroke of our flesh to know what true union feels like.

Share your darkness with me and I will show you I will still love you and accept you.

9-2-16

It's funny to me to see the spiritual community free themselves from one imprisonment of the mind only to get sucked into another.

To relieve your self of the many slaveries of the TV, media, religion.

To then give your "power" away and misplace your attention to Mercury Retrograde, to crystals, to wands, to alien language, to alien contact, to zodiacs, to astrology, to natural medicines like ayahausca, peyote, etc.

You are the one who makes the choice on what you want to experience. Not Because Mars "looks" like it is rotating backwards, not because this crystal give you the power you had in you the whole time, not because you are inclined to be a certain way due to your zodiac signs.

They are all templates used to remind you of your divinity, not to be always used because in it is where your power lies. NO, it has always been within you. These outside tools were just created for you to realize this.

Remind your self that everything you desire is WITHIN you. Not outside of you in the illusion itself. The moment you remember this is the moment you truly honor your power and honor what your purpose is here.

You only have to experience something one time to gain its strength and vibration. But we tend to forget that strength because we feel we are not worthy of it yet, so we keep going back to that tool until we believe we are and that is when we let go of the prop, and embody that within ourselves.

I love you.

9-3-16

I want to explore the darkness of your mind to shine a light on no man dared to before. They were too fixated on your outside illusion to notice the wisdom that you hold inside.

There will be times where you get messages about another person.
But it isn't the time to let them know that message, maybe it will never be. But that voice is a guiding voice for you to know how far you have come.

It is there to remind you the life times it has taken you to even get here.
That saying it takes 10,000 hours to master something. It isn't over a course of one human life. It is the course of all existence. We are already masters of all.

But some are not ready, they will fight tooth and nail because their belief is so imprinted. It is this way because they find significance in their story.

When in truth life is meaningless. We give it all the meaning we desire so that we can have fun and play in this playground. We keep returning to play the game of forgetting, we keep returning to see how deep into the forgetfulness we can really go.

It is a playful game and we have a lot of fun doing it and after all is said and done we discuss how great of an actor we were that we truly thought the world required saving, that other souls required saving.

Ask your self in any instance you do something to save a life form, a being, a soul , a water, a river why it is you do it?
Compassion? Significance? Self Worth? What is compassion really?
To me it is the understanding that all has a choice, that this has already played out in every single way and we are just going to certain points in time and realities to relive it because of how fun and memorable it was.

Compassion isn't feeling sorry or bad for something living out a story of fear or suffering. It is the understanding that they chose that suffering. Compassion is the holding of that space to allow them to experience their reality because they are learning a valuable lesson. One that they wanted to learn in this life time.

It is not to say that if you see a fellow soul with a tree on top of them and you go and say "Whelp, looks like you chose that. See you!"
No, you ask your self why would you support this fellow soul?

Aha, because they are an aspect of you, essentially they are you.
Understanding that they summoned you into their reality to assist in their growth and learning.

This same applies to every single thing that we feel requires saving. It is we have summoned ourselves to show us a different way. Not through violence but through simply being who you are. You do not have to protest. You simply just have to go out their and be you, shine your wisdom , share your experiences, be vulnerable!

Be that central hub for those who are seeking to find you as the beacon of light that you are so that you shine so brightly, you ignite the passion, that spark, that inspiration in another to then do the same thing as you.

This is how we will make the greatest impact. But most importantly in all of this...ask your self why you are doing the things you are doing.

The answer may surprise you.

A good majority may deny that they feel significant because of what they do, they feel like they are doing something. But when they are in the action they forget that the action is leading to the lesson they are to learn in the process.

Look at the lesson. This is Class Room : Earth after all.

Take a gander at your Soul Mates, as every single being here is your class mate.

9-4-16

Do things because you want to, not because it would satisfy someone else's desires. If it feels right and is aligned. You don't have to ever ask another person for their validation to do something.

9-5-16

If you feel that yearning in the heart, the one that draws you close to someone. Fear not that it will find a way to explore that feeling. Just ensure you do not stand in the way and pretend it is not there. Oh it will find a way.

9-12-16

It is within nature that you can reconnect to your self.
You feel the light coming through each object as a simple reminder and reflection to take time for your self.
To take those moments of silence as delicacies for the ears.

9-19-16

This is a reminder for you all. Take time today to honor your self where ever it is you are. You can always make time to sit down close your eyes and gather your thoughts.
You deserve this peace, as you are this peace.

9-28-16

I see my shadow and I now play with that aspect of my self. Understanding this entire time it was simply wanting my love and affection rather than my anger and resentment.
No matter where you travel to, its the same story. Just different physical bodies reenacting the drama of life.
Being actors in their own play, so they can heal an emotion or trauma that the other has not had the courage to heal.
So we keep coming back into these forms, taking on the new challenge to then heal that emotion or

trauma of our blood lines. Because we can, and we took that task on. Which is why we choose the parents we choose, we are able to know what they were not able to heal, and we then say to our selves. Alright, I got those ones, then the next blood line comes, and does the same for the next. Until all is healed.

One by one these blood lines heal, these "karmic" debts we agreed on. It is a game we enjoy to play when we transition.
We ask one another "So which emotions did you heal that life time?"

We always smile and laugh at the accomplishments of one another, because even in that realm we know we are just our selves talking to our selves.

This virtual reality of the physical is a fun one, have you found the easter eggs, the konami code yet? The answer lies in facing the shadow, to shine light on it. Go where the fear doesn't want you to.

That is the boss level. Expand, Expand, Expand.
9-29-16

Your power lies in your ability to be vulnerable. The freedom to express ones thoughts, without the fear of judgment. This is when you become free. Because you now allow a safe bridge for the other to cross.

10-1-16
When you think about what it is you want to create in this life, or maybe even this week.
There, in my experience anyways, seems to be an under lying fear, block, or wall that you hit.
When you come across it one of the many things can happen.

You look at it and observe it.
You pretend you have other things to do to avoid doing this one task that will propel you forward.
You don't do anything at all because anxiety gets to you and your mind rushes saying you have so many things to do.

It is in these moments it is the most critical to take time away from the task, center your self. Go take a bath, go breath outside. Then come back to that wall again and just do it.
Another way I have convinced my self to move passed that wall is to do another task, then in the middle of this task I immediately jump to the task I am hitting a wall with. So as to not give the mind or ego enough time to create an excuse as to not do the thing.

This generally has been working for me...sneak attacks.
10-3-16
Every day starts and ends with a choice.
What will yours be today?

When you tell me I can't do something.
That ignites my fire to do it so I can show what is possible.
Never will I ever allow my self to be limited by someone else's limitations.
I decide what limits me.
But by all means keep telling me I can't so I can gain more motivation and inspiration for it.

Rumors have always been hilarious to me.
To have someone speak about you in a way that is entirely not true and instead of going up to you an

asking you if it is.

In short...rumors are ways to know that people actually love you and admire you but are afraid of saying it, otherwise you wouldn't even be popping up on their minds.

10-4-16

Weekly Challenge:

The manifesting game. Think of some physical object that you believe is possible to create in your reality to manifest.

For example. I will create someone to gift me a banana.

The banana is the object. See how long it takes for this object to appear in your reality.

Ways to word it so it appears quicker:

1. I will create a someone to gift me a banana.
2. I am a banana making my way towards David.

Say this out loud and then let the idea of it go and continue on your day.

As you progress in this game, you will make further and further out requests, until you manifest some big things. Its all about creating the belief system, but in order to believe you must have an experience that solidifies that belief.

Step into your creator hood, and release the old paradigm of victim hood.

10-7-16

The phrase in the spiritual community that we say we live by is "We create our reality".

I see on my news feed a lot of you believe it. By taking ownership and responsibility of changing the course of the storm by just visualizing it move away.

However it is the same people that are taking ownership of something so vast that in other experiences they pretend they are a victim to circumstance and experience.

Why is it some of us will take credit for being gods and goddesses in our reality for some things and when it comes down to an experience that stirs up emotions in us we pass off the emotion on the experience rather then ourselves who are creating this experience?

Why is it only a convenient line to use when it caters to your story and not the hardships?
This isn't a mickey mouse phrase that we throw around just because it sounds awesome. "YEAH! I create my reality!"

No, it is a phrase to remember that literally every single experience you have in your life time is created solely by you, for you to experience the very same emotions you are passing off back to the experience it self.

It is designed to show you those emotions so that you can take ownership and responsibility for it to move forward in your spiritual evolution and to regain your power.

You will never regain your power by blaming an outside experience for the emotion you are feeling.

You will never fix an instance completely by "fixing" the outside experience that is showing you an emotion. You are merely placing a band-aid on it.

Instead ask your self, why would I have created this experience in the first place. There you will find the answer to many of your questions.

Most of which you have been running away from and afraid of because to truly take ownership and responsibility of everything, is to have to live the life you truly say you want to live.

And to some, that is scary because it is not the norm.

Just something to think about.

10-8-16

What will it take for you to see it was always just you that you were seeking...

When you begin to step into your power you will notice the universe conspires to leave bread crumbs for you. To show you which direction you can take your creative expressions.
However it is entirely up to you as you have free will to decide if you want to go that route.

Some side of you may say no, that is too risky, or no that sounds crazy. But, what if, you just took that leap and did it anyways?

As I step into my, how would I say this, wizardry...I receive reflections telling me affirmations for this and I begin to see the end goal and picture of what I am to become. I begin to receive items and artifacts to create things with and I step further into my unlimited creative expression. It may seem like a fairy tale to some. But when you begin to feel the power of belief mixed with creativity and science...

Your world will change because you now have created experiences to solidify the belief even further.

I am a Wizard, Harry.

Be the change you want to see in the world.
Is not a phrase to be said lightly. Literally, be the person you wish everyone else to be and they then can see what is possible when before they thought impossible.

10-11-16

When the fear wants to come at you.
Love it with yo heart, love it with yo heart.
When the fear give you attitude.
Love it from the heart, love it from the heart.

10-12-16

When you love in such a way that you feel the
focus of your love is the thing giving you the emotion.
That it is not just your self that has this love and that
you are no longer able to have a love like the one you
experience.

You then create attachments and it will make you
blind to any thing that doesn't fit inside the story of
what you are creating in the mind.
It is essential in these times that if you feel the
attachments to take a step back and analyze if you
have lost your self to the emotion.

To see if you are still providing that same love to
your self of which you are emanating out wards to the
object of focus.

By performing this you are now creating a healthy
emotional connection.

10-13-16

Seeds of manipulation towards a reality can only
affect the individual if they have not yet accepted the
outcome of what they feared.

10-15-16

To the untrained eye I am the just another human
in your tv show.
To the trained eye, those who wish to see beyond, I am

the soul you created to show you more of your own power and divinity.

If I am in your space, you have summoned me because you are ready.

Ready for what you ask?

Ready to see just how far we can take this exploration of self and beyond the limitations we have continued to place on our selves.

Ready to see just how creative we can be.

But you must ask the right questions for I will not give the knowledge so it can be heard upon deaf ears.

No If you are witnessing this, you are the ones who are ready to support the others.

You who have thought for so long you have been alone.

It is time to awaken from your slumber.

It is time to remember why you chose to return.

It is time to remember you are not the victims in your experiences.

It is time....What are you waiting for?

10-19-16

It wasn't until our hearts kissed that I remembered what I was holding was simply a version of me who wanted to further understand themselves.

It was at this moment I asked my self "How much further can I love?"

To which a response came through "As much as you so desire"

Constantly finding new versions of me to love because now it is coming from a genuine place rather than seeking something outside of my self to complete me.

It was my self sharing who I am to another version

of my self.

In this knowing I realized just how free I am to be without judgment.

Allowing safe space for exploration, without feeling a tug or drag or kenneled into. Just a sense of freedom because I have a choice.

Ready to see how deep the rabbit hole goes, whether or not the other felt it is of no matter because in that moment I felt more of my self. In that moment I saw how far the love I have can go because of a simple allowance and not an obligation.

10-22-16

Her scent is like tasting the sweetest honey
Waiting for the wind to escort it through the passages of the senses
Increasing the passion and blood flow through the body...
Now stimulated, primed and ready.
The thoughts begin to race of how and when to share each others flesh
Knowing we are in it to progress, to share information...
With a guided intention moving in harmony forward, plowing the fields of negativity.
It is as if a sudden surge of love mows those fields to make room for what there is to create.
No longer withholding...but now forgoing towards that unification of the energy.
Unlocking each others creative potential while raising the passion, the appetite.
Knowing how to mold and move the energy toward a common goal. Directing this unlimited force.
In it you begin to see the true selves, in it there is no

hiding.

As long as the eyes keep matching, as long as the intention holds.

The scene is set and now waiting to unfold....

Ready yet, here we go...

10-25-16

Remember Why You Chose To Return.

Stop Playing Small.

11-1-16

Stay on course, Stay on the path you see your self to be.

Distractions are of many. But distractions only show you the course of which to take after you realized it was a distraction.

Just as there are no such things as mistakes, or right or wrongs. As they are all still learning tools for you. Simply detours but still going towards the same direction.

Do you stay straight and on course or do you zig zag towards your destination?

That choice is always up to you but know in it you are still learning.

What a beautiful lesson it all is.

11-3-16

I had a dream where I was in a room with 32 small circles each filled with Tobacco around me burning. I was meditating inside the circle and the tobacco spoke to me letting me know it was time to begin working with the plant.

Think of all the ways you can brand and package your knowledge in such a way that upon reading what you have to offer others are lining up ready to learn from you.

Your life is absolutely unique to anyone else's, in such you have knowledge that others do not whether you believe it or not.

All of your experiences and wisdom are valid.

Otherwise you would not exist because you would have already experienced that existence.

Package what you know, the world is waiting to hear your wisdom.

11-4-16

Her scent was carried by the wind to deliver the message of her love to my senses.

11-5-16

When two souls decide to share their time with each other. The only true currency in which we have in this physical reality is time. It is then you give a portion of your self to yourself in exchange for deeper knowledge and understanding of who and what you are.

You begin to unlock more of your self by simply allowing a reflection to shine back to you and display all the things you have been refusing to see. In exchange you do the same for each other.

11-10-16

Wake up this day to know that just with a single choice you can turn your life into what you have always wanted.

11-14-16

Every touch of your skin brings me closer to the knowledge within. Ready to explore its secrets, no longer in fear because with you by my side as a reminder.

It is when you are in your own element and flow that you can only inspire others.
By shining as bright as you possibly can for others to recognize their own gifts and power.

11-17-16

She saw the light in me when others disregarded it.
She appreciated all of me and held space without judgment of my shadow.
She truly saw me past the walls I still had up.
She acknowledged my gifts when others were intimidated by them.

All because I began accepting my self.
In turn the universe brought this reflection to remind me and to keep pushing forward on my journey.

In this moment I am grateful for what has been created and will continue to cherish each moment to come.

11-23-16

As we take our first waking breathe of the day it is then we invite self awareness into this reality.

As we take our first sip, our first bite of food, It grounds us into this reality so that we do not shift into the others.

As our first thought begins to form and I turn over to see a physical reflection of my love beside me it is then I know I created this reality so that we may reflect to one another and grow together in truth.

No longer hiding in secrecy and withholding information because it may "hurt" the other person. In truth we know now that what is being done is we are allowing safe space for us to feel our emotions and develop emotional mastery to then wield the elements to be the greatest versions of our selves we can be in this time.

Our ripples in consciousness will expand out for others to recognize they too can do the same.

11-25-16

Let go of the way you think it has to be and embrace the way it currently is. That is when it will shift.

If you give someone true freedom and unconditional love. They will never have a reason to rebel you.

11-26-16

When will you allow your heart to open. To shine out that love you have to another without fear of it being hurt.

All this fear you have on thinking someone will hurt you is actually you creating someone to hurt you.

The moment you surrender to the endless possibilities of what can happen when you are truly authentic, truly open, truly expressive.

You too will then create a perfect reflection to show you how far you have come.

Let go, the only one that can ever hurt you is your self.

11-27-16

Your scent seduces me every time you are away. Lingering around using its ethereal fingers to pleasure my senses to leave me wanting more of you.

Is it all in my head, I ask?

Or is it me that truly am able to pick out your scent in an assortment of other smells that come from my space.

My nose at times wanting me to dabble in the deepest pools of love by igniting it at random. These pools of which we have no idea how deep they go, yet we are so eager to explore together. But I have been training my mind, body and soul to dive deeper each day.
Each new relationship leading me up to this one, training me to hold my breathe to see how deep I can truly dive to only realize it was never the breathe that I required to dive deep.

It was always just the trust that I will be safe enough to experience it, always safe in the pools of your infinite waters.

11-28-16

Not everyone is going to love you.
In fact some will downright despise you because you remind them or reflect to them aspects of them selves they have yet to accept or they feel they lack.

But you, the observer, can make a choice you can love everyone.

Especially during the moments in which you see aspects of your self wanting to deface you or attack you in certain manners.

These are the versions of your self surfacing to receive your acceptance into the oneness. These are the versions wanting your attention. The ones who you don't want to acknowledge.

Love your self there within, speak with that version of yourself and let it know You are sorry for not hearing its frequency earlier.

Now is the time.
I love you.
11-29-16
Finally a safe space...
A safe space to explore and be my self.
Allowing me to dive into my endless creativity in
ritual and magick.
Another vessel to share these intentions to see how
deep we can really go.
It was hard enough for my self to realize the things
flowing through my mind were actually insights into
other realms.
It was hard to get over the idea of me going crazy.
But for another to accept all of me, all of my crazy and
still yearn for the exploration of what is just beyond
those limits.
A safe space, one to explore, one to have fun
and know it's all just a game. Reminding one another
of the true intention of this recreation of selves.
We are the templates, the ones who will break past
the normal boundaries that have been setup.
We see beyond it and we see that fear and say oh,
there is more of me to face. Lighting the way for one
another.
Because we both feel safe to be our selves, to be true
to our emotions.
Holding on to the caduceus, both yin and yang
each one strand of the missing puzzle piece.
Every day is another chance to dive deeper into the
exploration because two are better then one, but
ultimately these same two will become one.
11-30-16
There are so many ways to love. But the love that I

have enjoyed the most so far, was the one in which I created you.

12-2-16
I am love which is a state of being that is the default setting before our minds get conditioned to others. Everything I do is made from unconditional love. Regardless of how you may perceive it.

Frequencies have huge influences on our state of being...and when you realize that everything has its own frequency....that's where the fun begins.

12-5-16
There is a light in each of us. You just have to open your eye to see it. In this space there is no fear. Because in the unknown is just more of you.

12-6-16
Learn to empower others. What you put fourth into the universe is rewarded back to you. Because for one, you are everything. Then two, Action and reaction, causality. Little by little your world shifts into a world of empowerment and then others will empower you.
Especially if you have a lover. It is vital to the relationship to empower one another and to continuously challenge one another for positive change and to remind one another who you are.
As to not get lost in the stories we tell ourselves. So when one forgets , the other reminds. It will be a perfect balance.
12-7-16
When you have that one thing in mind that you

have been putting off. Looking for anything and everything to distract from the thing you know could make a huge impact.

This is the moment that is showing you fear which is holding you back.

And the best thing about that fear, is that it is showing you the direction to go.

Research These

Listed below are the steps I took that allowed me to view the world How I do today, up until the point this book was released. In my coming books new modalities will be listed as well as entries.
I want this to be an ongoing thing where I share what flows through me.

1. Reiki Circles
2. Become vegetarian for a year, not to protect animals. Do it for your self.
3. Give up Alcohol, Marijuana for a year
4. Give up Porn for good, research how porn affects the mind
5. Reiki Attunement
6. Kundalini Yoga
7. Ashtanga Yoga
8. Ayahuasca Ceremony - Once a year
9. San Pedro Ceremony - Once a year
10. Water Fasting - Once a Year
11. Sensory Deprivation Tank
12. Build a Meditation Practice every day
13. Build a Breath work practice every day
14. Find a group of like minded people to meet with once a week
15. Research Tantra- Real Tantra, Not just having sex. Real Tantra is simple and the best teachers keep it simple. It is simply learning to direct ones energy towards what you want to manifest in life at the point of orgasm.
16. Research Sigils

17. Research ORMUS
18. Research The structure of Rituals

I am sharing this for when the other version of me comes across this they can reference this and begin the journey in their own way or this pathway.

Conclusion

Since the completion of this book there has been many events that have happened that I did not write in my journal.
Because I hit a threshold within my self and felt a ton of fear rising up in publishing this. One of the more profound experiences that happened was I began hearing voices in my head asking "Commander, What would you like us to do with the ships?" I at times play with the voice and play along and say to move them to certain areas.
There was one occasion I remember the voice coming through during a drum circle and I asked them to show a ship so I can see it. A ship flew above us very slowly a bright orange ball and from that point I realized this voice was real.

A few weeks had past since this experience and something inside me wanted to ask what my soul name was. It was told to me that it was Ashtar. I wondered oh wow what a funny name. I didn't think anything of it and was told that if I say this name I would feel the power of it. This was around the same time I began making Sirian Cosmic Head Bands, with the triskelion symbol. I never really knew why I was so drawn to this symbol until one day my friend Kevin showed me a tarot deck of cards that was supposed channeled by someone who received Sirian transmissions. On the cards was a triskelion, Triskelion symbol is an emblem

351

the sirians would use to identify themselves.

I was making these jewelry pieces intuitively, I never knew how to wire wrap but I was told to do so. So I did. Next comes the more profound part. I then wanted to research the name Ashtar to see what exactly the name referenced. I typed it into google and immediately Ashtar Command came up. He is the Commander of the Sirian Fleet, many channel him. I was in disbelief because why would my soul name be Ashtar. I thought it was coincidence and let it go. Then came a woman who was a channel, she found me somehow and pulled me aside and said to me. You are the physical embodiment of Ashtar. I could hardly believe the words came out of her mouth. Shortly after all of this, I let go of the thought because it seemed way to far fetched and I was having fear and doubts because of the responsibility involved in taking ownership of that. But I decided to have a channel session within my self and find out what the deal is and if I really am Ashtar.

I asked Ashtar Why am I the physical embodiment of you here on earth?

He answered "Because we have a contract with the Government to not interfere with humanity until it reaches a certain threshold or percentage of consciousness. So in turn I figured out a loop hole. The loop hole is simply I split my self into another being, which is you, and feed you information to create technologies that will empower humanity to raise the consciousness level to the one of which we can begin coming in to support. This water machine you are creating is one that we use, it is a different variation because your mind received slight distortions but it is essentially the same technology that programs the water to do many different tasks inside of our physical body. Little by little I will be in deeper communication with you to release certain pieces of information that you will then feed to the other light workers. This is a plan that has been planned out for a very long time now. You have been awakening many by your word as in each word you speak you are giving codes to their senses to remember who they were before they chose this physical body."

So this is what was spoken to me and ever since my depression I have heard a subtle voice always guiding me. It is the similar voice that speaks with me to transmit or transcribe my messages in my journal. I speak for many council members that wish to flow through on given days or I write based on experience.

There will be 2 more books based on journal entries that I will eventually publish. Then 5 other books which I have planned for to be under The Water Magister Series title. The first will be The Water Magister's: Empowering the Goddess, which will be free spoken words that flow out depending on the image that is captured on that Goddess. The Water Magister's: Plant Book, which will be a fictitious book where artist and friends, family can submit plants that do not exist just yet. The next book will be The Water Magister's: Sigil Book, which will feature many different sigils that have been channeled to me and to be used to empower others and used to create your reality. The last book will be The Water

Magister's: Metron's Meditations book which will feature the meditations I utilized and recorded during my first year of teaching meditation. The last book of the Series I wish to publish a book that is based on how this water machine came to be. These books will be published in no particular order.

It has been such an amazing journey so far since that depression. I am so grateful for it all and I will continue to remind my self to be in a state of gratitude.
In short this is for you, my self. So that you can continue on from where I left off in my understanding. I know it will continue to grow as we are still just learning to walk and create and realize we are creating all of our experiences. But once we master these emotions, we will begin to master the elements. We will literally be able to move objects, fly, use elemental magic. I for-see it happening, we will be Wizards and Sorceresses because we finally remember that this is a playground. But the trick of it all is to create rituals to allow the mind to slowly start to believe it. Until it is no longer required. Otherwise you will stay the same. Rituals are vital to your expansion if you do not believe the outcome to be true. Test your limits.

Now as for the Water Machine, I have been receiving many communications to begin the process of finding investors. I have the vision of what and how to make the machine. I see it being used in prison systems, and our agriculture industry to charge the foods and people who drink it with the highest resonance they can be at. If you are interested in supporting for the Water

Machine please contact me using my information in this book.

I love you.
-David Rodriguez , The Water Magister
Email: TheWaterMagister@gmail.com

Contacts Page

If you feel you would like to contact me you can do so by visiting:
Www.TheWaterMagister.com

Facebook: www.facebook.com/thewatermagister
Email: TheWaterMagister@gmail.com

Want to listen to my Tank Drum Music?

Visit:

https://momentology.bandcamp.com/album/remember-who-you-are-binaural-beat-meditations

May you begin to remember why you came back at this time.
You are what you have been looking for.

Poems

Poem 1

The following is poetry during the point in my life where I was still unconscious to my self yet I was still able to channel information as if I was sending messages to my self to read them now. These were during what I like to call my "Dark Stages of Life" But in truth it was such a beautiful time for my self and an even more amazing time reflecting on all of it.

This poem was written in 2003. It was based on a recurring dream that happened back when I was 18 after a dream I had where a vampire dog scratched my back and I awoke with scars on my back from it. It is about a vampire girl whom I first fell in love with in the dream world before any girl in the physical that I met. I wrote a script on this because for a full year I would have a recurring dream about her.

Poem Year 2003
I close my eyes and start to realize

I am drifting into a forever changing reality
The endless possibilities of each keeps me in awe
I dream of one category of dreams ever since that
day
The day I awoke to the marks on my back
But ever since that day I could control my dreams
I could do what I wanted and act how I wanted
I slip into unconsciousness and see the colors
I see beautiful colors mixing and twirling to form
The very first image of my dream within my mind
I see her now, she is clear as day
The vampire girl of my dreams
Which oddly enough has been the girl
I've had in every dream I've had, I walk with her
She is chained up because she is seen as a menace
A burden to everyone, I slit my wrist
I feed her hunger, she settles down
She is now in normal form, I sit next to her
She tells me about her life stories
Then she asks me if I would like to be one among
the night
I agree, I unchain her
She takes me in her arms and I feel bliss
Losing my life to a girl so beautiful and sweetly
evil
I now have seen bits and pieces of the truth
We always venture together now
But when will I meet her in this dream we call
"Reality"
I keep thinking of the girls I see in my life
Maybe one of them is her, but most likely not
They are all self indulged in doing things that
Does not involve a kind and caring person, instead

They surround themselves with people that are fake and treat

Them nice at first. Then use them and throw them aside.

When will they learn, when they do its already too late.

To you Vampire girl in my dreams this Rhapsody is to you.

When I dream I see you, I look forward to my dreams.

Put me out, turn me out, put me in a comatose state.

I'd rather be in a fantasy land then the reality of this Egoic,

Chaotic, dishonest, self importance world we call our home.

I gave up on this reality, I no longer care, my feelings, my emotions

Are all gone. The only feeling I have anymore int his reality is pity.

Time will tell what will come and what will go. But then again

There is no time back to my reality. Soon I'll be with the vampire

Girl. Once this day is over, Now I lay me down to sleep.

I'll dream of you until you come true.

Poem 2

This next poem was written during my first love's relationship in the physical.

Her name was Krista. A little bit about this before I go into this. I wanted to explain this relationship.

Because upon reminiscing it was about the first time I ever had my intuition speak to me so loudly. It was around 3 months into this relationship where I began having dreams. These dreams were extremely vivid and I work alot within my dream world as you will begin to read. In this particular dream I had with her, I was a video camera in her room watching her cheat on me with another man. Now mind you I have never been jealous or ever thought she would cheat on me. Nor did I ever consider cheating on her as well. So I found it very odd I had these dreams. After 3 days of having the same dream.

I asked her if she was, she denied it. 3 days more I had these dreams. I asked her once more, she denied it. I then got fed up and went onto my computer and went onto myspace when it used to be popular at the time. I had already known of her email but never her password. So I closed my eyes and the very first thing that came to my mind I typed it in. In complete shock it was her password and I was logged in.

I then saw a message from her and a man exchanging sexual talk. It was at this point my world was devastated.
I was suicidal and I did not want to live anymore.

How could anyone ever do this to someone? But as I remember now,
I was playing the victim. You are never a victim of any circumstance. I realize now I created this for my own self growth. I had to feel this pain. Thus it has led me to where I am now, and I am eternally grateful for her providing this service.

Now on to the poem.

-Stepping Stones- Year: 2004
The stepping stones of life
Are ordinarily full of strife
With the promise of something more
You tend to think life is a bore.

With each step you take
The more you try to be more awake
From the dream of a dream of a dream you know
We must endure the adventures and just "go" with the flow

You start to take another step in the right direction
Then you start to look all around to gain the right perception
The way we look at things day to day
We just look back and make sure you say to your self
Hey ....Is that okay?

The love we have between us cannot be mistaken
Because every day together is another blissful pill taken

Swallowed whole, it fills us, fuels us, feeds us
The emotions and wonderful intricacies of every
day life activities

Poem 3

This Poem is shortly after the breakup with Krista.
But the more I re read it I realize it can pertain to so
many beautiful souls out there hiding their potential.

-Smile You're living a lie- Year: 2004
Smile every day to hide the pain
When deep inside you know its all in vain
You go on your day as if all was norm
But you know you're hiding, buried inside

Through lies, deception, corruption our race has
progressed
We hide our pain through lies and go about our day
We smile to hide the pain
We know we hold guilt with us every day
No one to vent to, no one to go to

To relieve your lies, afraid of what they might
think
You became what you dislike in life
Justifying all your actions somehow making it
seem like its all ok

But it kills you inside, the more you hold it…
The more you hide it, the deeper it gets
The deeper it gets, the more it hurts
The more it hurts, the more guilt you feel
The more guilt you feel, it starts to numb

Then you do another harmful action

And so the cycle continues...
This is the lie we all live in, realize it
Stop your self, It isn't healthy for our society,
yourself, your loved ones.

Poem 4

It was here where I began to hold a lot of resentment for Krista. It began showing up in all areas of my life and my writings.

-Free from those shackles- Year: 2004

Finally free,
Free from those shackles
that were chained to my heart.

Each link rusting and breaking,
little by little gaining control
it has finally shattered
upon saying these words.

I don't trust you,
I don't respect you,
Nor Do I believe a single word
you say to me is true.

How does it feel?
Remember this feeling well,
Because it is quite similar to how you made me
I hope the wound was salted.

Remember this feeling,
Each tear freeing my bitter soul
Every drop like acid melting
these shackles that once tied my heart.

For now I've been free.
Remember this feeling well,
Let it burn you, fill you.
For it is only a fraction of what you did to me.

Poem 5

My soul begins to speak through to me after my heartbreak.

-If only you knew...- Year: 2004

If only you knew
my thoughts, my feelings
towards this wonderful world
You would think I'm askew.

Not right and not fit,
To be part of this world
Filled with a bunch of misfits
Not knowing to what to do so they do what there told.

Told to act and feel a certain way
Never thinking for yourself
even though you believe you are,
but you cant equate the solution to the problem within you.

Its all so easy if you set your mind aside,
We live in a world filled with destruction and demise
For once try and grasp the concept of true being that re-sides
Within your soul and you will find that you will surmise.

The power within you that you must utilize,
The real being your destined to see
not the selfish person we were taught to be
For when you do find it yourself, you too will
say...
If you only knew.....

Poem 6

This is more resentment being held for Krista. We would meet occasionally after the break up because I had a feeling of not being worthy so I kept coming back to her.

-Every little touch- Year: 2004

Every time we meet
Its never just a meet and greet
It always turns into more
And we know who's the whore.

Not even knowing how much it hurts me
Keeping my self at a distance 'cause i know it cant be
Trying not to get attached
All the while lifting the latch.

Little by little raising the gate
To the wall of my castle that I now call "Hate"
Each time it inches upward
Which is why I always seem to be distant and awkward.

You think I don't know about your other
You come to me when he seems to be a bother
Just run to me because your not satisfied
Just using me to achieve that little quick rise.

I can see in your eyes you do not care

Just in it because it gets you high and gets you by
I write to you because I know you wont dare
Ever try and tell me the truth about who you are.

I wonder sometimes if I ever did know you
But its just so sad that I could always see right
through you
Every word you say, I'm like the detector
I know you think your in control as the director.

Far be it to say your a great actor
But it's ok, Because I know what your after
Just in it for the blissful act never knowing that in
fact
It is hurting you more so then me, so I say to you
"Relinquish your selfish Acts".

Poem 7

-Target practice- Year: 2004

Ready, Aim, Fire
All around is always the desire
The urge and simplicity of the heart
Is never easy and never far apart

Many Decisions, Made within each moment
Never knowing what we would get from-it
Selfish acts and always superficial
Always asking what is beneficial

Never caring how it would hurt one another
Keep pushing forward and using each other
When do we realize it isn't what were after
When we do it just spells disaster

Killing yourself inside, Not even knowing
The consequences begin to start showing
Resentment, Remorse, Repentance
Are the feelings you feel while you go through
penitence.

Poem 8

This was my self attempting to let go of my heart ache.

-Never coming back- Year: 2004

Never coming back home
I've grabbed the lock and threw away the key
Face it, you used to have me
Now I'm realizing it was never ment to be
Or so you see, or think,
The truth is
You'll never know
Promises, I've made to myself are now at hand
A time to keep and uphold
It's alright you'll realize later the key has now been thrown
A little to late for you to gain back
Forever lost in the tears of sorrow it drowns
Sinking deeper into the void
Never looking back....
Never looking, Never turning back
Never coming back
Never coming back home.....

Poem 9

-Chasing the mythical white rabbit...- Year: 2004

As I start up at the starting line
I peer out to see my competition.
The shot is heard, they take off
I stay in the pen....running into the race late
I see all the jerks, fakes, chasing after the rabbit
I stop and stare, looking at them as they waste their energy.
I now begin the race, i run with all my might towards that goal.
I pass up, asshole slowly coming from behind on jerks.
I pass up dishonesty, all the while sneaking behind fakeness
I am now in second place, I see the major contender.
I am neck and neck towards manipulator, I stare him in the eye.
He stares back. we both head forward, towards the rabbit
I am outpacing him, he looses momentum....
I squeeze in ahead, still chasing my dreams and the white rabbit.
I cross the finish line, to hear the announcer say
" And the winner is, Mr. Nice guy"
I shall prevail and be a stronger person. Just wait and see,
This fuels me to become even more successful,

I will chase the rabbit until i finally do catch one to call my own.

Poem 10

This I wrote at a time in my life where I had just finished reading Conversations with God.
I was practicing the art of free writing. But through a keyboard, I realized that information channeled through me at such a rapid rate the only way I could keep up with it was to type it out. Luckily I type rather quickly! I was also influenced by watching the movie with Tom Cruise called "Vanilla Sky". It is one of my favorite movies to this day for the metaphors involved.

- Mask of Death- Year: 2004

These things shadowing your every move
You don't realize that you're in a grove
One that isn't you, a fake you
You take kind words like insults

These things they deny you from hearing the truth
That thing is the mask on your face, the perceived self.
You are a puppet to its bidding
Two personalities in one being
How ironic is it to be freed from guilt in a religion
Just to be in another cage in society
Filled with greed and irony and treachery.
Don't you see, you are brainwashed.
Your brain has been on autopilot!

These two personalities you have can you tell which is "real"?

Or are any real?
What is the truth you are seeking,
When will you realize the true friend behind all the
madness.
That mask has you zombiefied, petrified to all true
emotions and feelings

When you look at your self in the mirror what do
you see?
Do you see your self or do you see someone you
should be?
Do you see the person your trying to be?
That is the truth behind all this
You are not real
The real you is buried inside of you aching in
agony

Every-time you follow your mind and not your
soul.
It aches and gets buried further and deeper until
At one point it will overlap and you will become
Conscious of the truth, The Reality.

Poem 11

It was at this point I was felt hopeless with all the women in my life.
Immediately after this point I became a womanizer and read books on how to pick up women because I was not able to generate that love for my self yet.

-The Good guy- Year: 2005

In this day and time,
You say that good men are a rare find
That every man that drops lines
wants your body not your mind.
That none respect your spirit
and when you speak they don't hear it.
You are independent and they fear it
but when in those jeans they love how you wear it.
So they keep coming
Spitting their best game
but always end up running
As soon as you need funding
or actually start hoping to be something more...
More than an occasional fuck
or the arm trophy that keeps their ego up.
So we are all categorized as dogs and players
Automatically scrutinized
And every word labeled as lies
When we say you are the apple of our eyes.
The true men try to bare their souls
but almost always end up having to fold
Because they aren't skilled and bold

To fully play the cards they hold,
While the assholes with the better poker face take
the good guys place
Running far ahead in this race
Ruining the game.
The good guys deeds are easily erased and
replaced
With the stigma created by cunning guys
that are good with lies
So before you say good men are in short supply
open up your eyes.
Take a good look around at the guys you ignore
Overlook and put down
Because good guys are easily found
if you keep your eyes to the ground.
Don't get fooled by a handsome face
Or let "game" obscure your thoughts.
A good guy's game may not be appealing
but his words aren't from his dick
but from his heart.

Poem 12

I only have a few more entries of poems I wanted to share to lead you up to my most recent years.

-Moon Rise- Year: 2006

As the full moon rises up again
During the ever so clear night
I stare up to the glow and lights
On the waters edge to marvel and stare
Its such a site to see something so beautiful
Such things people take for granted
But to me, is the most beautiful thing.

Watching the glow shimmer from each wave
as it flows like blood from mother earth
Right up to the sandy shores of the beach
I cant help but wonder while sipping on my wine
If the one out there for me is too marveling
at the same wonderful site that is bestowed upon
me.

Even so, the full moon makes me happy
I like to go out and lay down while i drink on wine
Its a very relaxing feeling to feel the air
The air hit against your cheek as if a hand is
reaching to you
This may not make sense to most of you
It will one day, you will enjoy every day miracles.

The grass will be greener,
the sky will be bluer,
the clouds will smile at you,
the birds will fly around you
Why? Because you know the true miracles in life
are the ones
that you find in the moment, not the past or the
future.

So take the time for one day to just relax outside
and marvel
at the beauty that every human in existence tends
to
take advantage of, because you will never know
true beauty until you can see it everywhere within
everything.
Look as if you are seeing things for the first time
through a babies eyes...I read that somewhere.
Feel like you have never felt before.
Listen like you never knew what it sounded like.
This is the true beauty in life. Accept it.

Poem 13

As years inch closer to my awakening I begin receiving many subtle messages through my poetry for my self.

-Everlasting- Year: 2007

It is everlasting and going faster
every day people stepping back
but it all goes by in a blink of an eye
People wishing they didn't do the things they did
always wishing they could turn back the hands of
time

But I know as i watch them all
I know as I see them fall
They need to be picked up
because they seem to just be fed up

With this reality of lies we live in
Hoping to one day find that one person who
completes us
and makes us whole, when in fact
Without a doubt it just you on the inside that does

Always searching for the truth, but it seems
you are chasing a fairy tale, an idea, a thought
of one that was told to you when you were young
trying to believe so hard that what was told was
real

But what you were born into is lies, deceit, agony
Do you want to break out?
Do you want to break free?
Do you even know these tales that are being told?

I question every action, i analyze every person
Trying to be someone their not
I just wish i could show them to act their own way
Do not follow the media, do not follow the leader.

In truth, you are the leader of your world
You are the creator of worlds
You are the alpha and the omega
You are everything around you

I write this all not in poem,
But in verse, in thoughts of words
that flow through me like a never ending ocean
allow my fingers to type what they wish

I just step aside then read it all over and
am in shock at the things I write
I have not written or allowed my self free
To write in free verse
It has changed, i am now again able to flow words
through my ways, I see couples
I see relationships all being pushed into something
more,
All becoming nothing more then a fantasy play
land of fun

Poem 14

I remember asking in a note pad if I am losing my mind. This is what flowed out from asking that question.

-No, you haven't lost your mind- Year: 2008
Stop hiding

Well here we are feeling lost,
your hiding not wanting to crash and burn
one day the sun will shine on you
and no I wont think you lost your mind.

You can never wait for luck,
because so far the way the story goes
is just a repeat of living a life
of people saying you've lost your mind.

I cant take the game people play
hiding behind that veil of lies,
I don't mind, i wont care if only
you knew it was never to late to let go.

Let the past be forgotten,
it was never ment to be anyways
so as you say good night, good night
Remember, I wont think you have lost your mind.

Poem 15

11-1-13

In this day and age, we often lose sight of what really matters most in life. Due to all of the outside distractions that are constantly bombarding us from all
Angles, including but not limited to our own personal dialog that manifests in our thoughts.

The negative media, advertisements, society, pressure from work. We often lose ourselves and forget what it was we truly wanted in the first place.

But once you push all of that aside, what is left?
You realize all this time you were attempting to be something you are not and that is when you become you.
Peaceful, loving and always caring about others. That is who you are. Be the change you want to see in life.
The time is now to show the world how resilient we really are.

www.ingramcontent.com/pod-product-compliance
Lightning Source LLC
Chambersburg PA
CBHW031124090426
42738CB00008B/965